A DICTIONARY

OF

SELECT AND POPULAR

QUOTATIONS,

WHICH ARE IN DAILY USE:

TAKEN FROM THE

Latin, French, Greek, Spanish, and Italian

LANGUAGES:

TOGETHER WITH

A COPIOUS COLLECTION OF LAW-MAXIMS AND LAW-TERMS

TRANSLATED INTO ENGLISH,

WITH

ILLUSTRATIONS HISTORICAL AND IDIOMATIC.

SIXTH AMERICAN EDITION, CORRECTED, WITH ADDITIONS.

"He has been at a great feast of languages, and stolen all the scraps."
Shakspeare.

PHILADELPHIA:
CLAXTON, REMSEN & HAFFELFINGER,
624, 626 & 628 MARKET SEREET.
1873.

ADVERTISEMENT

TO THE

SIXTH AMERICAN EDITION.

The utility of the *Dictionary of Quotations* has been fully tested, by the publication of *five* editions of the work.

To each of these successive editions, the editor made copious additions; besides correcting and altering, in many instances, the translations, in order to give most clearly and obviously, the meaning and bearing of the passages quoted.

In preparing this *Sixth* edition for the press, care has been taken to give the work a thorough revision, to correct some errors which had before escaped notice, and to insert many additional quotations, Law Maxims, and Law-Terms.—In this state it is offered to the public, in the *stereotype* form.

Philad. March, 1831.

INDEX

TO THE ABBREVIATIONS.

GR. *Greek.*	TAC. *Tacitus.*
LAT. *Latin.*	CIC. *Cicero.*
SP. *Spanish.*	SEN. *Seneca.*
ITAL. *Italian.*	VIRG. *Virgil.*
FR. *French.*	LAB. *Laberius.*
FR. PROV. *French Proverb.*	OV. *Ovid.*
HOR. *Horace.*	LUCRET. *Lucretius.*
JUV. *Juvenal.*	CAT. *Catullus.*
CLAUD. *Claudian.*	MART. *Martial.*
LUC. *Lucan.*	PROP. *Propertius, &c.*

N. B. The passages in inverted commas, after each quotation, are in general a close if not a literal translation. What follows is a more diffuse explanation of its bearing and application, than a mere translation could possibly convey.—Where the sense is sufficiently clear, the explanation is of course omitted.

NOTICE. It is recommended to the general reader, if the quotation should not be found on a first reference, to drop the first Monosyllables, *at*, *car*, *et*, *id*, *il y a*, *nam*, *sed*, *ut*, which are variously used to link the quotation with the context. The second word, on referring to the alphabetical order, will generally be found, in these cases, to furnish the desired explanation.

DICTIONARY

OF

SELECT AND POPULAR

QUOTATIONS.

AB actu ad posse valet consecutio. Lat.—" The induction is good, from what has been to what may be."—By this logical maxim it is meant to state, that when a thing has once happened, it is but just to infer that such a matter may again occur.

Ab alio expectes, alteri quod feceris. Lat. LABERIUS. —" You may expect from one person, that which you have done to another."—Your conduct to others should form the measure of your own expectations.

A barbe de fol, on apprend à raire. French.—" Men learn to shave on the chin of a fool."—They love to make experiments at the expense of others.

Abatis. Fr. Milit. Term.—Trees felled and fastened together, to oppose the progress of an enemy.

Ab inconvenienti. Lat. Phrase.—" From the inconvenience."—*Argumentum ab inconvenienti.*—An argument to show that the result of a proposed measure will prove inconvenient, or unsuited to circumstances.

Ab initio. Lat. Phrase.—" From the beginning."—His proceedings were ill-founded *ab initio.*

A bis et à blanc. Fr. Prov.—" At the brown and the white."—By fits and starts.

Abnormis sapiens. Lat. HORACE.—" A person whose wisdom is not derived from instruction."—" A mother wit, and wise without the schools."

A bon chat, bon rat. Fr. Prov.—" To a good cat, a good rat."—The parties are well suited, or matched.

A bon chien il ne vient jamais un bon os. Fr. Prov.—

"A good bone does not always come to a good dog."—Merit does not always meet its due reward.

Ab origine. Lat.—"From the origin."

Aborigines. Lat.—The first inhabitants of a country—as the *Indians* in America.

Ab ovo usque ad mala. Lat. Phrase.—"From the eggs to the apples."—From the beginning to the end of the entertainment. These were the first and last articles served up at a Roman feast.

Absentem lædit cum ebrio qui litigat. Lat. SYRUS.—"He hurts the absent who quarrels with a drunken man."—You should consider your adversary as absent, when his senses are departed.

Absentem qui rodit amicum,
Qui non defendit, alio culpante—
Hic niger est; hunc tu, Romane, caveto. Lat. HOR.—He who attacks an absent friend, or who does not defend him when defamed by another—that man is a dark character; do you, Roman, beware of him."—The man who yields even a silent assent when his friend is calumniated, must be regarded as wholly unworthy of confidence or esteem.

Absit invidia. Lat.—"All envy apart."—Without being supposed to speak invidiously.

Abundat dulcibus vitiis. Lat. QUINTIL.—"He abounds with pleasing faults."—Spoken of an author, even in whose errors something pleasing is to be found.

Ab uno disce omnes. Lat. VIRG.—"From this single instance, you may learn the nature of the whole."—From this specimen of guilt, you may form a general inference of the criminality.

Ab urbe conditâ. Lat.—"From the time of the building of the city" (of Rome).—In general thus abridged, A. U. C. in the chronology of the Romans.

A capite ad calcem. Lat.—"From the head to the foot."—From the beginning to the end.

A causa persa, parole assai. Ital. Prov.—"When the

cause is lost, there is enough of words."—Do not discuss that which is already decided.

Accedas ad curiam. Law Lat.—"You may approach the court."—This name is given to a writ by which proceedings may be removed from an inferior to a superior court.

Acceptissima semper
Munera sunt, auctor quæ pretiosa fecit. Lat. Ovid.—"Those gifts are ever the most acceptable which the giver has made precious."—They derive frequently their value from our estimation of the donor.

Accusare nemo se debet, nisi coram Deo.—Lat. Law Maxim.—"No man is bound to accuse himself, unless it be before God."—No oath is to be administered, whereby any person may be compelled to confess a crime or accuse himself. The law will not force any man to say or show that which is against him.

Acerrima proximorum odia. Lat. Tacitus.—"The quarrels of relatives are the most violent."—The phrase may also be applied to that violence of rage which generally belongs to a civil war.

Ac etiam. Law. Lat.—"And also."—A clause added by recent custom, to a complaint of trespass in the Court of King's Bench, which adds "and also" a plea of debt. The plea of trespass, by fiction, gives cognizance to the court, and the plea of debt authorizes the arrest.

Acribus initiis, incurioso fine. Lat. Tacitus.—"Alert in the beginning, but negligent in the end."

A cruce salus. Lat.—"Salvation from the cross."

Acta exteriora indicant interiora secreta. Lat. Law Maxim.—"By the outward acts we are to judge of the inward thoughts."—We can only decide on men's intentions from their conduct.

Actio personalis moritur cum persona. Lat. Law Maxim.—"A personal action dies with the person."—In case of a trespass or battery, the death of the one or the other of the parties puts an end to the action.

Actis ævum implet, non segnibus annis. Lat. OVID. —"He fills his space with deeds, and not with lingering years."—Applied to a character distinguished for a number of brilliant actions accomplished in the course of a short life.

Actum est de Republicâ. Lat.—"It is all over with the Republic."—A phrase used to intimate that the constitution is in extreme danger.

Actum ne agas. Lat. TERENCE.—"Do not labour at what is already finished."

Actus Dei nemini facit injuriam. Law Max.—"No one shall be injured through the act of God."—As if a house be set on fire by lightning, the tenant shall not be responsible for the damage.

Actus legis nulli facit injuriam. Lat. Law Max.—"The act of the law does injury to no man."—If land, for instance, out of which a rent charge is granted, be recovered by elder title, the grantee shall have a writ of annuity, because the rent-charge is made void by course of law.

Actus, me invito factus, non est meus actus. Lat. Law Maxim.—"An act done against my will, is not my act."—If a person be compelled, for instance, through fear or duress, to give a bond or other writing, the deed is rendered void by the compulsion.

Actus non facit reum, nisi mens sit rea. Lat. Law Maxim.—"The act does not make a man guilty, unless the mind be also guilty."—Unless the intent be criminal, the deed can not be attainted of criminality.

A cuspide corona. Lat.—"A crown from the spear." —Honour earned by military exploits.

Ad calamitatem quilibet rumor valet. Lat.—"Any rumour is sufficient against misfortune."—When a man is unfortunate, a breath may complete his ruin.

Ad captandum vulgus. Lat.—"To ensnare the vulgar."—A lure thrown out to captivate the mobility.

Ad deliquium animi. Lat.—"Even to fainting."

A Deo et rege. Lat.—"From God and the king."

Adeo in teneris consuescere multum est. Lat. Virgil.—" So important is it to be accustomed in our tender years."—Such are the advantages of an early education.

Ad eundem. Lat.—" To the same."—In passing from one university or law society to another, it is said that he was admitted *ad eundem gradum*, to the same rank which he held in the association or corporation of which he was previously a member.

Ad finem. Lat.—" To the end."—Or the conclusion.

Adhuc sub judice lis est. Lat.—" The contest is still before the judge."—The affair is not yet decided.

Adieu la voiture, adieu la boutique. French Proverb. —" Farewell the carriage, and farewell the shop." —The affair is all over.

Ad infinitum. Lat.—" To infinity."—And thus the calculation proceeds *ad infinitum.*

Ad interim. Lat.—" In the meanwhile."

At Kalendas Græcas. Lat.—At the Greek Kalends." —The Kalends formed a division of the Roman month, which had no place in the Greek reckoning of time. The phrase was therefore used by the former to denote that the thing could never happen.

Ad libitum. Lat.—" At pleasure."—In music it is used to signify those ornamental graces which are left to the taste of the performer.

Ad nauseam. Lat.—" To disgust."—His attempts at wit were prolonged *ad nauseam*—until they excited disgust.

Ad nullum consurgit opus, cum corpore languet. Lat. Gallus.—" When the body is indisposed, it is in vain that we call on the mind for any strenuous application."

Ad ogni uccello—suo nido è bello. Ital. Proverb.— " With every bird its own nest is charming."

Adolescentem verecundum esse decet. Lat. Plautus. —" It becomes a young man to be modest."

Ad populum phaleras: ego te intus et in cute novi Lat. Persius.—" Away with those trappings to the vulgar; I know thee both inwardly and out wardly."—I know the man too well to be deceived by appearances.

Ad quæstionem juris respondeant judices, ad quæstionem facti respondeant juratores. Lat. Law Maxim.—"Let the judges answer to the question of law, and the jurors to the matter of fact."

Ad quod damnum. Law Lat.—"To what damage."—A writ which ought to be issued before the grant of certain liberties, such as a fair or market, ordering the sheriff to inquire what damage the county is liable to suffer by such grant. The same writ is also issued for a similar inquiry with respect to lands granted to religious houses or corporations, for turning highways, &c.

Ad referendum. Lat.—"To be farther considered."—A diplomatic phrase borrowed from the States of Holland, and now used proverbially to imply a slowness of deliberation and decision.

Adjustez voz flutes. French.—"Make your flutes agree."—Settle your differences by yourselves.

Adscriptus glebæ. Lat.—"Attached to the soil."—Disposable with the land. This is now the wretched description of the peasantry in Russia. It was formerly so in other countries.

Ad tristem partem strenua est suspicio. Lat. Syrus.—"Suspicion is ever strong on the suffering side."—When we play a losing game, we are apt to suspect all those who are around us of treachery.

Adulandi gens prudentissima laudat
Sermonem indocti, faciem deformis amici.
Lat. Juvenal.

"The skilful class of flatterers praise the discourse of the ignorant, and the face of the deformed friend."—They attack each man on his weak side.

Ad valorem. Lat.—"According to (or upon) the value."—An *ad valorem duty* is a per centage upon the *value*, or invoiced price, of the article imported.

Ægrescitque medendo. Lat. Virgil.—"By being cured he grows sick."—He undermines his constitution by too much care.

Ægri somnia vana. Lat. Horace.—"The idle

dreams of a sick man."—The fickle fancies of a distempered brain.

Ægroto dum anima est, spes est. Lat. Cicero.—"Whilst life remains to a sick man there is hope."—This has passed as a proverb into our own language.

Æqua lege, necessitas
Sortitur insignes et imos. Lat. Horace.
"Necessity, by an equal law takes the highest and the lowest.—"No rank can shield us from the impartiality of Death.

Æquam memento rebus in arduis
Servare mentem. Lat. Horace.
"Remember to preserve an equal mind in arduous ffairs."—Equanimity is the best support under difficulties.

Æquam servare mentem. Lat.—"To preserve an equal mind."

Æquanimiter. Lat.—"With equanimity."

Æqua tellus
Pauperi recluditur regumque pueris. Lat. Hor.
"The earth opens equally for the poor man and the prince."—The sentiment is precisely similar with that of the preceding quotation—*Æqua lege, &c.*

Æquè pauperibus prodest, locupletibus æquè.—Lat. Hor.—"Equally profitable to the rich and to the poor."

Æquitas sequitur legem. Lat. Law Maxim.—"Equity follows the law."—Equity can not however make a different rule from that which the law has established

Æquo animo. Lat.—"With an equal mind."

Æquum est
Peccatis veniam poscentem readere rursus.
Lat. Hor.
"The man who asks pardon for his own faults should forgive others."—Our charities and indulgences should be mutual.

Æs debitorum leve, gravius inimicum facit. Latin.

LABERIUS.—"A slight debt produces a debtor—a large one an enemy."

Ætas parentum pejor avis, tulit
Nos nequiores, mox daturos
Progeniem vitiosiorem. Lat. HORACE

"The age of our fathers, which was worse than that of our ancestors, produced us, who are about to raise a progeny even more vicious than ourselves."

A facto ad jus non datur consequentia. Lat. Law Maxim.—"The inference from the fact to the law is not allowed."—A general law is not to be trammeled by a specific or particular precedent.

Affirmatim. Lat.—"In the affirmative."

Afflavit Deus et dissipantur. Lat.—"The breath of God has issued, and they are dispersed."—This was the inscription of the medal struck in the reign of Queen Elizabeth, on the dispersion and destruction of the vaunted Spanish armada. It is now sometimes quoted to mark what is held to be a signal interference of Providence in discomfiting the views of an enemy.

A fin. French.—"To the end."

A fortiori. Lat—"With stronger reason."—If a weak man be dangerous, it follows, *a fortiori*, that a weak *and bad* man must be more dangerous.

A grands frais. French Phrase.—"At great expense."—Sumptuously.

Agnosco veteris vestigia flammæ. Lat. VIRGIL.—"I recognise some traces of my former flame."—I feel that my passion is not wholly extinguished.

Aide-toi, le ciel t'aidera. French. FONTAINE.—"Help yourself, and Heaven will help you."—Depend rather on your exertions than your prayers.

A la bonne heure. French.—"At a good hour."—This comes happily—it is well timed.

A la mode. French.—"According to the fashion."

Alere flammam. Lat.—"To feed the flame." To increase the tendency.

A l'extinction de la chandelle. French.—"To the extinguishing of the candle."—To the last extremity. It is also used to denote a sale by "inch of candle."

A l'extrémité. French.—"At the point of death."—Without resource.

Alia tentanda via est. Lat. VIRG.—"Another way must be tried."—We must diversify our means to attain our end.

Alias. Lat.—"Otherwise," as Robinson *alias* Robson. An *alias* is also a name given to a second writ, issuing after a first writ has been sued out without any effect.

Alibi. Lat.—"Elsewhere."—Law Term, for a defence where the culprit aims to prove his *absence* at the time and from the place where the crime was committed.

Aliena negotia curo, excussis propriis. Lat. HOR.—"I attend to other men's business, neglecting my own."—The quotation is used to mark an officious person.

Aliena nobis, nostra plus aliis placent. Lat. SYRUS.—"The things which belong to others please us more, and that which is ours, is more pleasing to others.

Alienâ optimum frui insaniâ. Lat.—"It is of the highest importance to be able to derive instruction from the madness of another."—It is true practical wisdom to make the faults of others serve as so many beacons to ourselves.

Alieni appetens, sui profusus. Lat. SALLUST.—"Coveting the property of others, and lavish of his own."—This, which was the historian's description of *Catiline*, has since been justly applied to other political adventurers.

Alieno in loco,
Haud stabile regnum est. Lat. SENECA.—"The sovereignty which is held over strange or remote territories is precarious."

Alii multa perficiunt; nos nonnulla conamur;
Illi possunt; nos volumus. Lat.—"Others accomplish many things; we endeavour to effect something: they have the power; we have the will."

A l'improviste. French.—" Unawares."—At an opportunity not foreseen.

A l'impossible nul est tenu. French.—" No man is bound to perform an impossibility."

Aliquis malo sit usus ab illo. Lat.—" Some use or benefit may possibly be derived from that evil."

Aliquis non debet esse judex in propria causa. Lat. Law Maxim.—" No man should be a judge in his own cause."

Aliquando bonus dormitat Homerus. Lat. HOR.—" Sometimes even the good Homer nods."—The greatest genius has its weaknesses and its failures.

Alitur vitium, vivitque tegendo. Lat. VIRGIL.—" Vice thrives and lives by concealment."—It is in the nature of foul deeds to delight in darkness.

Alium silere quod valeas, primus sile. Lat. SENECA.—" To make another person hold his tongue, be you first silent."—Do not irritate an idle dispute by fruitless perseverance.

Αλλων ιατρος, αυτος ελκεσι βρυων. GR. PLUTARCH.—*Allon iatros, autos elkesi bruon.*—" The physician of others, whilst he himself teems with ulcers."

Alma mater. Lat.—" A benign mother."—A name given by students to the university in which they were educated.

Alta sedent civilis vulnera dextræ. Lat. LUCAN.—" The wounds of civil war are deeply felt."

Alter ego. Lat.—" Another self."—Another person so like me in appearance, or in peculiarities of behaviour, as to be identified with me.

Alterius sic
Altera poscit opem res, et conjurat amice.
Lat. HORACE.
" Thus one thing demands the aid of the other, and both unite in friendly co-operation."

Alter idem. Lat.—" Another same."—A person or thing, very strongly resembling another.

Alter remus aquas, alter mihi radat arenas. Lat. PROPERTIUS.—" Let me strike the water with one oar, and with the other scrape the sands."—Let me never hazard my safety by getting out of my depth.

Alterum alterius auxilio eget. Lat. SALLUST.—"The one needs the assistance of the other."

Alumni. Lat.—Those who have received their education at a college, are called *alumni* (or *foster-children*) of that college.

Amabilis insania, et mentis gratissimus error. Lat. HORACE.—"A delightful insanity, and a most pleasing error of the mind."—These words are ironically applied to men who look with complacency on their own mistakes and errors.

Amantium iræ amoris redintegratio est. Lat. TERENCE.—"The quarrels of lovers is the renewal of love"

A ma puissance. French.—"To my power."

Amare et sapere vix Deo conceditur. Lat. LABERIUS.—"To love and to be wise is scarcely granted to the highest."—Love and prudence are absolutely incompatible.

Ambiguas in vulgum spargere voces. Lat. VIRG.—"To scatter doubtful rumours amongst the vulgar"—To endeavour to mislead the crowd by ambiguous intimations.

Ambiguum pactum contra venditorem interpretandum est. Lat. Law Maxim.—"An ambiguous deed or contract is to be expounded against the seller or grantor."—Thus if a man has a warren in his lands, and grants the same land for life, without mentioning the warren, the grantee will have it with the land.

Ame damnée, French.—"A d——d soul."—A tool, a drudge—one who will do any dirty work.

Ame de boue. Fr.—"A soul of mud."—A debased creature.

Amende honorable. Fr.—To make the *amende honorable,* is to confess the crime or offence, and ask pardon for the same.

A mensa et thoro Lat.—"From bed and board."

A merveille. Fr.—"To a wonder."—Rarely. He executed his part *à merveille.*

Amicitiæ sempiternes, inimicitiæ placabiles. Lat. —"Eternal friendships, placable enmities."

Amicitia semper prodest, amor et nocet. Lat. Laberius.—"Friendship is always profitable; Love is frequently injurious."

Amici vitium ni feras, prodis tuum. Lat. Syrus.—"Unless you bear with the faults of a friend you betray your own."—If you do not concede a little, you disclose your own want of temper or of friendship.

Amicum ita habeas, posse ut fieri hunc inimicum scias. Lat. Laberius.—"Be on such terms with your friend as if you knew that he might one day become your enemy."

Amicum perdere est damnorum maximum. Lat. Syrus.—"To lose a friend is the greatest of all losses."

Amicus certus in re incerta cernitur. Lat. Ennius. —"A sincere friend is discovered in a doubtful matter."—It is in situations of hazard that we can prove the sincerity of friendship.

Amicus curiæ. Lat.—"A friend of the court."—This appellation is given in courts of law, to the person who gives his advice or opinion, when not immediately concerned in the cause.

Amicus humani generis. Lat.—"The friend of the race."—The highest title which man can obtain, and which but few Franklins and Howards are found justly to claim.

Amicus Plato, amicus Socrates, sed magis amica veritas. Lat—"Plato is my friend, Socrates is my friend, but truth is more my friend."—By this quotation the speaker or writer intimates that he is not without his personal feelings and attachments, but that nothing can make him swerve from the sacred interests of truth.

Amicus usque ad aras.—"A friend even to the altar"

—One who will sustain his friendship even to the last extremity.

Amittit meritò proprium, qui alienum appetit Lat. PHÆDRUS.—"He deservedly loses his own property, who covets that of another."

Amo. Lat. "I love."

A moitiè de moitiè.—"From half to half."—By halves.

Amor patriæ. Lat.—"The love of our country."—The affection which the native of every climate bears to the soil which has given him birth.

Amoto quæramus seria ludo. Lat. HORACE.—"Setting raillery aside, let us now attend to serious matters."

Amphora cæpit
Institui; currente rotâ cur urceus exit? Lat. HOR.—"A large jar was begun to be formed; why, as the wheel goes round, does it turn out to be an insignificant pitcher."—The metaphor is taken from the potter's wheel. The quotation is applied to those, who, having promised a magnificent work, produce in the end something inadequate, and perhaps contemptible.

Αναγκη ουδε θεοι μαχονται.—*Ananchè oude theoi machontai.* Gr. Prov.—"The gods themselves do not fight against necessity."—They know that her force is resistless.

Anglicè.—"In English."—According to the English fashion.

Anguillam cauda tenes. Lat. Prov.—"You hold an eel by the tail."—You are engaged with an active and slippery opponent.

Anguis in herba. Lat.—"A snake in the grass."—A lurking danger, or one not actually foreseen.

Animal implume, bipes. Lat.—"An animal without feathers, and walking on two legs."—This is PLATO's imperfect definition of a man, which was so successfully ridiculed by DIOGENES, who brought a *plucked cock* into the school, and scornfully asked, "if that was PLATO's man?"

Animi cultus quasi quidam humanitatis cibus. Lat.

Cicero.—"Cultivation is as necessary to the mind, as food is to the body."

Animis opibusque parati. Lat.—"Ready (to defend it) with our lives and our property."—This, on one shield, and the words *Dum spiro spero. Spes* "While I live I hope. Hope"—on another, are the mottos of the state of South Carolina.

Animo et fide. Lat.—"By courage and faith."

Animo non astutiâ. Lat.—"By courage not by craft."

Animo vidit, ingenio complexus est, eloquentiâ il luminavit. Lat. Paterc. of Cicero.—"These subjects he saw by the power of his mind, he comprehended by his understanding, and enlightened by his eloquence."

Animoque supersunt
Jam prope post animam. Lat. Sidon. Apoll.
"Their spirit seems even to survive their breath."

Animum picturâ pascit inani. Lat. Virgil.—"He fills his mind with a vain or idle picture."—This is sometimes applied in ridicule to *dilettanti*, or picture-fanciers.

Animus furandi. Law Lat.—"The intention of stealing."—He took the goods *animo furandi*—with a felonious design.

Animus quod perdidit optat.
Lat. Petron. Arbiter.
"The mind still wishes for what it has lost."

An nescis longas regibus esse manus? Lat. Ovid.—"Do you not know that kings have long hands?"—"It were to be wished," says Swift, "that they had as long ears."

Anno Domini. Lat.—"In the year of our Lord."

Anno mundi. Lat.—"In the year of the world."

Anno urbis conditæ. Lat.—"In the year of the building of the city" (of Rome).

Annus mirabilis. Lat.—"The wonderful year."—The year of wonders.

An præter esse reale actualis essentiæ, sit aliud esse necessarium, quo res actualiter existat? Martinus Scriblerus "Whether, besides the *real being* of *actual being*, there be any other *being* necessary to cause a thing to *be?*"—A question humorously put to ridicule the absurdity of metaphysics run mad.

An quisquam est alius liber, nisi ducere vitam Cui licet, ut voluit. Lat. PERSIUS. "Is there any man free, except him who has the power of passing his life in what manner he pleases?" —It is the very essence of freedom, that each man shall do whatever he likes, without injury to another.

Ante bellum. Lat.—"Before the war."

Ante tubam trepidat. Lat.—"He trembles before the trumpet or charge is sounded."—His fears anticipate the danger.

Antiquâ homo virtute ac fide. Lat. TERENCE.—"A man of ancient virtue and fidelity."—Of that honesty and good faith which is represented in all ages, as belonging solely to the elder times.

Antiquam obtinens. Lat.—"Possessing antiquity."

A outrance. Fr.—"To the utmost."—*Combat à outrance*, a desperate battle.

A parte antè. Lat.—Relating to something which preceded.—Eternity *a parte antè*, "a past eternity."

A pas de geant. Fr.—"With a giant's stride."

A peindre. Fr.—"A model for a painter."

Apertè mala cùm est mulier, tum demum est bona. Lat. Prov.—"When a woman is openly bad, she then is at the best."—Her avowal is preferable to her hypocrisy.

Aperto vivere voto. Lat. PERSIUS.—"To live with every wish expressed."

Apparent rari nantes in gurgite vasto. Lat. VIRGIL.—"They appear thinly scattered and swimming in the vast deep."—This phrase, originally used to describe the mariners surviving a shipwreck, is now critically applied to a work where the few thoughts of value are nearly whelmed in a mass of baser matter.

Appetitus rationi parent. Lat.—"Let the appetite or desire be obedient to reason."

A posteriori. Lat.—"From the latter," and,

A priori. Lat.—"From the former"—in the first instance.—Phrases which are used in logical argument, to denote a reference to its different modes. The schoolmen distinguish them into the *propter quod*, wherein an effect is proved from the next cause, as when it is proved that the moon is eclipsed, because the earth is then between the sun and the moon. This second is the *quia*, wherein the cause is proved from a remote effect, as that plants do not breathe because they are not animals; or that there is a God from the works of the creation. The former of these is called demonstration *a priori*, the latter demonstration a *posteriori.*

Appuyé. Fr. Milit. Term.—"The point to lean on."—The support, the strength, the defence.

Apropos. Fr.—"To the purpose; seasonably."—It has struck me *apropos.*

Apropos de rien. Fr.—"Apropos of nothing."—An absurd allusion.

Aptat se pugnæ. Lat. Virgil.—"He prepares himsel for the battle."

Apud fimum odorum vaporem spargis. Lat. Prov. "You sprinkle your odours over the dunghill."—You labour to adorn a subject unworthy of the pains.

Aqua fortis.—"Strong water,"—*Aqua regia.*—"Royal water."—Two chemical preparations well known for their solution of metals. The latter (which is a compound of the nitric and muriatic acids) is so called, because it will dissolve gold, which has been termed a royal metal.

Aquila non capit muscas. Lat. Prov.—"An eagle does not catch flies."—A great mind does not stoop to low, or little pursuits.

Aranearum telas texere. Lat.—"To weave a spider's web."—Metaphorically taken—to maintain a sophistical argument.

Arbiter elegantiarum. Lat.—"The arbitrator of the elegancies"—The person whose judgment decides on all matters of taste and form. A judge of propriety—a master of ceremonies.

Arbore dejectâ, quivis ligna colligit. Lat. Juv.—"When the tree is thrown down, any person may gather the wood."—It is in the power of the meanest to triumph over fallen greatness.

Arcades ambo,
Et cantare pares, et respondere parati.
Lat. Virgil.
"Both Arcadians, and both equally skilled in the opening song and in the response."—The poet speaks of two contending shepherds. The quotation is applied however to disputants of another description, either to intimate that they are closely matched, or that they are playing, as the phrase is, into each other's hands.

Arcana imperii. Lat.—"State secrets."—The mysteries of government.

Arcanum. Lat.—"A Secret."—The grand *arcanum*—the philosopher's stone.

Arcanum demens detegit ebrietas. Lat. Virgil.—"Mad drunkenness discloses every secret."—All reserve is laid aside in moments of intoxication.

Αρχη ημισυ παντος. *Arche hemisu pantos.* Gr. Hesiod.—"The beginning is the half of the whole."

Arcum intensio frangit, animum remissio. Lat. Syrus.—"Straining breaks the bow, and relaxation the mind."

Ardentia verba. Lat.—"Glowing words."—Expressions of uncommon force and energy.

A rez de chaussée. Fr.—"Even with the ground."

Argent comptant. Fr. "Ready money."—For immediate payment.

Argilla quidvis imitaberis udâ. Lat. Horace.—"You will easily model any thing from the moist clay."—This is one of the numerous apophthegms which insist on the advantage of early impressions

Argumentum ad crumenam. Lat.—"An argument to the purse."—An appeal to our interest.

Argumentum ad hominem. Lat.—"An argument to the man."—An argument which derives its strength from its personal application.

Argumentum ad ignorantiam. Lat.—An argument founded on the ignorance of facts or circumstances, shown by your adversary.

Argumentum ad judicium. Lat.—"An argument to the judgment."—An appeal made, according to LOCKE, to proofs drawn from any of the foundations of knowledge.

Argumentum ad verecundiam. Lat.—"An argument to the modesty."—An appeal to the decency of your opponent.

Argumentum baculinum. Lat.—"The argument of the staff."—Club law.—Conviction *per* force.

Αριϛον μετρον. Gr. *Ariston metron.*—"A mean is best in every thing."—This was the saying of CLEOBULUS, one of the seven wise men of Greece.

Arma tenenti omnia dat, qui justa negat. Lat. LUC.—"He who refuses justice to the defenceless, will make every concession to the powerful."

Armati terram exercent, semperque recentes
Convectare juvat prædas, et vivere rapto.
Lat. VIRGIL.

"In arms they ravage the earth, and it is their delight to collect the recent spoil, and live on plunder."

Ars est celare artem. Lat.—"The art is to conceal the art."—In every practical science, as in painting or acting, for instance, the great effort of the artist is, to conceal from the spectator the means by which the effect is produced.

Ars est sine arte, cujus principium est mentiri, medium laborare, et finis mendicare. Lat.—This is a most happy definition of the business of alchemy, or the vain search after the philosopher's stone.—"It is an art without art, which has its beginning in falsehood, its middle in toil, and its end in poverty."

Artes honorabit. Lat.—"He will honour the arts."

Asperæ facetiæ, ubi nimis ex vero traxere, acrem sui memoriam relinquunt. Lat. Tacitus.—"A bitter jest, when the satire comes too near the truth, leaves a sharp sting behind."

Asperius nihil est humili, cum surgit in altum. Lat. Claudian.—"Nothing is more disagreeable than a man of mean origin raised into power."

Aspettare, e non venire,
Stare in letto, e non dormire,
Servire, e non gradire,
Son tre cose di far morire. Ital. Prov.—
"To expect one who does not come—to lie a-bed and not to sleep—to serve and not to be advanced, are three things enough to kill a man."

Aspirat primo fortuna labori. Lat. Virgil.—"Fortune smiles upon our first attempt."

Assumpsit. Law Term.—"He assumed—he took upon him to pay."—An action on a verbal promise.

Astra castra, numen lumen. Lat.—"The stars my camp, the Deity my light."

Astra regunt homines, sed regit astra Deus. Lat.—"The stars govern men, but God governs the stars."

A tâtons. Fr.—"Groping."

A tort et à travers. Fr.—"At wrong and across."—At random.

Atria hominibus plena sunt, amicis vacua. Lat Sen.—"The courts of kings are filled with *men*, but are entirely without *friends*."—They are hot houses of intrigue and ambition, in which sincere friendship never flourishes.

At pulchrum est digito monstrari et dicier hic est. Lat. Persius.—"It is pleasing to be pointed at with the finger, and to have it said, There goes the man."—In our several pursuits we are all actuated by a wish for notoriety.

At qui sunt ii qui Rempublicam occupavere? Hom-

ines sceleratissimi, immani avaritiâ, nocentissimi, iidemque superbissimi. Lat. SALLUST.—"But who are those that have seized on the commonwealth?—Men the most profligate, of insatiable avarice, and whose guilt is only equalled by their insolence."

At spes non fracta. Lat.—"But hope is not broken."

Au bon droit. Fr.—"To the just right."

Au bout du compte. Fr.—"At the end of the account."—After all.

Auctor pretiosa facit. Lat.—"The giver makes the gift more precious."

Aucun chemin de fleurs ne conduit à la gloire. Fr. LA FONTAINE,—"The path that leads to glory is never strewed with flowers."

Audaces fortuna juvat timidosque repellit. Lat.—"Fortune assists the bold, and repels the coward."

Audacter et sincerè. Lat.—"Boldly and sincerely."

Audax omnia perpeti,
Gens humana ruit per vetitum nefas.
Lat. HORACE.

"Daring to every extent of guilt, the human race rushes to perpetrate every thing that is wicked and forbidden."—This often forms a motto to some discourse or *tirade* against the wickedness of the age.

Aude aliquid brevibus Gyaris et carcere dignum,
Si vis esse aliquis—Probitas laudatur et alget.
Lat. JUVENAL.

"Dare to do something worthy of transportation and imprisonment, if you mean to be of consequence.—Virtue is praised, but freezes."

Audendo magnus tegitur timor. Lat. LUCAN.—"Fear is often concealed by a show of daring."—The coward blusters to disguise his terrors.

Audentes fortuna juvat. Lat. VIRGIL.—"Fortune assists the bold."—Intrepidity will generally insure success.

Audi alteram partem. Lat. Prov.—"Hear the other party."—Listen to what is said on both sides.

Audire est operæ pretium. Lat. HORACE.—"It is

worth your while to hear."—What I am about to disclose is worthy of your attention.

Auditâ querelâ. Lat. Law phrase.—"The complaint being heard."—A writ which lies where a person has any thing to plead, without having a day in court to make his plea.

Auditque vocatus Apollo. Lat. VIRGIL.—"And Apollo hears when called upon."—When the God of poesy has not been fruitlessly invoked.

Au fait. Fr.—"Skilful, competent to."—He is *au fait* in that matter—he is well skilled in it, or master of it.

A fond. Fr.—"To the bottom."—I knew the man *à fond*—I understand his character thoroughly.

Aula Regis. Lat.—"The King's court."—A court which accompanied the king wherever he travelled. This was the original of the present Court of King's Bench.

Au pis aller. Fr.—"At the worst."—Let the worst come to the worst.

Au plaisir fort de Dieu. Fr.—"At the strong disposal of God."

Aura popularis. Lat.—"The popular gale."—The favouring breeze of public approbation.

Aurea mediocritas. Lat.—"The golden mean."—The happy intermediate state between pomp and poverty.

Auream quisquis mediocritatem
Diligit, tutus caret obsoleti
Sordibus tecti; caret invidendâ
Sobrius aula. Lat. HORACE.—
"Whoever is fond of the golden medium, is serene, and exempted equally from the filth of an old mansion, and from the cares of an envious court."—The greatest share of human happiness is placed in the condition of mediocrity.

Auribus teneo lupum. Lat. TERENCE.—"I hold a wolf by the ears."—I know not how to quit or to retain my hold with safety.—This is similar to our English phrase of "catching a Tartar."

Auri sacra fames. Lat. VIRGIL.—"The accursed thirst of gold."—See the phrase at length, *Quia non mortalia pectora &c.*

Auro pulsa fides, auro venalia jura;
Aurum lex sequitur, mox sine lege pudor.
Lat. PROP.—

"By gold all good faith has been banished; by gold our rights are abused: the law itself follows gold, and soon there will be an end of every modest restraint."—The spirit of venality appears to have loosened all the bonds of society.

Aurum e stercore.—"Gold from dung."—Valuable knowledge extracted from literary rubbish.

Aurum omnes, victa pietate, colunt. Lat. PROP.—"All men now worship gold, all other reverence being done away."—The age is become so venal, that nothing is respected but wealth and its possessors.

Aurum potabile. Lat.—"Liquid, or drinkable gold."—Some quacks in ancient times pretended that they could form by a solution of this metal, a *panacea*, or medicine which should cure all diseases.

Auspicium melioris ævi. Lat.—"A pledge of better times."

Aussitôt dit, aussitôt fait. Fr. Prov.—"No sooner said than done."

Aut amat, aut odit mulier; nil est tertium. Lat. SYRUS—"A woman either loves or hates; there is no medium."—Her passions are ever in extremes.

Autant en emporte le vent. Fr.—"So much the wind carries away."—This is all idle talk.

Aut Cæsar, aut nullus Lat.—"He will be CÆSAR or nobody."—Equivalent to "neck or nothing."

Aut insanit homo, aut versus facit. Lat. HORACE.—"The man is either mad, or he is making verses."

Aut nunquam tentes aut perfice. Lat.—"Either never attempt, or accomplish what you undertake."

Auto de fè. Sp.—"An act of faith."—The name given, in Spain and Portugal, to the broiling of Jews and heretics for the love of God!

Autrefois acquit. Fr.—"Formerly acquitted."—A plea by which the culprit states that he has been tried before for the same offence, and found *not guilty*.

Autumnus libitinæ quæstus acerbæ. Lat. Juv.—"The autumn is the harvest of greedy death."—It has always been considered as the most unhealthy season.

Auxilia humilia firma consensus facit. Lat. Lab.—"Union gives firmness and solidity to the humblest means."—Small states, when they coalesce with unanimity, are strong.

Avalanche. Fr.—A large mass of snow and ice—such frequently detach themselves, and slide or roll down the sides of the Alps, and other high mountains, sometimes burying whole villages with their inhabitants.

Avant courier. Fr.—"A forerunner."

A verbis legis non est recedendum. Lat. Law Maxim.—"There is no departing from the words of the law."—The judges are not to make any interpretation contrary to the express words of the statute.

Aviendo pregonado vino, venden vinagre. Sp. Prov.—"After having cried up their wine, they sell us vinegar."

A vinculo matrimonii. Lat.—"From the chain or tie of marriage."—A final divorce.

Avi numerantur avorum. Lat.—"They exhibit a long line of ancestors."

Avise le fin. Fr.—"Consider the end."

Avito viret honore. Lat.—"He flourishes with hereditary honours."—With honours transmitted from his ancestry.

A vostra salute. Ital. } "To your health."
A votre santé. Fr. }

Aymez loyauté. Fr.—"Love loyalty"

B

Bas bleu. Fr —"A blue-stocking."—A female who plunges into literature and criticism, to the neglect of the other duties of her sex."

Basis virtutum constantia. Lat.—"Steadiness is the foundation of all virtue."

Bastardus nullius est filius, aut filius populi. Lat. Law Maxim.—"A bastard is the son of no man, or the son of the people."—A bastard being born out of marriage, his father is not known by the law. He is therefore in law as no man's issue, it being regarded as uncertain from whom he is descended.

Beau idéal. Fr.—"Ideal beauty."—A species of beauty created by fancy, and existing in the imagination alone.

Beau monde. Fr.—"The gay world."—The world of fashion.

Beaux esprits. Fr.—"Gay spirits."—Men of wit."

Bella femina che ride, vuol dir, borsa che piange. Ital. Prov.—"The smiles of a pretty woman are the tears of the purse."—The latter must be drained to insure the continuance of the former.

Bella! horrida bella! Lat.—"Wars! horrid wars!"

Bella matronis detestata. Lat. Horace.—"Wars detested by matrons"—by orphans, widows, &c.—by all but ambitious ministers, commissaries, contractors, *et id genus omne.*

Bellum internecinum. Lat.—"A war of mutual destruction."—A war to be continued until one or other of the contending parties be ruined or exterminated.

Bellum lethale. Lat.—"A deadly war."—The sense is nearly similar to that of the preceding phrase.

Bellum nec timendum, nec provocandum. Lat. Pliny.—"War is neither to be timidly shunned, nor unjustly to be provoked.

Bellum pax rursus. Lat. Ter.—"A war and again a

peace."—Alternate warfare and reconciliation—applied by the author to the disputes between lovers.

Beneficia dare qui nescit, injustè petit. Lat. Prov.—"He who knows not how to confer a kindness is unworthy to receive one."

Beneficium accipere libertatem vendere est. Lat. LABERIUS.—"To accept of a benefit is to sell your liberty."

Benigno numine. Lat.—"By the favour of Providence."—This is the motto of the first founder of the house of CHATHAM.

Benignus etiam dandi causam cogitat. Lat. Prov. —"The benevolent man even seeks for an opportunity of giving."

Ben trovato. Ital.—"Well found."—An ingenious solution—a happy suggestion.

Ben vienes, si vienes solo. Spanish Prov.—"Thou comest well, if thou comest alone."—Spoken of a misfortune.

Bis dat, qui cito dat. Lat. Prov.—"He gives twice, who gives soon."—A promptitude in giving heightens a favour which may be depreciated by delay.

Bis est gratum quod opus est, si ultro offeras. Lat. Prov.—"That which is necessary is doubly grateful, if you offer it unsolicited."—Spontaneous bounty is ever most acceptable.

Bis peccare in bello non licet. Lat. Prov.—"It is not permitted to err twice in war."—In hostile operations, an error is to be prevented by as much caution, as if it were irretrievable.

Bis vincit, qui se vincit in victoria. Lat. SYRUS.—"He conquers twice, who restrains himself in victory."—He subdues his enemy by his valour, and himself by his moderation.

Bœotûm in crasso jurares aëre natum. Lat. HOR.—"You would swear that he was born in the thick air of the Bœotians."—The people of the Greek province of Bœotia were proverbially remarkable for their stupidity.

Bona fide. Lat.—" In good faith."—Actually, in reality.

Bona malis paria non sunt, etiam pari numero. Lat. Pliny.—" The enjoyments of this life are not equal to its evils, even if equal in number."

Bonarum rerum consuetudo pessima est. Lat. Syrus. —" The too constant use even of good things is hurtful."—We should restrain ourselves so as to *use*, but not to *abuse* our enjoyments.

Bon avocat, mauvais voisin. Fr. Prov.—" A good lawyer is a bad neighbour."—One of the popular satires on the professors of the law.

Bon grè, mal grè. Fr.—" With a good or ill grace."—Whether the party wills it or not.

Bonhommie. Fr.—" Goodnature."

Boni pastoris est tondere pecus, non deglubere. Lat. Suetonius.—" It is the part of a good shepherd to shear his flock, but not to flay them."

Bon jour, bonne œuvre. Fr.—" A good day, a good work."—This corresponds with the English proverb—" The better day, the better deed."

Bonis nocet, quisquis pepercerit malis. Lat. Syrus.— " He injures good men, who spares the wicked."

Bonis quod benefit, haud perit. Lat. Plaut.—" The kindness, which is bestowed on the good, is never lost."

Bon mot. Fr.—" A good word."—A witticism.

Bonne bouche. Fr.—" A nice morsel—a delicate bit." —Something reserved as a gratification.

Bonne et belle assez. Fr.—" Good and handsome enough."

Bonne renommée vaut mieux que ceinture dorée. Fr. Prov.—" A good name is better than a girdle of gold."—Is preferable to wealth or splendour.

Bonos viros sequar, etiamsi ruant. Lat. Cic.—" I will adhere to the counsel of good men, although misfortune or death should be the consequence."

Bonum est fugienda aspicere in alieno malo. Lat. Syrus.—" It is well for those who can infer from the misfortune of others what are the things which they should avoid."

Bonum, magis cărendo, quam fruendo, cernitur. Lat. Prov.—" That which is good is descried more strongly in its absence than in its enjoyment."

Bonum summum, quo tendimus omnes. Lat. LUCRETIUS.—" That supreme good to which we all aspire."

Bonum virum facile dixeris—magnum libenter. Lat.—" You would readily pronounce him a good man, and willingly, a great one."

Bonus Lat.—A consideration for something received. This is usually applied to the monies, &c. paid by banks or other corporate bodies for their charters.

Bonus Textuarius est bonus Theologus. Lat.—" A good Textuarist is a good Theologian."

Boutez en avant. Fr.—" Push forward."

Brevis esse laboro, obscurus fio. Lat.—" I labour to be short, and I become obscure."—A phrase applied to authors, who, aiming at terseness, leave so much unexplained as to become obscure to their readers.

Brutum fulmen. Lat.—" A harmless thunderbolt." —A loud but ineffectual menace. A law which is not respected or obeyed. His discourse was a mere *brutum fulmen*—" it was full of sound and fury, signifying nothing."

C

Cacoëthes. Gr.—Literally, an evil habit or custom. It is never quoted alone, but always in combination with some other word, as in the three instances which follow.

Cacoëthes carpendi.—" A rage for collecting."—Also for censuring.

Cacoëthes loquendi.—" A rage for speaking."—A wish or itching frequently to speak in public.

Cacoëthes scribendi.—" An itch for writing."—He has the *Cacoëthes scribendi*—He is an arrant scribbler.

Cadit quæstio. Lat.—" The question falls or drops to

the ground."—If matters be as stated, *cadit quæstio*,—the point at issue will not admit of a farther discussion.

Cæca invidia est, nec quidquam aliud scit quam detrectare virtutes. Lat. LIVY.—"Envy is blind, and she has no other quality than that of detracting from virtue."

Cæca regens vestigia filo. Lat. VIRGIL.—"Directing his doubtful steps by a thread."—Theseus, by means of a *clue of thread*, furnished by Ariadne, penetrated the Cretan Labyrinth, and killed the Minotaur. The phrase is generally used with reference to a person engaged in an intricate and cautious business.

Cætera desunt. Lat.—"The remainder is wanting."

Cæteris paribus. Lat.—"All other things being equal."—The circumstances being the same in both cases.

Calamitosus est animus futuri anxius. Lat. SENECA.—"Dreadful is the state of that mind which is deeply concerned for the future."

Canaille. Fr.—"The rabble—the multitude."

Candida pax homines, trux decet ira feras. Lat. OVID.—"Fair peace becomes men; ferocious anger should belong to beasts."

Candidè et constanter. Lat.—"Candidly and constantly."

Candor dat viribus alas. Lat.—"Truth gives wings to strength"

Canes timidi vehementius latrant. Lat. Proverb.—"Cowardly dogs bark the most loudly."

Cantabit vacuus coram latrone viator. Lat. JUV.—"The pennyless traveller will sing before the robber."

Cap à pié. Norm. Fr.—"From head to foot."

Capias. Law Lat.—"You may take."—A writ to authorize the capture or taking of the defendant. It is divided into two sorts, *viz.*

Capias ad respondendum.—"You take to answer."—A writ issuing to take the defendant for the purpose of making him answerable to the plaintiff; and,

Capias ad satisfaciendum.—"You take to satisfy." —A writ of execution after judgment, empowering the officer to take and detain the body of the defendant until satisfaction be made to the plaintiff.

Captum te nidore suæ putat ille culinæ. Lat. JUVENAL.—"He thinks that you are taken with the smell of his kitchen."—He is inclined to regard you as a parasite.

Caput mortuum. Lat.—"The dead head."—In chemistry, the ashes remaining in the crucible.—Figuratively, "the worthless remains."

Caret initio et fine. Lat.—"It wants both beginning and end"—both head and tail.—It is a sheer absurdity.

Caret periculo, qui etiam tutus cavet. Lat. SYRUS.—"He is most free from danger, who, even when safe, is on his guard."—A proverb which very happily illustrates the advantages arising from vigilance.

Carpe diem, quam minimè credula postero. Lat. HOR.—"Enjoy the present day, distrusting that which is to follow."—This is one of the maxims of the *Epicurean* school, which recommended the immediate enjoyment of pleasure in preference to remote speculation.

Carpere et colligere. Lat.—"To pluck, and bind together."

Carte blanche. Fr.—"A blank sheet of paper."—To give a *carte blanche,* is when one party is so far reduced as to sign his name to a blank paper, and to leave the other to prescribe the conditions. It imports of course, an "unconditional submission."

Car tel est notre plaisir. Fr.—"For such is our pleasure."—This was anciently the form of a regal ordinance, under the Norman line. It is now used, but in an ironical sense, to mark some act of despotic authority.

Cassis tutissima virtus. Lat. HOR.—"Virtue is the safest helmet."—the most secure defence.

Castigat ridendo mores. Lat.—" It corrects our morals, by holding up to ridicule our vices and follies."

Castrant alios, ut libros suos, per se graciles, alieno adipe suffarciant. Lat. Jovius.—" They castrate the books of other men, in order that with the fat of their works they may lard their own lean volumes."—Applied to plagiarists, in whose works whatever is good is found to be stolen.

Casus fœderis. Lat.—" An extinction of the league or agreement."

Casus omissus. Law Lat.—" An omitted case."—A contingency not provided for by law.

Casus, quem sæpe transit, aliquando invenit. Lat. Prov.—" Him whom chance frequently passes over, it at some time finds."—The continuance of good fortune forms no ground of ultimate security.

Catalogue raisonnée. Fr.—A catalogue of books, or other articles, giving a somewhat detailed description of each, with an estimate of its merit or value.

Causa et origo est materia negotii. Lat. Law Max.—" The cause and beginning is the matter of the business."—Every man has a right to enter into a ta vern, and every lord to distrain his tenant's beasts; but if in the former case a riot ensues, or if in the latter the landlord kills the distress, the law will infer that they entered for these purposes, and deem them trespassers from the beginning.

Causa latet, vis est notissima. Lat.—" The cause is unknown, but the effect is most powerfully felt."

Cave à signatis. Lat.—" Beware of those who are marked."

Caveat actor. Lat. Law Maxim.—" Let the actor or doer beware."—Let him look to the consequences of his own conduct. If a landlord gives an acquit tance to his tenant for the rent which is last due, the presumption is, that all rent in arrear has been duly discharged.

Caveat emptor. Lat.—" Let the buyer beware."—Let the person concerned be on his guard.

Cave quid dicis, quando, et cui. Lat.—"Be cautious what you say, when, and to whom."

Cavendo tutus. Lat.—"Safe by caution."

Cavendum est ne major pœna, quam culpa, sit; et ne iisdem de causis alii plectantur, alii ne appellenter quidem. Lat. CICERO.—"Care should be taken in all cases, that the punishment do not exceed the guilt; and also that some men may not suffer for offences, which others commit with impunity."

Cedant arma togæ, concedat laurea linguæ. Lat.—"Let arms yield to the gown, and the laurel give way to the tongue."—The power of eloquence is sometimes superior to military force.

Cede Deo. Lat. VIRGIL.—"Yield to Providence."—Submit, where all opposition must be vain.

Cede repugnanti, cedendo victor abibis. Lat. OVID—"Yield to the opposer, by yielding you will obtain the victory."—There are circumstances, under which, a prudent concession is equal to an advantage gained over your opponent.

Cedite Romani scriptores, cedite Graii. Lat.—"Yield, ye Roman, and yield, ye Greek writers." Yield to a competitor who outweighs you all. This is a quotation generally employed in an ironical sense.

Cela va sans dire. Fr.—"That passes without comment."—It follows of course.

Celui qui se défait de son bien, avant que de mourir, se prépare à bien souffrir. Fr.—"He that parts with his property before his death, prepares himself for much suffering."—He will have to encounter a degree of insolent neglect, which he might have avoided by keeping his property at his own disposal.

Ce monde est plein de fous, et qui n'en veut pas voir,
Doit se renfermer seul, et casser son miroir.
Fr. BOILEAU.—
"This world is full of fools, and he who would not wish to see one, must not only shut himself up alone, but also break his looking glass."

Ce qu'on nomme liberalité, n'est souvent que la vanité de donner, que nous aimons mieux que ce que nous donnons. Fr. Rochefoucault.—"That which is called liberality is frequently nothing more than the vanity of giving, of which we are more fond than of the thing given."

Celui qui a trouvé un bon gendre, a gagné, un fils; mais celui qui en a rencontré un mauvais, a perdu une fille. Fr.—"The man who has got a good son-in-law, has gained a son; but he who has found a bad one, has lost a daughter."

C'en est fait. Fr.—"It is all over."—*C'en est fait de lui.* He is a ruined man.

Ce n'est pas être bien aise que de rire. Fr. St. Evremond.—"Laughing is not always a proof that the mind is at ease, or in composure."

Cent' ore di maliconia non pagano un quattrino di debito. Ital. Prov.—"An hundred hours of vexation will not pay one farthing of debt."

Ce qui vient par la flute, s'en va par le tambour. Fr. Prov.—"What comes by the flute, goes away by the tabourin."—Easy got—easy gone.

Ce qui manque aux orateurs en profondeur,
Ils vous le donnent en longueur.
Fr. Montesquieu.—
"What our orators want in *depth*, they give you in *length*."

Cernit omnia Deus vindex. Lat.—"There is an avenging God who sees all."

Certiorari. Law Lat.—"To be made more certain."—A writ issuing to order the record of a cause, to be brought before a superior court.

Certum pete finem. Lat.—"Keep a certain end in view."

Ces discours, il est vrai, sont fort beaux dans un livre. Fr. Boileau.—"All this would do very well for a book." *i. e.* It is very showy in theory, but not reducible to practice.

Ce sont toujours les avanturiers, qui font des grandes choses, et non pas les souverains des grandes empires. Fr. MONTESQUIEU.—"It is only adventurers that perform great actions, and not the sovereigns of large empires."

Cessante causa, cessat et effectus. Lat. Law Maxim. —"When the cause is removed, the effect must cease also."—Thus the release of a debt is a discharge also of the execution.

C'est le crime qui fait la honte, et non pas l'échafaud. Fr. CORNEILLE.—"It is the guilt, not the scaffold, which constitutes the shame."—These were the last words of the heroine CORDET, when, by depriving the miscreant MARAT of life, she had ridden the earth of a monster.

C'est le ton qui fait la musique. Fr.—"It is the tone that makes the music."—By this it is intimated, that as much depends on the *tone* and manner in which words are employed, on certain occasions, as on the words themselves.

C'est la prosperité qui donne les amis, mais c'est l'adversité qui les épreuve Fr.—"It is prosperity that gives us friends, but it is adversity that tries them."

C'est là le diable. Fr. Phrase.—"There is the devil." —There lies the whole difficulty.

C'est une grande habilité que de savoir cacher son habilité. Fr. ROCHEFOUCAULT.—"The greatest skill is shown in disguising our skill."—See "*Ars est celare artem.*"

C'est une grande folie de vouloir être sage tout seul. Fr. ROCHEFOUCAULT.—"It is a great folly to think of being wise alone."—None but a fool can suppose that he has a monopoly of good sense.

C'est le père aux écus. Fr. Phrase.—"He is the father of the crowns."—He is the monied man.

C'est pour l'achéver de peindre. Fr. Phrase—"This is to finish his picture."—This is to complete his ruin.

C'est une autre chose. Fr. Phrase.—"It is quite a different thing."—The facts completely differ from the statement.

C'est une bague au doigt. Fr. Phrase.—"It is a ring on your finger."—It is as good as ready money.

C'est un sot à vingt-quatre carats. Fr. Phrase.—"He is a fool of twenty-four carats."—His folly is absolutely without any *alloy.*

Ceux qui n'aiment pas, ont rarement de grandes joyes; ceux qui aiment ont souvent de grandes tristesses. Fr. Prov.—"Those who do not love, seldom feel great enjoyments; those who do love, are frequently liable to deep sorrows."

Chacun à son gout. Fr. Phrase.—"Every man to his taste."—A proverbial remark in every language, on the prevailing diversity of choice and opinion.

Chacun dit du bien de son cœur, et personne n'en ose dire de son esprit. Fr. ROCHEFOUCAULT.—"Every man speaks of the goodness of his heart, but no man dares to speak in the same manner of his wit."

Chaque oiseau trouve son nid beau. Fr. Phrase.—"Every bird thinks his own nest handsome."—We are all most inclined to commend that which is our own.

Chasse-cousin. Fr.—"Chase-cousin."—Bad wine, such as is given for the purpose of driving away poor relations.

Chat échaudé craint l'eau froide. Fr. Prov.—"A scalded cat dreads cold water."—This is a saying rather more pregnant than the English—"A burnt child dreads the fire."

Chef d'œuvre. Fr.—"A master-piece."—An unrivaled performance.

Che sarà sarà. Ital. Prov.—"Whatever will be, will be."

Chevalier d'industrie. Fr.—"A knight of industry."—A man who lives by ingenious and persevering fraud.

Chevaux de frize. Fr. Milit. Term.—Stakes sharpened at each end, and fastened by the middle across each other to stop the progress of cavalry.

Chi non sa niente, non dubita de niente. Ital. Prov —"He who knows nothing, doubts of nothing."

Chi t'ha offeso non te perdonera mai. Ital. Prov.—"The man who has offended you will never forgive you."

Cicerone. Ital.—A name given, in Italy, to those who accompany strangers to view the curiosities of a city.

Ciencia es locura si buen senso no la cura. Span Prov.—"Science or learning is of little use, if it be not under the direction of good sense."

Cineres credis curare sepultos? Lat.—"Do you think that the ashes of the dead can by this be affected?"—Do you think that they feel sensible of the regard or contempt of the living?

Citius venit periculum cum contemnitur. Lat. LABERIUS.—"The danger arrives the sooner which is despised."—The false contempt of an enemy naturally leads to insecurity.

Civitas ea autem in libertate est posita, quæ suis stat viribus, non ex alieno arbitrio pendet. Lat. LIVY.—"That state alone is free which rests upon its own strength, and depends not on the arbitrary will of another."

Clair-obscur. Ital.—In painting, the art of distributing the lights and shadows to produce the most pleasing effect.

Clarior è tenebris. Lat.—"More bright from obscurity."

Clarum et venerabile nomen gentibus, et multum nostræ quod proderat urbi. Lat.—"An illustrious and venerable name among the nations, and which was eminently useful to our country."—This eulogium, though spoken of another, could never have been more applicable than to our Washington and Franklin.

Clausum fregit. Law Lat.—"He broke through the enclosure."—A name given by a fiction of law to an action for debt, in which such a trespass is supposed to have taken place

Clericus clericum non decimat. Lat.—"A clergyman does not take tythes from a clergyman."

Cœlum non animum mutant, qui trans mare cur runt. Lat. HORACE. "Those who cross the seas change their climate, but not their mind."—That maxim of the poet is meant to enforce, that weak minds can derive but little advantage from the survey of foreign countries—or, in another sense, that the guilty can not leave *themselves* behind.

Cogenda mens est, ut incipiat. Lat. SENECA.—"Compulsion must be used on the mind to impel it to exertion."

Cogi qui potest, nescit mori. Lat. SENECA.—"The man who can be compelled, knows not how to die."—He who is fearless of death may smile at the menace of compulsion.

Cognovit actionem. Lat. Law Maxim.—"He has acknowledged the action."—This in law is where a defendant confesses the plaintiff's cause of action against him to be just and true; and after issue, suffers judgment to be entered against him without trial.

Colubrum in sinu fovere. Lat. ÆSOP.—"To cherish a snake in your bosom."—To suffer a secret enemy to partake of your confidence.

Comes jucundus in viâ pro vehiculo est. Lat. PUBL. SYR.—"An agreeable companion on a journey serves in the place of a carriage."—His conversation will shorten the way, and beguile the fatigue.

Comitas inter gentes. Lat.—"Politeness between nations."—That mutual consideration which is due from one civilized nation to another, which interferes even in their conflicts, and mitigates the asperities of warfare.

Comme le voilà accommodé. Fr. Prov.—"How finely he is fitted!"—What a pickle he is in!

Comme il faut. Fr.—"As it should be."—It is done *comme il faut,* it is neatly or properly executed.

Comme je fus. Fr.—"As I was."

Commune bonum.—"A common good."—A matter of mutual or general advantage.

Commune periculum concordiam paret. Lat.—"A common danger produces unanimity."

Communia propriè dicere. Lat. HORACE.—"To express common-place things with propriety."—This is stated by the poet to be the great difficulty of the dramatic author, whose scenes are drawn from middle life.

Communibus annis. Lat.—"One year with another."—On the annual average.

Communi consensu. Lat.—"By common consent."

Communitur bona profundere Deorum est. Lat.—"It is the province of the gods to confer benefits impartially upon all."

Compendiaria res improbitas, virtusque tarda. Lat.—"Wickedness takes the shorter road, and virtue the longer."

Componere lites. Lat.—"To settle the dispute."

Componitur orbis
Regis ad exemplum; nec sic inflectere sensus
Humanos edicta valent, quam vita regentis.
Lat. CLAUDIAN.

"The people are fashioned according to the example of their king; and edicts are of less power than the model which his life exhibits."—The fashions and models take their progress downward, and every thing depends on high example.

Compositum miraculi causâ. Lat. TACITUS.—"A narrative made up only for the sake of the wonder which it may occasion."—One of those fictions, the object of which is less to inform than amaze the reader.

Compos mentis. Law Lat.—"A man of a sound and *composed* mind."—A man in such a state of mind as to be qualified legally to execute a deed.

Comptant comté. Fr.—"The ready money being paid down."

Con amore. Ital.—"With love."—He entered on the

business *còn amore*—with an earnest and particu lar zeal.

Concordia discors. Lat.—" A jarring concord, or dissonant harmony."—Applied to an ill-suited junction of things or persons.

Concordiâ res parvæ crescunt, discordiâ maximæ dilabuntur. Lat. SALLUST.—" By union the smallest states thrive and flourish, by discord the greatest are wasted and destroyed."

Condo et compono quæ mox depromere possim. Lat. HOR.—"I compose and lay up what I may hereafter be able to bring forward."—In my hours of leisure I form those sketches, which study may afterwards improve.

Congè d'èlire. Fr.—" A leave to elect."—The king's permission to a dean and chapter, giving them leave to choose a bishop. This is so far a mere form, as it is always accompanied by a letter, naming the person whom *they must* of course elect.

Conjunctio maris et fœminæ est de jure naturæ. Lat. Law Maxim.—" The conjunction of man and wife is by the law of nature."

Consequitur quodcunque petit. Lat.—" He attains whatever he pursues."

Conscia mens recti, famæ mendacia ridet. Lat. OVID.—" The mind which is conscious of innocence despises the lies of rumour."

Consensus facit legem. Law Maxim.—" Consent makes the law."—When the parties make an agreement, the terms are of their mutual willing, and are no longer a matter of legal consideration, if not against the law.

Consilio et animis. Lat.—" By wisdom and courage."

Constantia et virtute. Lat.—" By constancy and virtue."

Constans et lenis, ut res expostulet, esto. Lat. CATO. —" Be firm or mild, as the occasion may require." —Suit your conduct to the circumstances.

Consuetudo manerii et loci est observanda. Lat. Law

Maxim.—"The custom of the manor and of the place is to be observed."

Consuetudo pro lege servatur. Lat. Law Maxim.—"Custom is to be held as a law."—This and the preceding maxim only go to show the principle that where customs have prevailed from time im memorial, they have obtained the force of laws.

Contemni est gravius stultitiæ, quam percuti. Lat. —"To folly it is more grievous to be despised, than to be struck."—Weak minds will sooner bear an injury than a reproach.

Conte bleu. Fr.—"An idle tale."—A story of a cock and a bull.

Contigit ex merito tibi honor. Lat.—"A well deserved honour has been conferred upon you."

Contra bonos mores. Lat.—"Against good manners or morals."—This quotation is generally used in legal discussions. If the act be not against law, it is an encroachment upon morality.

Contra malum mortis, non est medicamen in hortis. Lat.—"There is no remedy in the apothecary's shop against the disease of death."

Contra stimulum calces. Lat. Terence.—This is best translated by the phrase of St. Paul.—"You kick against the pricks," *i. e.* you attempt a vain opposition.

Contractata jure, contrario jure pereunt. Lat.—"The right or immunity established by one law is subverted by a subsequent and contrary law."

Contre fortune bon cœur. Fr.—"A good heart against fortune."—A common phrase of admonition, to buoy up the spirits in case of disaster.

Contre-temps. Fr.—"A disappointment—a mischance."

Conventio privatorum non potest publico juri derogare. Lat. Law Maxim.—"An agreement between individuals can not set aside the public law."

Coram domino rege. Lat.—"Before our lord the king."

Coram nobis. Lat.—"Before us."—The vulgar say

he was on his *coram nobis*—that is, he was brought before persons of authority.

Coram non judice. Lat.—"Before one who is not a judge."—The matter was *coram non judice*—it was before an improper tribunal.

Cordon. Fr. Milit. Term.—"A line,"—on which troops act and support each other.

Corona civica. Lat.—"A civic crown," or garland of oak, given by the Romans to him who saved the life of a citizen.

Corpora lentè augescunt, cito extinguuntur. Lat. TACITUS.—"Bodies are slow of growth, but are rapid in their dissolution."

Corps diplomatique. Fr.—"The diplomatic body."—The ambassadors of several courts, acting under the *diplomas* which invest them with that character. It is sometimes used in a broader sense, to describe those men who are best acquainted with the diplomatic forms.

Corpus delicti. Law Phrase,—"The body of the crime."—The whole nature of the offence.—The *corpus delicti* in many cases, as in that of a forged promissory note, is especially stated upon the record.

Corpus onustum
Hesternis vitiis, animum quoque prægravat unà. Lat. HORACE.
"The body loaded with yesterday's excess, also bears down the mind."—The effect of dissipation is not only felt corporally, but mentally.

Corpus sine pectore. Lat. HORACE.—"A body without a soul."—A dull and inanimate being.

Corrumpunt bonos mores colloquia prava. Lat. Prov.—"Depraved conversation will corrupt the best morals."—Or, as in the English maxim—"Evil communication &c."

Corruptio optimi pessima Lat.—"The corruption of the best is productive of the worst."

Corruptissimâ in republicâ, plurimæ leges. Lat

Tacitus.—"When the state is most corrupt, then are laws most multiplied."

Cor unum, via una. Lat.—"One heart, one way."

Cosa fatta capo ha. Ital. Prov.—"A thing which is done has a head."

Couleur de rose. Fr.—"Of the colour of the rose"—of the most pleasing nature.

Coup d'essai. Fr.—"A first essay."—An attempt.

Coup de grace. Fr.—"A stroke of mercy."—The stroke which finished the sufferings of those who had been broken on the wheel.

Coup de main. Fr.—"A sudden or bold enterprise."

Coup d'œil. Fr.—"A quick glance of the eye."

Coup de pied. Fr.—"A kick."

Coup de soleil. Fr.—"A stroke of the sun."—An injury done to the head by exposure to the sun.

Courage sans peur. Fr.—"Courage without fear."

Coûte qui coûte. Fr.—"Let it cost what it may."—At any èxpense.

Craignez honte. Fr.—"Fear shame."

Craignez tout d'un auteur en courroux. Fr. Boileau.—"You are to apprehend the worst from an enraged author."—The irritable temper of authors has long been a matter of notoriety.

Cras credemus, hodie nihil. Lat. Prov.—"To-morrow we may believe it, but not to day."—Let us see what time may produce, for we can not credit the present assertion.

Credat Judæus Apella. Lat. Horace.—"Let the circumcised Jew believe it."—A phrase of contemptuous incredulity. The Jews, when this was written, were treated pretty nearly as they are now; they were regarded as the outcasts of every community.

Crede quôd habes, et habes. Lat.—"Believe that you have it, and you have it."

Credite posteri? Lat.—"Will posterity believe?"—Can they be led to think that such absurdities were accredited by their forefathers?

Credo quia impossibile est. Lat.—"I believe it, because it is impossible."

Credula res amor est. Lat. Ovid.—"Love is an affair of credulity."—Those who are in love, believe every idle tale which flatters their expectations.

Crescentem sequitur cura pecuniam,
Majorumque fames. Lat. Hor.—
"The accumulation of wealth is followed by an increase of care, and by an appetite for more."

Crescit amor nummi quantum ipsa pecunia crescit. Lat. Juvenal.
"The love of pelf increases with the pelf."

Crescite et multiplicamini. Lat.—"Increase and multiply."

Crescit eundo. Lat.—"It increases in its course."

Crescit indulgens sibi dirus hydrops. Lat. Hor.—"The fatal dropsy gains on the patient from his gratifying his thirst."

Crescit sub pondere virtus. Lat.—"Virtue grows under the imposed weight."—The idea is taken from the received opinion of the palm-tree, which is said to grow the faster in proportion to the incumbent weight.

Cretâ an carbone notandum. Lat.—"Whether to be marked with chalk or charcoal."—It was in this manner that the superstitious Romans distinguished the lucky and unlucky days.

Crimen falsi. Lat.—"Falsehood, perjury."

Crimen læsæ majestatis. Lat.—"The crime of wronging or injuring majesty."—The guilt of high treason.

Crimina qui cernunt aliorum, non sua cernunt:
Hi sapiunt aliis, desipiuntque sibi. Latin.—
"There are those who can see the faults of others, but who can not discern their own.—Such men are wise for others, and fools to themselves."

Crimine ab uno,
Disce omnes. Lat. Virgil.
"From a single offence, you may learn the nature of them all."

Cruci dum spiro fido. Lat.—"Whilst I breathe, I trust in the cross."

Crudelem medicum intemperans æger facit. Lat. Syrus.—"A disorderly patient makes the physician cruel."—He compels him to use restraints, which would otherwise be unnecessary.

Crux. Lat.—"A cross."—Any thing particularly tormenting or vexatious; thus,

Crux criticorum, medicorum, mathematicorum, &c. —"The greatest difficulty which can occur to critics, physicians, or mathematicians, &c."

Crux est si metuas, quod vincere nequeas. Lat. Auson.—"It is a tormenting thing to fear what you can not overcome."

Cucullus non facit monachum. Lat.—"The cowl does not make the friar."—We are not to judge of the man from his disguise or assumed character.

Cui bono?—"To what (or for whose) good," will it tend?—What is to be the advantage resulting from the measure which you propose?

Cuicunque aliquis quid concedit, concedere videtur et id, sine quo res ipsa esse non potest. Lat. Law Maxim.—"To whomsoever a man grants a thing, he grants that, without which the thing can not be enjoyed."—A person, for instance, selling the timber on his estate, the buyer may cut down the trees and convey them away without being responsible for the injury which the grass may sustain, from carts, &c. during the necessary time of conveyance.

Cui fortuna ipsa cedit. Lat. Cic.—"To whom fortune herself gives way."—Who surmounts every obstacle.

Cuilibet in arte suâ credendum est. Lat. Proverb.—"Every man is to be trusted in his own art."—We should, in general, give credit to men for superior skill in that art, or science, which they have made their peculiar study.

Cui licet quod majus, non debet quod minus est non licere. Lat Law Maxim.—"He to whom the greater thing is lawful, has certainly a right to do the lesser thing."—Thus, if a man has an office to himself and his heirs, he may make an assignee, and, *a fortiori*, he may appoint a deputy.

Cui malo? Lat.—"To what evil" will it tend?—What, or where is the mischief likely to arise from the measure proposed?

Cui prodest scelus, is fecit. Lat. SENECA.—"He has committed the crime, who has derived the profit." —This as a general maxim is true, but not without some exceptions.

Cuivis in arte sua credendum est. Lat.—See "*Cuilibet in arte sua,*" *&c.*

Cujus est solum, ejus est usque ad cœlum. Lat. Law Maxim.—"He who has the property in the soil, has the same up to the sky."—His neighbour must not therefore offend by making any improper projections to impend over his land or tenement.

Cujuslibet rei simulator atque dissimulator. Lat. SALLUST, of CATILINE.—"A man who could, with equal skill, pretend to be what he was not, and not to be, what he really was."—A person deeply versed in the acts of hypocrisy.

Cul de sac. Fr.—"The bottom of a bag."—A difficulty.—An apparent passage but closed at the end.

Cum corpore mentem,
Crescere sentimus, pariterque senescere.
Lat. LUCRET.

"We find that as the mind strengthens with the body, it decays with it in like manner."

Culpa sua damnum sentiens, non intelligitur damnum. Law Lat.—"He who suffers by his own fault, is not to be deemed a sufferer."

Cum fortuna manet, vultum servatis, amici;
Cum cedit, turpi vertitis ora fugâ. Lat. OVID.

"Whilst fortune continues favourable, you have always the countenance of friends; but when she changes, they then turn their backs in shameful flight."

Cum grano salis. Lat.—"With a grain of salt."—

The statement is to be received *cum grano salis,* with some allowance, or in a qualified sense.

Cum licet fugere, ne quære litem. Lat. Prov.—"Do not seek the quarrel or the suit, which there is an opportunity of escaping."—Where there is an outlet, go neither to law nor to logger-heads.

Cum multis aliis, quæ nunc præscribere longum est. Lat.—"With many other matters which it would be now tedious to state."—A summary which is generally placed at the end of a beadroll of indifferent *items,* and in an ironical sense.

Cunctando restituit rem. Lat. ENNIUS.—"He restored his cause by delay."—See "*Unus homo nobis,*" *&c.*

Cupido dominandi cunctis affectibus flagrantior est. Lat. TACITUS.—"The lust of power is the most violent of all the affections of the mind."

Curæ leves loquuntur, ingentes stupent. Lat. SENECA.—"Light griefs may speak, deep sorrow's tongue is bound."—The anguished sufferer is silent, when complaints of a nature less severe are vented most loudly.

Cur ante tubam tremor occupat artus? Lat. VIRG.—"Why should a tremor seize the limbs before the trumpet sounds?"—Wherefore those marks of trepidation before the danger is actually announced?

Curatio funeris, conditio sepulturæ, pompæ exequiarum, magis sunt vivorum solatia, quam subsidia mortuorum. Lat. AUGUSTUS.—"The care of the funeral, the place of burial, and the pomp of obsequies, are consolations to the living, but of no advantage to the dead."

Cur ego amicum offendam in nugis? Lat.—"Why should I offend a friend for a trivial reason?"

Curiosa felicitas. Lat.—These words do not admit of a *literal* translation—they are applied to "a felicity of expression," which belongs only to the poet of nature, and in some fortunate moments.

Cur omnium fit culpa, paucorum scelus? Lat.—"Why should the wickedness of a few be laid to the account of all?"

E

Currente calamo. Lat.—"With a running pen."—Applied to works written with fluency and expedition.

Curtæ nescio quid semper abest rei. Lat. HORACE.—"A nameless something is always wanting to our imperfect fortune."—The most opulent and happy in the eyes of the world, if brought to a frank confession, would acknowledge that they felt some want or deficiency.

Custos morum. Lat.—"The guardian of morality."—Every judge and magistrate is said, and ought, to be a *custos morum.*

Custos rotulorum. Lat.—"The officer who has the custody of the rolls and records of the sessions of peace."

D

Dabit Deus his quoque finem. Lat. VIRGIL.—"Providence will also put an end to these."—Generally spoken of public calamities or inflictions.

Dabitur licentia sumpta prudentur. Lat. HOR.—"An indulgence will be granted, if prudently used."

D'accord. Fr.—"Agreed."—In tune.

Da locum melioribus. Lat. TERENCE.—"Give place to your betters."—Let a due deference be shown to rank, to sex, and to superior station.

Damna minus consueta movent Lat. JUVENAL.—"The afflictions or losses to which we are accustomed affect us less deeply."

Damnant quod non intelligunt. Lat. CIC.—"They condemn what they do not even understand."

Damnosa quid non imminuit dies? Lat. HORACE. "What does not destructive time diminish and impair."—Every work of art and every production of nature is equally liable to injury from the lapse of ages.

Damnum absque injuriâ. Law Lat.—"A loss without an injury."—Thus, the erection of a mill or the establishment of a school in any given place, may occasion a loss to others, but an action for damage can not be maintained.

Damnum appellandum est cum malâ famâ lucrum. Lat.—"The gain which is made at the expense of reputation should rather be set down as a loss."

Dans l'art d'interesser consiste l'art d'écrire. Fr. Delille.—"In the art of interesting, consists the art of writing."

Dans un pays libre, on crie beaucoup quoiqu'on souffre peu; dans un pays de tyrannie, on se plaint peu quoiqu'on souffre beaucoup. Fr. Carnot.—"In a free country there is much clamour with little suffering; in a despotic state there is little complaint, but much grievance."

Dare pondus idonea fumo. Lat. Persius.—"To give weight to smoke."—To give to trifles an air of moment.

Da spatium tenuemque moram; male cuncta ministrat impetus Lat. Statius.—"Allow an interval for deliberation; all things are done badly, that are done with violence and precipitancy."

Data. Lat.—"Things granted."—He proceeds on certain *data*—on premises which have been previously admitted.

Data fata secutus. Lat.—"Following his revealed destiny."

Dat Deus immiti cornua curta bovi. Lat.—"God gives short horns to the mischievous ox."—Providence so curtails the means of the malicious, as to make them fall short of their end.

Date obolum Belisario. Lat.—"Give a farthing to Belisarius."—This great general was reduced to beg in his old age. The phrase is therefore sometimes applied to fallen greatness.

Dat veniam corvis, vexat censura columbas. Lat. Juv.—"Censure pardons the crows, whilst it harasses the doves."—This is a phrase of general use and application. The censorious too often fasten on the innocent, whilst the guilty are suffered to escape.

Davus sum, non Œdipus. Lat. TERENCE.—"I am Davus (a simple servant), and not an Œdipus."—I am not enough of a conjuror to divine the solution of your riddle. Œdipus, according to the Greek fables, had solved the enigma of the Sphinx.

Debito justitiæ. Lat. Law Phrase.—"By debt of justice."—By a claim justly established.

De bonis non. Law Lat.—"Of the goods which have not" been before administered on. An *administrator de bonis non,* is one who is appointed to the administration of such part of an estate as is left unsettled by a removed or deceased executor or administrator.

De bon vouloir servir le roy. Fr.—"To serve the king with good will."

Debouchure. Fr. Military Term.—"The mouth or opening of a strait or river."

Début. Fr.—"First appearance"—on the stage, in public life, &c. &c.

Deceptio visus. Lat.—"A deceiving of the sight."—An illusion practised on the eye.

Decies repetita placebit. Lat HORACE.—"It will continue to please, though ten times repeated."

Decipimur specie recti. Lat. HORACE.—"We are deceived by the appearance of what is right—of rectitude."—Fair appearances are necessary to the purposes of deception.

Decipit
Frons prima multos. Lat. JUVENAL.
"The first appearance deceives many."

Decori decus addit avito. Lat.—"He adds an honour to those of his ancestors."

De die in diem. Lat.—"From day to day."

Dedimus potestatem. Lat.—"We have given power."—A writ in law whereby commission is given to one or more private persons, to assist for the expedition of some act belonging to the judge. The words are used also to denote the commission of a justice of the peace, which begins in the same manner.

Dediscit animus sero quod didicit diu. Lat. Seneca. —"The mind unlearns with difficulty what it has long learned."—Impressions long entertained are not easily erased.

De facto. Lat. Law Phrase.—"From the fact," and,

De jure. Idem.—"From the law."—These opposite phrases are best explained together. In some instances, the penalty attaches on the offender at the instant when the *fact* is committed; in others, not until he is convicted by *law* In the former case, he is guilty *de facto;* in the latter, *de jure.* So, also, a king is said to be such, *de facto*, when *in possession* of the throne (however obtained); and, *de jure*, when he has the hereditary *right*, or is a *legitimate.*

Défaut de la cuirasse. Fr.—"The defective part of the armour,—or, for want of armour."—He was taken *défaut de la cuirasse:* he was attacked on his weak side.

De fide et officio judicis non recipitur quæstio. Lat. Law Maxim.—"No question can be entertained respecting the good intention and duty of the judge."—No presumption against him can be received in the first instance. There must be strong and full proof of malversation.

Degeneres animos timor arguit. Lat. Virgil.— "Fear indicates a degenerate mind."

De gustibus non est disputandum. Lat.—"There is no disputing about tastes."—They are too many, and too various, to be the objects of rational discussion.

De haute lutte. Fr.—"By a violent struggle."—By main force.

De hoc multi multa, omnis aliquid, nemo satis. Lat. —"On this subject, many persons have said much, every body something, and no man enough."

Dei gratia. Lat.—"By the grace of God."—An addition sometimes made by kings to their titles.

Dejeuner à la fourchette. Fr.—"A meat-breakfast."

De jure.—See *De facto.*

De lanâ caprinâ. Lat.—"About goat's wool,"—A dispute, *de lanâ caprinâ,* respecting a matter not worth discussion.

De la Vanite nait la Honte. Fr.—"Vanity is the parent of shame."

Del credere. Italian, for the word *guarantee,* or *warranty,* as applicable to factors; who, for an additional premium, become bound when they sell goods upon credit to warrant the solvency of the parties. This is called a *Commission del credere.*

Delectando pariterque monendo. Lat. HORACE.—"By giving equal pleasure and instruction."—This best praise of an author, this great master has given elsewhere in other words—"*Miscuit utile dulci.*"—He combined that which was *pleasurable* with what was *useful.*

Delenda est Carthago Lat.—"Carthage must be destroyed."—The oft-repeated phrase of a *Roman* senator, tending to provoke the destruction of that rival city.

Deliberandum est diu, quod statuendum semel. Lat. SYRUS.—"That should be maturely considered, which can be decided but once."—Every precaution is necessary where the deed is irrevocable.

Deliberat Roma, perit Saguntum. Lat.—"Rome deliberates, and Saguntum perishes."—We are slow to resolve, whilst our allies are in the extremity of danger.

Deliramenta doctrinæ. Lat.—"The wild speculations or wanderings of learned men."—The fantasies of those whom "too much learning hath made mad."

Délirant reges, plectuntur Achivi. Lat. HORACE.—"When monarchs err, the Greeks (*i. e.* the people) are punished."

Delphinum sylvis appingit, fluctibus aprum.
Lat. HORACE.
"He paints a dolphin in the woods, and a boar in the waves."—He introduces objects which are unsuited to the scene.

De mal en pis. Fr.—"From bad to worse."

De medietate linguæ. Law Lat.—A jury *de medietate linguæ*, is one composed, one half of citizens, and the other of foreigners, for the purpose of trying an alien or foreigner.

De minimis non curat lex. Lat. Law Maxim.—"The law does not regard very minute or trivial affairs."

De monte alto. Lat.—"From a high mountain."

De mortuis nil nisi bonum. Lat.—"Of the dead, let nothing be said but what is *favourable.*"—This long-received maxim is by some not improperly amended by substituting *verum*, for *bonum.*—"Let nothing be said but what is *true.*"

De non apparentibus, et non existentibus eadem est ratio. Lat.—"The reasoning must be the same with respect to things which do not *appear*, as to those which do not *exist.*"

De novo. Lat.—"Anew."—To commence *de novo*—to begin again at the beginning—to do all over again.

Denoûement. Fr.—"The catastrophe, the clearing up of a plot, &c."

Deo adjuvante, non timendum. Lat.—"God assisting, there is nothing to be feared."

Deo date. Lat.—"Give to God."

Deo duce, ferro comitante. Lat.—"My God my guide, and my sword my companion."

Deo favente. Lat.—"With God's favour."

Deo juvante. Lat —"With God's assistance."

Deo volente. Lat.—"God willing."—So many phrases intimating a hope of the aid, or a submission to the will of Providence.

Deo non fortunâ. Lat.—"From God, not fortune."

Deo Opt. Max. An abbreviation of *Deo optimo maximo.* Lat.—"To the most holy and almighty God."

Depôt. Fr. Military Term.—"A store or magazine."

Depressus extollor. Lat.—"Having been depressed, I am exalted."

Dernier resort. Fr.—"The last resource."

Desideratum. Lat.—"A thing desired."—Such a work is a *desideratum* in that branch of literature.

Desinit in piscem, mulier formosa supernè. Lat. Hor.—"A woman elegantly formed above, ending in nothing but a fish."—The idea is taken from the mermaid. The application is to literary works which give the fairest opening promise, and terminate in defect, and deformity.

Désordre de pensées. Fr.—"Confusion of thought, or ideas."

Desperandum. Lat.—"A thing, or event to be despaired of."—Something not to be expected.

Desunt cætera. Lat.—"The remainder is wanting."—Placed at the end of an imperfect work.

Desunt inopiæ multa, avaritiæ omnia. Lat. Syrus.—"Poverty is in want of much, but avarice of every thing."

Deteriores omnes sumus licentia. Lat. Ter.—"We are all the worse for unrestrained indulgence."

Détour. Fr. Military Term.—"A circuitous march."

Detur aliquando otium quiesque fessis. Lat. Sen.—"Let ease and rest be sometimes granted to the wearied."—Let there be due alternations of labour and repose.

Detur dignissimo. Lat.—"Let it be given to the most worthy."

Detur pulchriori. Lat.—"Let it be given to the fairest."—This was the inscription on the apple which fable tells us was adjudged by *Paris* to the goddess *Venus*, to the mortification of *Juno* and *Minerva*.—Let the prize be given to the most deserving.

Deus hæc fortasse benignâ
Reducet in sedem vice. Lat. Horace.
"Perhaps Providence by some happy change will restore things to their proper places."

Deus nobis hæc otia fecit. Lat. Virgil.—"God has given to us this peace or leisure."

De vitâ hominis nulla cunctatio longa est. Lat. Law Maxim.—"When the life of a man is at stake, no delay that is afforded can be too long."—By this humane maxim, it is intimated, that as the effect of a rash sentence can not be recalled, we should pause and deliberate, before we consign a fellow-creature to death.

Dextra dare. Lat.—"To interchange right hands.— To give each other the most solemn assurance either of mutual support, or of mutual reconciliation.

Dictum de dicto. Lat.—"Report upon hearsay."— Vague report.

Dies datus. Lat. Law Term.—"The day given."— The day or time appointed for the answer of the tenant or defendant.

Dies faustus. Lat.—"A lucky day," and,

Dies infaustus. Lat.—"An unlucky day."—These were marked by the superstitious Romans, the former with a *white*, and the latter with a *black* stone.

Dies juridici. Lat. Law Term.—"Court days," or, days on which the law is administered, and,

Dies non. (The word *Juridici* being understood.)— "The *days* on which *no* legal proceedings can take place." These are (in the British courts) all Sundays in the year; the *Purification*, in Hilary term; the *Ascension*, in Easter term; the festival of St. *John* the Baptist, in Trinity term; and those of *All Saints*, and *All Souls*, in Michaelmas term.

Dieu defend le droit. Fr.—"God defends the right."

Dieu et mon droit. Fr.—"God and my right."— The motto of the sovereigns of Great Britain.

Dieu me conduisse. Fr.—"May God conduct me."

Difficile est longum subito deponere amorem. Lat. CATULLUS.
"It is difficult, at once, to relinquish a confirmed passion."

Difficile est satiram non scribere. Lat. JUVENAL.— "It is difficult not to write a satire;"—the times being such as to call for its severest correction.

Difficilem oportet aurem habere ad crimina. Lat. SYRUS.—"One should not lend an easy ear to criminal charges."—To attack is so much more easy than to repel, that an accuser should ever be listened to with distrust.

Difficilis, querulus, laudator temporis acti. Lat. HOR.—"Peevish, complaining, and the eulogist of the times which are past."—This, generally speak ing, is the just character of an old man. Age, we know, is querulous, and delights in the retrospect of its early enjoyments.

Digito monstrari et dicier hic est. Lat. PERSIUS.—"To be pointed at by the finger, and have it said, there goes the man."—Such is the ambition of many to be notorious.

Dignum laude virum Musa vetat mori. Lat. HOR.—"The muse forbids the virtuous man to die."—She consecrates his name at least to immortality.

Dignus vindice nodus. Lat. HOR.—"A knot worthy to be untied by such hands."—A difficulty which calls for the highest interference.

Dii talem avertite casum. Lat. VIRGIL.—"May the gods avert so great a misfortune."

Dii penates. Lat.—"The household gods" among the ancients. The difference between them, and *dii lares* was, that each house had its particular *dii penates,* to which their influence was limited; while the *dii lares* presided over individuals, houses, towns, &c. in general, though each of them had its own.

Diis aliter visum. Lat. VIRG.—"It has seemed otherwise to the gods."—Providence has disposed of the matter in a different way.

Diis proximus ille est
Quem ratio, non ira movet; qui facta rependens,
Consilio punire potest. Lat. CLAUDIAN.
"He is next to the gods, whom reason, and not passion, impels; and who, after weighing the facts, can measure the punishment with discretion."—This is a pleasing picture of a mild governor.

Dilutiones in lege sunt odiosæ. Lat. Law Maxim.—"Delays in the law are odious."—This is a maxim, it is to be feared, *rather belied in the practice*

It can now go only to intimate that a dilatory plea can not be received, unless the matter be supported by an affidavit.

Dimidium facti qui cæpit, habet. Lat. HORACE.—This is literally translated by our own proverb—"What's well begun is half done."

Diruit, ædificat, mutat quadrata rotundis. Lat. HOR.—"He pulls down, he builds up, he changes the square into the round."—He is perpetually changing, merely to gratify his own caprice.

Discipulus est prioris posterior dies. Lat. SYRUS.—"Each succeeding day is the scholar of that which preceded."—The errors which we commit on one day, should teach us to conduct ourselves more wisely on those which follow.

Discite justitiam moniti, et non temnere divos. Lat. VIRG.
"Learn justice, being admonished, and not to despise the gods."—Learn from affliction, the sense of justice, and the respect which is due to heaven.

Diseur des bons mots. Fr.—"A sayer of good things."—A would-be wit.

Disjecta membra poetæ. Lat. HOR.—"The scattered remains of the poet."—Distort a truly poetical passage as you will, there will still be found a remainder of poetic spirit.

Disponendo me, non mutando me. Lat.—"By disposing of me, not by changing me."

Distrahit animum librorum multitudo. Lat. SEN.—"A multitude of books distracts the mind."—But little of solid acquirement is to be expected from promiscuous reading.

Distringas. Law Phrase.—"You may distrain."—A writ to empower the sheriff to that effect.

Dives agris, dives positis in fœnore nummis. Lat. HOR.—"A person rich in lands, and in money placed at usury."—Used to describe a man of immense property.

Dives fieri qui vult,
Et cito vult fieri. Lat. JUVENAL.

"A man who wishes to become rich, and to acquire riches soon."—A desperate adventurer.

Divide et impera. Lat.—"Divide and govern."—This is the Machiavelian policy of almost all governments.

Divisum imperium. Lat.—"A divided, or mutual authority."—Alternate jurisdiction.

Dociles imitandis
Turpibus et pravis omnes sumus. Lat. JUV. "We are all easily taught to imitate that which is base and depraved."

Doctrina sed vim promovet insitam. Lat. HORACE. "Learning serves to bring forward the natural powers of the mind."

Doctus iter melius. Lat.—"Being taught a better course."

Doctus utriusque juris. Lat.—"Learned in either department of the law."

Dolce cose a vedere, è dolci inganni. Ital. ARIOSTO "Things sweet to see, and sweet deceptions."—A phrase frequently applied to specious, but deceitful appearances.

Doli capax. Lat.—"Competent to discern evil"—and, consequently, to commit a crime.

Dolore affici, sed resistere tamen. Lat. PLINY.—"To be affected by grief, but still to resist it."—This, that finished philosopher observes, is the incumbent duty of man.

Dolus an virtus quis in hoste requirat. Lat. VIRG. "Who should ask of an enemy whether he succeeded by stratagem or by valour?"—Either mode may be adopted in cases of avowed hostility.

Dolus versatur in generalibus. Lat. Law Maxim.—"Fraud lurks in loose generalities."—It is its nature, to deal in broad and general statements, without coming to close and tangible assertions: or, in other terms, general propositions, without modification, often lead to very erroneous conclusions.

Domine, salvum fac regem! Lat.—"O lord, preserve

the king!"—An inscription upon some of the French coins.

Domini pudet, non servitutis. Lat. SENECA.—"I am ashamed of my master, and not of my servitude."—There is no disgrace in obeying those who are worthy of command.

Dominium à possessione cæpisse dicitur. Lat. Law Maxim.—"Right is said to have its beginning from possession."—This maxim goes to prevent the disturbance of titles to estates. But if there be proof of record established, it outweighs the memory of man, which by the statute 32 Henry VIII. is fixed at sixty years.

Dominus providebit. Lat.—"The Lord will provide."

Dominus vobiscum. Lat.—"May the Lord be with you."—This is the benediction of the priests, in the Roman churches, to the congregation;—the response is, *et cum spiritu tuo,*—"and with thy soul."

Donec eris felix, multos numerabis amicos. Lat. OVID.—"Whilst you are prosperous you may count on having many friends."

Dormitur aliquando jus, moritur nunquam. Lat. Law Maxim.—"A right sometimes sleeps, but never dies."—A right to land, for instance, it is understood can not die. If a man releases his right it is extinguished for the time: but this is understood only of the right of the person making the release.

Dormiunt aliquando leges, nunquam moriuntur. Lat. Law Maxim.—"The laws sometimes sleep, but they never die."

Dos d'âne. Fr.—"The ass's back."—A military phrase used to describe a shelving ridge.

Dos est magna parentum virtus. Lat.—"The virtue of parents is in itself a great portion."—No inheritance can be more valuable than that of a fair fame transmitted from our ancestors.

Double entendre. Fr.—"A double meaning."—It is

generally used to mark an obscene illusion in disguise, or, as the phrase is, wrapt up in clean linen.

Douceur. Fr.—" Sweetness, gentleness"—generally used to denote a bribe, a compensation, an inducement.

Doux yeux. Fr.—" Soft glances."—To make the *doux yeux*—to interchange tender looks.

Droit d'aubaine. Fr.—" The right of escheat."—By this law, which expired with the French monarchy, in 1793, the personal property of every foreigner, dying within the king's dominions, escheated to the crown.

Droit des gens. Fr.—" The law of nations."

Droit et avant. Fr.—"Right and forward."

Dubiam salutem qui dat afflictis, negat. Lat. Sen.—" He who holds out a doubtful safety to the afflicted, denies all hope."

Duces tecum. See *Subpœna, &c.*

Ducis ingenium, res
Adversæ nudare solent, celare secundæ.
Lat. Horace.

" Misfortunes display the skill of a general, prosperous circumstances conceal his weakness."—It is less difficult, for instance, to gain a battle, than to conduct a retreat, or govern a nation.

Ducit amor patriæ. Lat.—" The love of my country leads me."

Du fort au foible. Fr.—"From the strong to the weak."—One with another.

Dulce bellum inexperto. Lat.—" War is sweet to him who has not tried it,"—who is ignorant of its desolating effects.

Dulce est desipere in loco. Lat. Hor.—" It is pleasant to play the fool in a proper place."—There are seasons when it is permitted that wisdom may take the garb of frivolity, and without incurring any reproach.

Dulce et decorum est pro patria mori. Lat. Hor.—" It is pleasant and honourable to die for one's country."—This is an apophthegm cited in all wars, and in all ages.

Dulcique animos novitate tenebo. OVID.
"I will arrest their attention by a pleasing novelty.

Dulcis inexpertis cultura potentis amici:
Expertus metuit. Lat. HORACE.
"Those who are unacquainted with the world take pleasure in the intimacy of a great man; those who are wiser dread its consequences."

Dum deliberamus quando incipiendum, incipere jam serum fit. Lat. QUINTILIAN.—"Whilst we consider when we are to begin, it is often too late to act."—Deliberation protracted is, on some occasions, as dangerous as precipitancy.

Dum de te loqueris, gloria nulla tua est.
Lat. VERINUS.
"When you speak in your praise, you add nothing to your reputation."

Dum in dubio est in animus, paulo momento huc illuc impellitur. Lat. TERENCE.—"Whilst the mind is in a state of uncertainty, the smallest impulse directs it to either side."

Dum lego, assentior. Lat.—"Whilst I read, I assent." —I yield implicitly to the writer's opinions. This was used emphatically by *Cicero*, on reading *Plato's* arguments on the immortality of the soul.

Dum spiro, spero. Lat.—"Whilst I breathe, I hope."

Dum vires annique sinunt, tolerate laborem;
Jam veniet tacito curva senecta pede. Lat. Ov.
"Whilst your strength and years permit, you should endure and encounter labour: remember that crooked age, with silent steps, will soon arrive."

Dum vitant stulti vitia, in contraria currunt. Lat. HORACE.—"When fools seek to avoid one error, they fall into its opposite."—They are ever in extremes.

Dum vivimus, vivamus. Lat.—"Whilst we live, let us live."—We only live whilst we enjoy life; let us therefore enjoy it as long as we can.

"Live while you live," the epicure would say,
"And seize the pleasures of the present day."

"Live while you live," the sacred preacher cries,
"And give to God each moment as it flies."
Lord, in my views let both united be;
I live in *pleasure*, when I live in *Thee*.

Doddridge.

Duos qui sequitur lepores, neutrum capit. Lat. Prov.—"He who follows two hares is sure to catch neither."—When the attention of a man is divided between two objects, he rarely attains either of them.

Durante bene placito. Lat.—"During our good pleasure."—By this tenure, the judges in England, once held their seats, at the will of the sovereign. They are now held more properly, *Quamdiu se bene gesserint*—"As long as they shall conduct themselves well;"—that is to say, during life, unless a criminal charge shall be made and proved against them.

Durante vita. Lat.—"During life."—A clause in letters patent.

Durate, et vosmet rebus servate secundis. Lat. Virg.—"Hold out, and preserve yourselves for better circumstances."—The hope of better times is the strongest argument which can be used to inspirit the drooping resolution.

Durum! sed levius fit patentia,
Quicquid corrigere est nefas. Lat. Horace.
"It is hard!—But that, which it is impossible to correct, becomes more light by patience."

Durum telum necessitas. Lat. Prov.—"Necessity is a hard weapon."—It is dangerous to oppose those whom necessity has driven to extremity.

Dux fæmina facti. Lat. Virg.—"A woman was the leader to the deed."—This is a quotation often used, because it frequently happens that female spirit takes the lead in the greatest enterprises.

E

Ea sub oculis posita negligimus; proximorum incuriosi, longinqua sectamur. Lat. Pliny.—"We neglect the things which are placed before our eyes, and regardless of what is within our reach, we pursue whatever is remote."

Eau bénite de cour. Fr.—"The holy water of the court."—*i. e.* Court-promises.

E cœlo descendit Γνωθι σεαυτον.—"From heaven the precept, '*know thyself*,' came down."

Ecce homo. Lat.—"Behold the man."—The French say, *Il a l'air d'un ecce homo.*—He appears to be in a deplorable condition.

Ecce signum. Lat.—"Behold the sign or badge."

Eclat. Fr.—"Splendour, pomp, glory, brilliancy,"—also, rumour, noise, talk.

E contrario. Lat.—"On the contrary."

E converso. Lat.—"Reversing the order" of a proposition.

E flamma cibum petere. Lat. TER.—"To get one's bread out of the fire."—To obtain a livelihood by the most desperate means.

Εγγυα παρα δ'ατη. Gr. *Engua para d'ate.*—"Promise; and mischief is near."—This was the saying of THALES, one of the seven sages of Greece. Nothing can lead into greater hazards than promises hastily and incautiously made.

Ego et rex meus. Lat.—"I and my king."—This insolent transposition is attributed to Cardinal WOLSEY. It is sometimes quoted to mark an extraordinary instance of impertinent assumption.

Ego spem pretio non emo. Lat. TERENCE.—"I do not buy hope with money."—I do not purchase expectation at so dear a rate.

Eheu fugaces, Posthume, Posthume,
Labuntur anni; nec pietas moram
Rugis et instanti senectæ
Afferet, indomitæque morti. Lat. HOR.

"Alas! Posthumus, our years are few and fleeting; nor can even piety delay the wrinkles of approaching age, or the progress of resistless death."

Eheu! quam brevibus pereunt ingentia causis. Lat. CLAUDIAN.—"Alas! by what slight means are great affairs brought to destruction."

Elegit. Law Lat.—"He has chosen."—A judicial writ directed to the sheriff, empowering him to seize for damages recovered.

Elige eum, cujus tibi placuit et vita et oratio. Lat. SENECA.—"Choose that man of whose *life*, as well as whose *eloquence*, you can approve."

Embonpoint. Fr.—"Good plight of body, plumpness."

Empta dolore docet experientia. Lat. Prov.—"Experience bought by suffering is instructive."

En ami. Fr.—"As a friend."

En avant! Fr.—"Forward!—March on!"

En barbette. Fr. Mil. Term.—Said of a battery, when the cannon are higher than the breast-wall.

En Dieu est ma fiance. Fr.—"In God is my trust."

En Dieu est tout. Fr.—"In God is every thing."

Enfans perdus. Fr.—"Lost-children."—Those troops which are stationed at the advanced or dangerous posts; in English termed the *forlorn hope* of the army.

Enfant gaté. Fr.—"A spoiled child."

Enfant trouvé. Fr.—"A foundling."

Enfermer le loup dans la bergerie. Fr. Prov.—"To shut up the wolf in the sheepfold."—Metaphorically, to patch up a disease.

Enfilade. Fr. Mil. Term.—"A row."—Where a battery is placed so that it can fire along a pass, it is said to *enfilade* that pass. The troops within its range are *enfiladed.*

En flute. Fr.—A large vessel is said to be *en flute,* when she carries only her upper tier of guns; her hold being filled with stores.—She is then only a transport of greater force.

En habile homme.—"Like a skilful man."

En habiles gens. Fr.—"Like able men."

En la rose je fleuris. Fr.—"I flourish in the rose."

En masse. Fr.—"In a body."—*En foule.*—"In a crowd."

En parole je vis. Fr.—"I live in the word."

En plein jour. Fr.—"In open day."

En revanche. Fr.—" In return."—To make amends or requital.

Ense petit placidam sub libertate quietem. Lat.—" He seeks, with his sword, for peace and liberty." —Motto of the state of MASSACHUSETTS.

Ens rationis. Lat.—" The creature of reason."—The conclusion obtained by long and abstract ratiocination.

En suivant la vérité. Fr.—" In following the truth."

Entre chien et loup. Fr.—" Between dog and wolf." —Or, as we say in English—" Between hawk and buzzard."—Twilight.

Entre deux feux. Fr.—" Between two fires."

Entre deux vins. Fr.—" Between the two vines."—Neither absolutely drunk nor sober.

Entre nous. Fr.—" Between ourselves."

Eödem collyrio mederi omnibus. Lat.—" To cure all by the same salve."—To play the quack, and vend a *panacea* for the cure of all disorders.

Eo instanti. Lat.—" At that instant."

Eo magis præfulgebat quod non videbatur. Lat. TACITUS.—" He shone with the greater splendour, because he was not seen."—This expression is used by the historian when speaking of the statue of a great man, which was invidiously removed from the view of a popular procession.

Eo nomine. Lat.—" By that name."—Under that description.

Epicuri de grege porcus. Lat. HOR.—" A swine belonging to the herd of Epicurus."

E pluribus unum. Lat.—" One of many."—The motto of the United States of America.—The allusion is to the formation of *one* federal government by the several constituent states.

Ergo agite, et lætum cuncti celebremus honorem. Lat. VIRGIL.—" Come on then, and let us all celebrate this joyous festival."

Eripuit cœlo fulmen, sceptrumque tyrannis. Lat.—" He snatched the thunder from heaven, and the sceptre from tyrants."—This was the exergue of a medal struck in honour of our late Dr. BENJAMIN FRANKLIN, when ambassador from the United States to France. The allusion is to his discovery of the identity of electrical fire with that of lightning; and to the eminent share which he had in establishing the independence of his native country.

Erratum. Lat.—"An error."—*Errata.*—"Errors"—a list of typographical errors.

E se finxit velut araneus. Lat.—"He spun from himself like a spider."—He had nothing to depend on but his own resources.

Espérance et Dieu. Fr.—"Hope and God."

Esprit de corps. Fr.—"The spirit of the body."—That zeal for their mutual honour which pervades every collective body, such as the gentleman of the army, the bar, &c.

Esse quam videri malim. Lat.—"I should wish to *be*, rather than to *seem.*"—I should prefer *to be* in fact estimable, to being merely *regarded* as such by the world.

Est demum vera felicitas, felicitate dignum videri. Lat. PLINY.—"To appear worthy of being happy, constitutes true happiness."

Est modus in rebus; sunt certi denique fines,
Quos ultra citraque nequit consistere rectum.
Lat. HORACE.

"There is a *medium* in all things. There are certain limits, beyond, or at this side of which, propriety can not exist."—This is a very popular quotation; it is used to illustrate the position, that every virtue consists in the middle course.

Esto perpetua. Lat.—"Be thou perpetual."—May this institution be permanent.

Esto quod esse videris. Lat.—"Be what you seem to be."

Esto ut nunc multi, dives tibi, pauper amicis. Lat. JUV.—"Be, as many in the world now are, rich to yourself, and poor to your friends."

Est profecto Deus, qui quæ nos gerimus auditque videt. Lat. TERENCE

"There is certainly a God who sees and hears all that we do."

Est proprium stultitiæ aliorum cernere vitia, oblivisci suorum. Lat. CICERO.—"It is the peculiar faculty of fools, to discern the faults of others at the same time that they forget their own."

Est quædam flere voluptas;
Expletur lachrymis, egeriturque dolor. Latin. OVID.—"There is a certain pleasure in weeping; grief finds in tears both a satisfaction and a cure."—There is, as SHAKSPEARE has it, "a luxury in grief."

Est quôdam prodire tenus, si non datur ultra. Lat. HOR.—"It is something to have progressed thus far, if it is not permitted to go farther."—That industry is to be approved, which advances in a certain degree, though it fails of its proposed object.

Est quoque cunctarum novitas carissima rerum. Lat. OVID.—"Novelty is also the most delightful of all things."

Esurienti ne occurras. Lat.—"Do not encounter a hungry man."—Risk not a contest with desperate necessity.

Et cætera. Lat.—"And the rest."

Et credis cineres curare sepultos? Lat. VIRG.—"Do you think that the ashes of the dead are to be affected by the affairs or passions of the living?"

Et cui per mediam nolis occurrere noctem. Lat.—"And he is one whom you would be unwilling to meet at midnight,"—With whom it might not be safe to trust yourself alone.

Et decus et pretium recti. Lat.—"The ornament and the reward of virtue."

Etenim omnes artes, quæ ad humanitatem pertinent, habent quoddam commune vinculum, et quasi cognatione quâdam inter se continentur. Lat. CIC. *pro* ARCHIA.—"All the arts which belong to polished life are held together by some common tie, and connected, as it were, by some intimate relationship."—Such for instance, is the relation between Painting, Poetry, and Music.

Et genus et formam regina pecunia donat. Lat. Hor.—"All-powerful money gives both birth and beauty."

Et genus et proavos, et quæ non fecimus ipsi,
Vix ea nostra voco. Lat. Ovid
"For birth and ancestry, and what we have not ourselves achieved, we can scarcely call our own."—This is frequently employed as being a just satire on the pride of birth, when not sustained by personal achievements.

Et genus et virtus, nisi cum re, vilior algâ est. Lat. Hor.—"Both virtue and birth, unless sustained by riches, are held more cheap than the sea-weed."

Etiam fortes viros subitis terreri. Lat. Tacitus. "Even bold men are to be shaken by sudden events."—The strongest mind is not proof against influence of surprise.

Etiam oblivisci quod scis, interdum expedit. Lat. Syrus.—"It is sometimes expedient to forget what you know."—It is useful to dissemble, and to withhold even the positive knowledge of facts, when one has to deal with an artful adversary.

Et male tornatos incudi reddere versus. Lat. Hor.—"And to return verses, which have been ill-formed, to the *anvil*," for revision.

Et meæ, si quid loquar audiendum,
Vocis accedet bona pars. Lat. Horace.
"And if any opinion of mine is worthy of attention, it shall be given freely in his favour."

Et mihi res, non me rebus, submittere conor. Lat. Hor.—"I endeavour to make circumstances submit to me, not to submit myself to circumstances."—This line describes very strongly a mind where firmness and vigour are united.

Et minimæ vires frangere quassa valent. Lat. Ovid, *de Tristibus.*—"A little force will break that which has been cracked before."—When a man's spirits are once broken, he is easily subdued by the slightest occurrence.

Et nati natorum, et qui nascentur ab illis.
Lat. Horace.

"And the children of our children, and those wh. shall be born of them."—These things we shall fee, and remember, and our *nati natorum*, &c. to our posterity to the last period.

Et nos quoque tela sparsimus. Lat.—"And we too have flung our weapons."

Et quæ sibi quisque timebat,
Unius in miseri exitium conversa tulere. Lat. VIRG.—"And what each man feared for himself was easily borne, when it was turned to the destruction of a single wretch!"—The circumstance to which the poet alludes is this—one man out of an army was to be sacrificed, the lot being drawn, each man cheerfully submitted to the decision which removed his individual apprehensions.

Et quiescenti agendum est, et agenti quiescendum est. Lat. SENECA.—"The active should occasionally rest, and the inactive should apply to labour."—The mind as well as the body requires alternate action and repose.

Et qui nolunt occidere quenquam,
Posse volunt. Lat. JUVENAL.
"Even those who do not wish to kill a man, are willing to have the power of doing it."

Etre pauvre sans être libre, c'est le pire état où l'homme puisse tomber. Fr. ROUSSEAU.—"To be poor without being free, is the worst state into which man can fall."

Etre sur un grand pied dans le monde. Fr. Prov. "To be on a great foot (or footing) in the world."—This proverb originated at the time when a man's rank was known by the size of his shoes. Those of a prince measured two feet and a half—a plain cit was allowed only twelve inches.

Et sic de similibus. Lat.—"And so of the like."—What is said of this will apply to every thing similar.

Etsi non prosunt singula, juncta juvant. Lat.—"Although, taken individually, their effect is trifling, when combined, it is powerful."

E variis sumendum est optimum. Lat. Cic.—"We should select the best from various sources."

Ex. Lat.—"Out."—*Ex-minister,* a minister out of office.

Ex abundanti cautela. Lat.—"From excessive caution."

Ex abusu non arguitur ad usum. Lat. Law Max.—"No argument can be drawn from the abuse of a thing against its use."—If a principle or practice be perverted from its right meaning or end, no solid argument against either can be drawn from such perversion. We have heard of debtors made the victims of personal spleen by their creditors; but it would not be fair to argue, on this ground alone, against the practice of imprisonment for debt.

Ex animo. Lat.—"From the fullest conviction of the mind"—with the whole intention.

Ex cathedrâ. Lat.—"From the chair."—An ordinance, *ex cathedrâ,* pronounced from high authority.

Excelsior. Lat.—"More elevated."—Motto of the state of New York.

Exceptio probat regulam. Lat. Law Maxim.—"The exception proves the existence of the rule."

Excerpta. Lat.—"Extracts."—Abridged notices taken from a work.

Excessus in jure reprobatur. Lat. Law Maxim.—"All excess is condemned by the law."—Whatever the law ordains must be within tne rules of reason. Thus the law awards liberal, but it by no means, allows excessive damages.

Excitari non hebescere. Lat.—"To be spirited, not inactive."

Ex concesso. Lat.—"From what has been granted."—Arguments, *ex concesso,* from admissions made by an adversary.

Ex confesso. Lat.—"Confessedly."

Ex curiâ Lat.—"Out of court."

Excusatio non petita fit accusatio manifesta. Lat.

—" An exculpation which is not called for, betrays the guilt of him who makes it."

Ex debito justitiæ. Lat.—" From what is due to justice."

Ex delicto. Lat.—" From the crime."

Exeat aulâ qui vult esse pius. Lat. LUCRET.—" Let him, who will be good, retire from the court."—The satirists of very early days have noticed courts as hot-beds of immorality.

Exegi monumentum ære perennius. Lat. HOR.—" I have erected a monument more lasting than brass." —This phrase is justly applied by the poet to his own works. It is now generally used in an ironical sense.

Exempli gratia. Lat.—" As an example,—for instance." Usually abbreviated, *ex. gr.*

Exemplo plus quam ratione vivimus. Lat.—" We live more by example than by reason."—Most men act rather upon the precedents set by others, in like cases, than on their individual judgment.

Exemplo quodcunque malo committitur, ipsi
Displicit auctori. Lat. JUVENAL.
" Whatever is committed from a bad example, is displeasing even to its author." We hate those faults in others, of which we have ourselves set the example.

Ex facto jus oritur. Lat. Law Maxim.—" The law arises out of the fact." Until the fact be settled, the law can not apply.

Exigui numero, sed bello vivida virtus. Lat. VIRG. —" Small in number, but of tried and war-proof valour."—A quotation not seldom resorted to, for the purpose of encouraging the lesser to resist the greater force.

Ex mero motu. Lat.—" From a mere motion."—From a man's own free will, without suggestion or constraint.

Ex necessitate rei. Lat.—" From the necessity of the case."—" Arising from the urgency of circumstances.

Ex nihilo nihil fit. Lat.—"Nothing can come of nothing."—No beneficial result can be expected where the basis is unsolid.

Ex officio. Lat.—"By virtue of his office."—As a matter of duty.

Ex parte. Lat.—"On one side."—*Ex parte* evidence, is that testimony, which, as before a grand jury, is delivered in only on the side of the prosecution.

Ex pede Herculem. Lat.—Judge of the size of the statue of "*Hercules* from that of the foot."—Decide upon the whole from the specimen which is furnished.

Experimentum crucis. Lat.—"The experiment of the cross."—A bold and decisive experiment.

Experimentum in corpore vili. Lat.—"An experiment made upon a thing of no value."

Experto crede. Lat. VIRG.—"Believe one who has experience to justify his opinion."

Expertus metuit. Lat. HORACE.—"The man who has experience dreads it."—The original application was to the friendship of the great. The phrase however is often and variously applied.

Explorant adversa viros. Lat.—"Adversity tries men."

Ex post facto. Lat.—A law made to punish an act *previously committed* and which was innocent at the time of its commission; or, raising the grade of an offence, making it greater than it was when committed; or changing the punishment after the commission of the offence, making it more severe than it was when committed; or, finally, altering the rules of evidence so as to allow different, or less evidence to convict the offender than was required when the offence was committed. Such a law is termed *ex post facto,* and is expressly prohibited by the constitution of the United States.—This prohibition, however, applies only to *criminal* or *penal* cases, and does not extend to *civil* cases.

Expressio unius est exclusio alterius. Lat. Law Max

—"The naming of one man is the exclusion of the other."

Expressum facit cessare tacitum. Lat. Law Max — "A matter expressed causes that to cease which, otherwise, by intendment of law, would have been implied."—An express covenant qualifies the generality of the law, and restrains it from going further than is warranted by the agreement of the parties.

Ex principiis nascitur probabilitas; ex factis vero veritas. Lat.—"From principles is derived probability; but truth (or certainty) is obtained only from facts."

Ex quovis ligno non fit Mercurius. Lat. Prov,—"A Mercury is not to be carved out of every wood."—This corresponds with the homely proverb.—"You can not make a silk purse, &c."

Ex tempore. Lat.—"Out of hand—without delay, or premeditation."

Extinctus amabitur idem. Lat. Hor.—"The same man when dead shall be beloved."—Envy pursues the living. No man can expect to share the honours which are due to merit, until after his decease.

Extra flammantia mænia mundi. Lat.—"Beyond the flaming boundaries of the world."—A strong hyperbolic effusion.

Extremis malis extrema remedia. Lat.—"To desperate evils, desperate remedies" must be applied.

Ex uno disce omnes. Lat.—"From one you may learn all."—From this specimen you may judge of the remainder.

Ex vi termini. Lat.—"By the meaning, or force of the expression."

Ex vitio alterius, sapiens emendat suum
Lat. P. Syrus.
"From the errors of others, a wise man corrects his own."

F

Faber suæ fortunæ. Lat.—"The framer of his own fortune."

Facetiarum apud præpotentes in longum memoria est. Lat. Tacitus.—"The powerful hold, in deep remembrance, an ill-timed pleasantry."—It is dangerous to sport with the feelings of the great.

Facies non omnibus una,
Non diversa tamen, qualem decet esse sororum.
Lat. Ovid.

"The face was not the same with all. It was not however materially different: the resemblance was such as should appear between sisters."—These lines, which were originally used to express a family-likeness, are now employed to mark those political circumstances, which from their similitude bespeak the same political parent.

Facile est inventis addere. Lat.—"It is easy to add to, (or make improvements upon) things already invented."

Facile evenit quod diis cordi esset. Lat. Livy.
"Those events which are pleasing to the gods, are readily and certainly produced."

Facilè omnes, cum valemus, recta consilia
Ægrotis damus. Tu, si hic sis, aliter sentias.
Lat. Terence.

"We can all, when we are well, give good counsel to the sick. Were you in my place, you would feel otherwise."—We think and feel for others, differently from what we should do for ourselves, were we in a similar situation.

Facilè princeps. Lat.—"The admitted chief."—The first man, without dispute.

Facilis descensus Averni:
Sed revocare gradum, superasque evedere ad [auras,
Hoc opus, hic labor est. Lat. Virgil.

"The descent into hell is easy, but to recall your steps, and reascend to the upper skies, forms the difficulty and the labour."—The poet speaks of the descent of Æneas into the infernal regions. In its general application, it means that it is much easier for a man to get into, than to extricate himself from, any difficulty, or danger.

Facilius crescit quam inchoatur dignitas. Lat. LAB —" It is more easy to obtain an *accession* of dignity, than to acquire it in the first instance."

Facinus quos inquinat, æquat. Lat. LUCAN. " Those whom guilt stains, it makes equals."—The expression is nervous and happy. Nothing can be so great a leveller as the mutual consciousness of criminality.

Facit indignatio versus. Lat.—" The verses flow from indignation."—My strong feelings impel me to write.

Façon de parler. Fr.—" A manner of speaking."—*C'est ma façon de parler.*—" It is the mode in which I choose to express myself."

Fac simile. Lat.—" Do the like."—A close imitation. —An engraved resemblance of a man's hand-writing, &c.

Fæx populi. Lat.—" The dregs of the people."—Contemptuously applied to the lower classes.

Faire l'homme d'importance. Fr.—" To assume a consequence."

Faire sans dire. Fr.—" To act without ostentation."

Faire mon devoir. Fr.—" To do my duty."

Fallacia alia aliam trudit. Lat. TERENCE.—" One imposture or fallacy produces another."—Any one falsehood or deceit is naturally the parent of many others.

Fallentis semita vitæ. Lat. HORACE.—" The deceitful path of life."

Fallit enim vitium, specie virtutis et umbra. Lat. JUVENAL.
" Vice can deceive under the guise and shadow of virtue."

Fallitur egregio quisquis sub principe credit
Servitium. Nunquam libertas gratior extat
Quam sub rege pio. Lat CLAUDIAN.
" That man is deceived who thinks it slavery to

live under an excellent prince.—Never did liberty appear in a more gracious form, than under a pious king."—This once was poetic incense offered to an emperor. It is now quoted as an axiom by the advocates for absolute monarchy.

Falsus honor juvat, et mendax infamia terret Quem, nisi mendosum et mendacem? Lat. Hor. "False honour aids, and calumny deters, none but the vicious and the liar."—The man of spirit and integrity, will equally despise the encomium and the aspersion which are founded upon falsehood.

Falsus in uno, falsus in omnibus. Lat.—"He who is false in one particular, will be so in all."—This is a maxim which, though sometimes true, can not be of general application.

Famæ damna majora, quam quæ estimari possint. Lat. Livy.—"An injury done to character is so great, that it can not possibly be estimated."

Fari quæ sentiat. Lat.—"To speak what he thinks."

Fas est et ab hoste doceri. Lat.—"It is fair to derive instruction even from an enemy."—He, who notices the mistakes of a foe, gains from thence a lesson of advantage.

Fastidientis est stomachi multa degustare. Lat. Seneca.—"It proves a squeamish stomach to taste of many things."—A weak appetite, taken in any sense, is only to be allured by variety.

Fata obstant Lat.—"The fates oppose it."—It is in the destiny of things that the matters should be otherwise settled.

Fata viam invenient. Lat.—"The fates will find their way."—It is in vain to oppose our destiny.

Fata volentem ducunt, nolentem trahunt. Lat. Horace.—"The fates lead the willing, and drag the unwilling."

Fatetur facinus is qui judicium fugit. Lat. Law Maxim.—"He confesses his crime who flies from judgment."—His flight is a tacit admission of his guilt.

Faux pas. Fr.—" A false step."—A mistake, a deviation from rectitude.

Favete linguis. Lat.—" Favour by your tongues."—Give attention whilst the business proceeds. A solemn admonition repeatedly given whilst the superstitious rites of the Romans were in the act of being performed.

Fax mentis incendium gloriæ. Lat.—" The torch of the mind is the flame of glory."

Felices ter et ampliùs
Quos irrupta tenet copula; nec malis
Divulsus querimoniis,
Supremâ citiùs solvet amor die. Lat. Hor.
" Happy and thrice happy are those, who enjoy an uninterrupted union, and whose love, unbroken by any sour complaints, shall continue till death."—There is no happiness on earth exceeding that of a reciprocal satisfaction in a conjugal state.

Felicitas multos habet amicos. Lat.—" Happiness has many friends."—All men court the intercourse of the prosperous.

Felicitas nutrix est iracundiæ Lat. Prov.—" Prosperity is the nurse of anger."—It leads men to indulge their passions and forget themselves.

Felix quem faciunt aliena pericula cautum. Lat.—" Happy are they who can learn prudence from the dangers of others."

Felix qui nihil debet. Lat.—" Happy is the man who owes nothing."

Felix qui potuit rerum cognoscere causas. Lat. Virg.—" Happy is the man who is skilled in tracing effects up to their causes.

Felo de se. Law Term.—" A felon of himself."—A person of sound mind who voluntarily puts an end to his existence.

Femme couverte. Fr.—" A married woman."

Femme sole. Fr.—" A spinster—woman unmarried."

Feræ naturæ. Lat.—" Of a wild nature."—This phrase is generally used to describe those animals, which being of a wild and savage nature, are the common property of all. Tame animals, on the other hand, which are the absolute property of man, are called *Mansueta*, from *manui assueta*, "accustomed to the hand," or, *domitæ naturæ*, "of a tamed and subdued nature."

Ferme ornée. Fr.—"A decorated farm."—A farm in which, though ornament be introduced, its useful purposes are not overlooked.

Fertilior seges est alienis semper in agris,
Vicinumque pecus grandius uber habet.
Lat. OVID.
"The crop is always greater in the lands of another, and the cattle of our neighbour are deemed more productive than our own."—Such is the envious nature of man.

Fervet olla, vivit amicitia. Lat. Prov.—"While the pot boils, friendship lasts."

Festina lente. Lat. AUGUSTUS CÆSAR.—"Hasten slowly."—Do not let impetuosity betray you into imprudence.

Festinare nocet, nocet et cunctatio sæpe:
Tempore quæque suo qui facit, ille sapit.
Lat. OVID.
"It is injurious to be precipitate, and delay is also frequently injurious.—That man is wise, who does every thing in its proper time."

Festinatio tarda est. Lat.—"Haste is slow."—Precipitancy seldom attains its object.

Fête champêtre. Fr.—"A rural feast."—An entertainment, with rustic sports, given in the open air.

Fiat. Lat.—"Let it be done."—A word used to signify a peremptory and decisive order.

Fiat justitia, ruat cœlum. Lat.—"Let justice be done, though the heavens shall fall."—Though ruin should ensue, let justice take its course.

Fiat lux. Lat.—"Let there be light."

Ficta voluptatis causâ sint proxima veris.
Lat. HORACE.
"Let the feigned sources of pleasure be as near as possible to truth."—This is a judicious advice to

poets. In indulging the imagination, let not the departure be too great from probability.

Fide et amore. Lat.—"By faith and love."

Fide et fortitudine. Lat.—"By faith and fortitude"

Fide et fiduciâ. Lat.—"By faith and courage."

Fidei coticula crux. Lat.—"The cross is the touchstone of faith."

Fideli certa merces. Lat.—"The faithful are certain of their reward."

Fidelis ad urnam. Lat.—"Faithful to the ashes."

Fideliter. Lat.—"Faithfully."

Fides probata coronat. Latin.—"Approved faith crowns."

Fides sit penes auctorem. Lat.—"Let the faith be with the author."—A phrase often used, when a writer citing a supposed fact, chooses to cast the responsbility on the person who had previously given it to the public.

Fidus et audax. Lat.—"Faithful and intrepid."

Fieri facias. Law Lat.—"Cause it to be done."—A judicial writ addressed to the sheriff, empowering him to levy the amount of a debt, or damages recovered.

Filius nullius, or, *Filius populi.* Lat.—"The son of nobody."—A bastard, so called, because, by common law, he can not have an inheritance.

Fille de chambre. Fr.—"A chambermaid."

Fille de joie. Fr.—"A daughter of pleasure."—A prostitute.

Finem imponere curis. Lat. VIRG.—"To put an end to one's troubles."

Finem respice. Lat.—"Look to the end."

Finis coronat opus. Lat.—"The end crowns the work."—It is impossible to decide on the merits of an affair, until it is completely terminated.

Fit fabricando faber. Lat.—"A mechanic becomes skilful by labouring in his calling."—Practice alone in any profession makes a man master of his business.

Flagrante bello. Lat.—"Whilst the war is raging."—During hostilities.

Flagranti delicto. Lat.—"In the commission of the crime."—A person apprehended *in flagranti delicto,* with full evidence of his guilt.

Flebile ludibrium. Lat.—"A sad mockery."—A derision, to be lamented, of something highly just and respectable.

Flebit, et insignis totâ cantabitur urbe. Lat. HOR.—"He shall regret it, and become the sad burden of some merry song."—Spoken of any one who shall provoke the indignation of the poet.

Flèche. Fr. Mil. Term.—"An arrow."—A small fort open to your army, but with a ditch and breast-work towards the enemy. It is so called from its resemblance to that weapon.

Flectere si nequeo superos, Acheronta movebo.
Lat. VIRG.
"If I can not influence the gods, I will move all hell."—Acheron, a river of the infernal regions, in the Pagan mythology, is here put figuratively for the whole.—"If I can not succeed by fair means, I will attempt it by foul."

Flecti non frangi. Lat.—"To bend not to break."

Floriferis ut apes in saltibus omnia limant.
Lat. LUCRET.
"As bees taste of every thing in flowery lawns." They collect the most precious juice of every flower.—The motto is generally chosen by selectors, who either cull, or affect to cull, the beauties of many authors.

Flotsam. See *Jetsam.*

Fœcunda culpæ sæcula, nuptias
Primùm inquinâvere, et genus, et domos.
Lat. HORACE.
"This age, fertile of guilt, has first polluted the marriage bed, and with it our houses and our race."

Fœcundi calices quem non fecêre disertum? Lat. HOR.—"Whom has not the inspiring bowl made eloquent."

Fœdum crimen servitutis. Lat.—"The foul crime of servitude,"—or "of servility."

Fœnum habet in cornu. Lat. Prov.—"He carries hay upon his horn."—It was the custom of the ancients to put a wisp of hay about the horns of a mad bull. He bears evident signs of madness.

Formidabilior cervorum exercitus, duce leone, quam leonum, cervo. Lat. Prov.—"An army of stags is more to be feared under the command of a lion, than an army of lions led by a stag."

Formosa facies muta commendatio est. Lat. Lab.—"A pleasing countenance is a silent recommendation."

Forsan et hæc olim meminisse juvabit:
Durate, et rebus vosmet servate secundis.
Lat. Virgil.
"Perhaps the remembrance of these events may prove a source of future pleasure. Endure them, therefore, and reserve yourselves for more prosperous circumstances."

Forsan miseros meliora sequentur. Lat. Virg. "Perhaps a better fate awaits the afflicted."—A topic of consolation similar to the preceding.

Fort. Fr.—"Chief excellence."—That quality, or that department of his profession, in which any one excels.

Fortem posce animum. Lat.—"Wish for a strong mind."

Fortes creantur fortibus. Lat. Hor—"The brave are descendants of the brave."

Forte scutum salus ducum. Lat.—"A strong shield is the safety of commanders."

Fortes fortuna juvat. Lat.—"Fortune assists the bold."—Vigorous enterprise is commonly successful.

Forti et fideli nil difficile. Lat.—"Nothing is difficult to the brave and faithful."

Fortior et potentior est dispositio legis quam hominis. Lat. Law Maxim.—"The disposition of the law is of greater force and potency than the disposition of man."—Thus a man, having granted a lease for years, can not overthrow this grant by any surrender of his interest.

Fortis cadere, cedere non potest. Lat.—"The brave man may fall, but can not yield."

Fortis sub forte fatiscet. Lat.—"A brave man will yield to a braver man."

Fortiter et rectè. Lat.—"Courageously and honourably."

Fortiter in re. Lat.—"Firm in acting."

Fortiter geret crucem. Lat.—"He will bravely support the cross."

Fortitudine et prudentia. Lat.—"By fortitude and prudence."

Fortuna non mutat genus. Lat. Hor.—"Wealth can not change your origin."

Fortunæ cætera mando. Lat.—"I commit the rest to fortune."—I have made the wisest arrangements in my power, but I still know that I am not beyond the reach of accident.

Fortunæ filius. Lat. Hor.—"A son of fortune."—A person highly favoured by that blind deity.

Fortunæ majoris honos, erectus et acer. Lat. Claud. —"A man who reflects honour on his distinguished situation: of an erect and bold spirit."

Fortuna multis dat nimium, nulli satis. Lat. Mart. —"Fortune gives too much to many, but to none enough."

Fortuna, nimium quem fovet, stultum facit. Lat. Prov.—"Fortune, when she caresses a man too much, makes him a fool."

Fortuna opes auferre, non animum potest. Lat. Seneca.—"Fortune can take away riches, but can not deprive of courage."

Fortuna sequatur. Lat.—"Let fortune follow."

Fortuna vitrea est, tum cum splendet frangitur. Lat. Syrus.—"Fortune is made of glass, when she shines she is broken."—She has all its splendour and all its brittleness.

Foy pour devoir. Fr.—"Faith for duty."

Foy en tout. Fr.—"Faith in every thing."

Fragili quærens illidere dentem,
Offendet solido. Lat. HORACE.
"He (my adversary) in seeking to fasten on a weak part, shall find a firm resistance."—If his malice be directed towards me, he shall meet with an unlooked for and plenary punishment.

Fraises. Fr.—Pointed stakes used in fortification.

Frangas non flectas. Lat.—"You may break, but not bend me."

Fraus est celare fraudem. Lat. Law Max.—"It is a fraud to conceal a fraud."—On such a concealment devolves a share in the guilt.

Fraudare eos qui sciunt et consentiunt, nemo videtur. Lat. Law Maxim.—"A fraud committed upon those who are aware of it and consent to it, is not deemed a fraud."

Fronti nulla fides. Lat.—"There is no trusting to the countenance."—We can not judge by appearances.

Fruges consumere nati. Lat.—"Men who are only born to devour provisions."—The worthless who live and die without having rendered a service to society.

Fruitur fama. Lat. TAC.—"He enjoys his renown." —He lives to witness the glorious results of his labours.—To no one perhaps has this ever happened in a more eminent degree, than to the great and virtuous *Lafayette.*

Frustra fit per plura, quod fieri potest per pauciora Lat.—"That is idly done by many, which may be done by a few."—This maxim, though it may be variously applied, is generally used to enforce the position—that it is better to proceed by negotiation than warfare.

Frustra laborat, qui omnibus placere studet. Lat. Prov.—"He labours vainly, who endeavours to please every person."—Exemplified in the popu lar fable of the old man, his son, and the ass.

Fugam fecit. Lat. Law Phrase.—"He has taken to

flight."—Used, when it is found by inquisition, that a person has fled for felony, &c.

Fuge magna: licet sub paupere tecto,
Reges, et regum vitâ præcurrere amicos.
Lat. Horace

"Avoid greatness; in a cottage there may be found more real happiness, than kings or their favourites enjoy in palaces."

Fugiendo, in media sæpe ruitur fata. Lat. Livy.—"By flying, men often meet the very fate which they wish to avoid."

Fugit hora. Lat.—"The time passes over."

Fugit irreparibile tempus. Lat.—"Time flies, and can not be recalled."

Fuimus. Lat.—"We have been."

Fuit Ilium. Lat. Virg.—"Troy *has* been."—That which was the object of contention exists no more.

Fulcrum. Lat.—"Prop or support—the point on which a lever turns."

Functus officio. Lat.—"Discharged of duty."—He is *functus officio*—his official power no longer exists.

Fungar inani munere. Lat. Virgil.—"I shall discharge an unavailing duty."—This is a common prefix to an elegy on a deceased friend.

Fungar vice cotis, acutum
Reddere quæ ferrum valet, exsors ipsa secandi.
"I shall perform the office of a whetstone, which can make other things sharp, though it is itself incapable of cutting."

Furiosus furore suo punitur. Lat. Law Max.—"A madman or lunatic is punished by his own madness."—If a madman kill any person, he shall not suffer for the act, because being deprived of memory and understanding by the hand of God, he is regarded as having broken the mere words of the law, but not the law itself.

Furor. Lat.—"A rage."—*Furor loquendi,* an eagerness for speaking—*Furor scribendi* an itch for writing.—Vide *Cacoëthes.*

Furor arma ministrat. Lat. VIRG.—"Their rage supplies them with weapons.

Furor fit læsa sæpius patientia. Lat. Prov.—"Patience when too often outraged is converted into madness."—There is a certain degree of irritation which is beyond all endurance.

Fuyez les dangers du loisir. Fr.—"Avoid the dangers of idleness."

Fuyez les procès sur toutes choses: la conscience s'y intéresse, la santé s'y altère, les biens s'y dissipent. Fr. LA BRUYERE.—"Avoid lawsuits beyond all things; they influence your conscience, impair your health, and dissipate your property.

G

Gaiété de cœur. Fr.—"Gaiety of heart."—Sportiveness. High animal spirits.

Garde fou. Fr.—"Fool-preserver."—Parapet of a bridge.

Gardez la foi. Fr.—"Guard the faith."

Gardez la foy. Fr.—"Keep the faith."

Garrit aniles ex re fabellos. Lat. HOR.—"He tells an old wife's tale rather pertinently."—This is sometimes addressed to one who is possessed of more anecdote than argument.

Gaudetque viam fecisse ruinâ. Lat. LUCAN.—"He rejoices to have made his way by ruin."—This is the character given by the poet to Cæsar. It will equally suit any other ambitious despot, who, in the pursuit of his object, is regardless of the havoc which he may occasion among the human race.

Gaudet tentamine virtus. Lat.—"Virtue rejoices in temptation."

Gaulois. Fr.—"Old French."

Gens d'armes. Fr.—"Guards."

Gens de condition. Fr.—"People of rank.

Gens d'église. Fr.—"Churchmen.'

Gens de guerre Fr. Military men."

Gens de peu. Fr.—" The mean sort of people."

Genus ignavum, quod tecto gaudet et umbra. Lat. Juv.—" A lazy race, who love the house and the shade."

Genus irritabile vatum. Lat.—" The irritable tribe of Poets."—Proverbially used, in consequence of the acrimony which generally enters into any contest between writers of this class. An English poet has described, in terms still more forcible,
" The jealous, waspish, wrong-head, rhyming race."

Gibier de potence. Fr.—" Game for the gallows."—Anglicè, *Newgate birds.*

Gladiator in arena consilium capit. Lat.—" The gladiator takes counsel on the stage where he is to fight."—The man asks for that advice in the very hour of danger, which he should previously, and in a cooler moment have solicited.

Gloria virtutis umbra. Lat.—" Glory is the shadow (or the companion) of virtue."

Γνωθι σεαυτον. *Gnothi seauton.* Gr.—" Know thyself." —The saying of Solon, one of the seven wise men of Greece. A precept at once the most necessary, and difficult to be obeyed.

Gobe-mouche. Fr.—" A fly-catcher."—One who eagerly listens to every idle report.

Gorge. Fr. Mil. Term.—" A strait or narrow pass."

Goutte à goutte. Fr.—" Drop by drop."

Græculus esuriens ad cœlum, si jusseris, ibit. Lat. Juv.—" A poor hungry Greek, if you order him, will even go to heaven."—That is, will attempt a thing the most difficult.—This was the reproach of Imperial Rome to the natives of the Greek provinces who resorted to that metropolis.

Gram. loquitur, Dia. vera docet, Rhe. verba colorat, Mu. canit, Ar. numerat, Geo. ponderat, As. docet astra. Lat.—" This is a definition given by the schoolmen in verse, to assist the memory, of what are called, the seven liberal sciences.— " *Grammar* speaks, *Dialectics* teach the truth, *Rhetoric* gives colouring to our speech, *Music* sings, *Arithmetic* numbers, *Geometry* weighs, and *Astronomy* teaches the knowledge of the stars."

Grammatici certant, et adhuc sub judice lis est. Lat. HOR.—"Grammarians dispute, and the controversy still remains undecided."

Grata superveniet, quæ non sperabitur, hora. Lat.—"The hour of happiness shall come, more gratifying when it is not expected."—This is a general topic of consolation to the unfortunate.

Gratior ac pulchro veniens in corpore virtus. Lat. VIRGIL. "Even virtue is more fair, when it appears in a beautiful person."—Beauty lends a grace even to intrinsic worth.

Gratis. Lat.—"For nothing."—Free of cost.

Gratis anhelans, multa agendo nil agens. Lat. PHÆDRUS.—"Panting without a cause, and in affecting to do much, really doing nothing."—The description of a busy, pompous blockhead.

Gratis dictum. Lat.—"Said for nothing."—Spoken of a transitory observation which makes nothing to the argument.

Grave virus munditias pepulit. Lat. HORACE. "The virulence of the poison has destroyed all that was sound and healthy."—This phrase is often used to mark some spreading cancer in the political world.

Graviora manent. Lat.—"Greater afflictions await us."

Graviora quædam sunt remedia periculis. Lat. Prov —"Some remedies are worse than the disease."

Gravis ira regum semper. Lat. SEN.—"The anger of kings is always severe."—Those who possess unlimited power are vindictive from habit.

Grossièreté. Fr.—"Grossness."—Rudeness in conversation.

Guerre à mort. Fr.—"War till death."

Guerre à outrance. Fr.—"War to the uttermost."—Or, a war of extermination.

Gutta cavat lapidem, non vi, sed sæpe cadendo. Lat

Prov.—"The drop hollows the stone, not by its force, but by the frequency of its falling."—An allusion to the power of perseverance.

H

Habeas corpus. Law Lat.—"You may have the body." This is the great writ of personal liberty. It lies where a person being indicted and imprisoned, has offered sufficient bail, which has been refused, though the case be bailable; in this case he may have an *habeas corpus* out of the proper court, in order to remove himself thither, and to answer the cause at the bar of that court.

Habeas corpus ad prosequendum. Law Lat.—"You may have the body in order to prosecute."—A writ for the removal of a person for the purpose of prosecution and trial in the proper county.

Habeas corpus ad respondendum. Law Lat.—"You may have the body to answer."—A writ to remove a person confined in any other prison, to answer to an action in the court.

Habeas corpus ad satisfaciendum. Law Lat.—"You may have the body to satisfy."—A writ which lies against a person in prison, &c. to charge him in execution.

Habemus confitentem reum. Lat. Cic.—"We have before us a criminal who confesses his guilt."

Habemus luxuriam atque avaritiam, publicè egestatem, privatim opulentiam. Lat. Sallust.—"We have luxury and avarice, public debt and private opulence."—This is the description of Rome. put by the historian in the mouth of Cato.

Habere facias possessionem. Lat. Law Term.—"You shall cause to take possession."—This is a writ which lies where a man has recovered a term for years in an action of ejectment, and it is directed to the sheriff, in order to put the plaintiff into possession.

Habere facias visum. Law Lat.—"You shall cause a view to be taken."—This is a writ which lies in several cases as in Dower, Formedon, &c. where a view is to be taken of the lands or tenements in question.

Habet aliquid ex iniquo omne magnum exemplum, quod contra singulos, utilitate publicâ rependitur. Lat. TACITUS.—"Every example of punishment has in it some tincture of injustice, but the sufferings of individuals are compensated by the promotion of the public good."

Hæc generi incrementa fides. Lat.—"This faith will furnish new increase to our race."—This faith will be of service to our descendants.

Hæc olim meminisse juvabit. Lat. VIRG.—"It will be pleasing to recollect these things hereafter."—There is a melancholy pleasure in the recollection of past misfortunes.

Hæc placuit semel; hæc decies repetita placebit. Lat. HORACE. "That pleased once; this will afford pleasure if ten times repeated."

Hæc studia adolescentiam alunt, senectutem oblectant, secundas res ornant, adversis solatium et perfugium præbent, delectant domi, non impediunt foris, pernoctant nobiscum, peregrinantur, rusticantur. Lat. CICERO.—"These (literary) studies are the food of youth, and the consolation of age; they adorn prosperity, and are the comfort and refuge of adversity; they are pleasant at home, and no incumbrance abroad: they accompany us at night, in our travels, and in our rural retreats."

Hæ nugæ in seria ducent mala. Lat.—"These trifles will lead into serious mischief."—That which is considered as mere sport may have a ruinous tendency.

Hæredis fletus sub persona risus est. Lat. Prov.—"The weeping of an heir is laughter under a mask."—He affects to mourn in order to conceal his secret joy."

Hæres jure representationis. Lat.—"An heir by the right of representation."—This is spoken of a grandson, who shall inherit from his grandfather, because in such case he represents and stands in place of his father.

Hæres legitimus est quem nuptiæ demonstrant. Lat. Law Max.—“He is the lawful heir, whom marriage points out to be such.”—A child born within wedlock, be it ever so soon after, is in law legitimate, and heir to the husband of its mother.

Hæret lateri lethalis arundo. Lat. Virgil.—“The deadly arrow still sticks in his side.”—Applied to persons continually pursued by their passions or remorses.

Hæ tibi erunt artes. Lat. Virg.—“These shall be thy arts.”—These are the pursuits to which you should direct your attention.

Hæ tibi erunt artes; pacisque imponere morem,
Parcere subjectis et debellare superbos.
Lat. Virgil.

“These shall be thy arts; to impose the conditions of peace, to spare the lowly, and pull down the proud.”—This is the character of a beneficent conqueror.

Hanc veniam petimus damusque vicissim. Lat. Hor. “We give this privilege and receive it in return.”

Haro. Fr.—“Hue and cry.”

Haud facile emergunt, quorum virtutibus obstat
Res angusta domi. Lat. Juvenal.

“Those rise with difficulty, whose virtues or talents are encumbered or depressed by poverty.

Haud ignara mali, miseris succurere disco. Lat. Virg.—“Having experienced misfortune myself, I have learned to sympathize with the wretched.”

Haud inscia ac non incauta futuri. Lat. Virgil.—“Neither ignorant nor careless with respect to the future.”—A motto not unfairly taken by a person informed on the subject in controversy, and who has well weighed its consequences.

Haud passibus æquis. Lat. Virg.—“Not with equal steps.”—This, which was used literally by the poet to mark the unequal paces with which *Æneas* and his infant son *Iulus* issued from burning Troy, is now metaphorically applied to two men who pursue the same objects, but with powers of attainment altogether different.

Hauteur. Fr.—" Height."—Metaphorically used, "Haughtiness."

Haut goût. Fr.—"High flavour."—As in venison, &c. long kept. By the vulgar it is used to denote a near approach to putrescency.

Helluo librorum. Lat. Cic.—" A literary glutton—a great reader."

Heu! me miserum! Lat.—" Ah! miserable man that I am!"

Heu! quam difficile est crimen non prodere vultu! Lat. Ovid.—"Alas! how difficult it is to prevent the countenance from betraying guilt."

Heu quam difficilis gloriæ custodia est! Lat Syrus. —" How difficult, alas! is the custody of glory!" How much more easy is it in many cases, to attain than preserve a high reputation!

'Ευρηκα. Gr. *Hureka.*—" I have found it."—This was the exclamation of *Archimedes*, the Syracusan, when on immersing his body in the bath, he discovered the means of ascertaining the purity of the golden crown made for Hiero, from the space which it would occupy in water.—It is now used mostly in ridicule, to mark an affected importance annexed to an insignificant discovery.

Heu! totum triduum. Lat. Terence.—" What! three whole days."—Can you be absent from your mistress for such a term?—A satire on the impatience of lovers.

Hiatus maxime (or *valde*) *deflendus.* Lat.—" A chasm (or deficiency) very much to be lamented." This phrase is often to be found in the editions of the ancient classics, to mark some loss sustained through the ravages of time. It is now sometimes used in ridicule, to mark some passage omitted through design.

Hic est aut nusquam, quod quærimus. Lat.—" Wha

we seek is either here or nowhere."—In our search after happiness, we miss the good which is immediately before us, and direct our inquiries to that which either does not exist, or is unattainable.

Hic et ubique. Lat.—"Here and there and every where."—Used to mark a perpetual change of place.

Hic finis fandi. Lat.—"Here was an end to the discourse,"—or, here let the conversation terminate.

Hic jacet. Lat.—"Here lies"—the initial words of Latin epitaphs.

Hic murus aheneus esto,
Nil conscire sibi, nullâ pallescere culpa.
Lat. HORACE.
"Let this be thy brazen wall of defence, to be conscious of no guilt, and not to turn pale on any charge."—The consciousness of innocence forms our best security.

Hic niger est; hunc tu, Romane, caveto. Lat. HOR. "That man is of a black character; do you, Roman, beware of him."—The word "black," was used by the Latins to mark every thing which they deemed either wicked or unfortunate.

Hic patet ingeniis campus: certusque merenti
Stat favor: ornatur propriis industria donis.
Lat. CLAUDIAN.
"Here is a field open for talent;—here merit wil' have certain favour—and industry its due reward."—Such a field but rarely presents itself. The quotation often presents itself to projectors whose hopes are bolder than their expectations.

Hic vivimus ambitiosâ
Paupertate omnes. Lat. JUVENAL.
"We all live here in a state of ostentatious poverty."—With most men it is the business of their life to conceal their wants.

Ἱερα πικρα. *Hiera picra.* Gr.—"The sacred bitter."—A medicine well known.

Hi motus animorum, atque hæc certamina tanta.
Lat. VIRG.

"These movements of the soul, and these violent contests."

Hinc illæ lachrymæ. Lat.—"From hence proceed those tears."—This is the secret or remote cause of the discontents which have been expressed.

Hinc subitæ mortes, atque intestata senectus. Lat. JUVENAL.—"Hence proceeds the number of sudden deaths, and of old men dying without a will." The poet is speaking of luxury, which abridges the life of man, and most frequently takes off the hoary epicure by surprise.

His nunc præmium est, qui recta prava faciunt. Lat. TERENCE.
"Now, those are rewarded who make a right conduct appear in a wrong point of view."

His saltem acumulem donis, et fungar inani munere. Lat. VIRGIL.—"I may at least bestow upon him these last offerings, and perform a vain and unavailing duty."

Hoc age. Lat.—"Do, or mind this."—Attend without distraction to the object immediately before you.

Hoc erat in votis. Lat. HORACE.—"This was in my wishes."—This was the chief or immediate object of my desire.

Hoc est vivere bis,
Vita posse priore frui. Lat. MARTIAL.
"It is to live twice when you can enjoy the recol lection of your former life."

Hoc fonte derivata clades,
In patriam, populumque fluxit. Lat. HOR
"From this source has the destruction flowed which has overwhelmed the country and the people."

Hodie mihi, cras tibi. Lat.—"To day to me, to-mor row it belongs to you."—A phrase very happily descriptive of the vicissitude of human affairs.

Homine imperito nunquam quidquid injustius,
Qui, nisi quod ipse facit, nil rectum putat. Lat. TERENCE.
"Nothing can be more unjust than the ignorant man, who thinks that nothing can be done rightly

or perfectly, but that which is executed by him self."

Hominem pagina nostra sapit. Lat. MARTIAL. "Our page relates to man."—Our themes are drawn from observation, and are intended for the practical use of mankind.

Homine replagiendo. Law Lat.—The name of a writ for replevying a person illegally detained by another.

Homines ad Deos nullâ re propius accedunt, quam salutem hominibus dando. Lat. CIC.—"Men in no particular approach so nearly to the gods, as by giving health (or safety) to their fellow men."

Homines amplius oculis quam auribus credunt. Lat. SENECA.—"Men trust rather to their eyes than their ears."

Homines, nihil agendo, discunt malè agere. Lat. CATO.—"Men by doing nothing, learn to do ill."—Idleness is the parent of almost every vice.

Hominis est errare, insipientis vero perseverare. Lat. —"It is common to man to err, but it is the characteristic of a fool to persevere in error."

Homo extra est corpus suum, cum irascitur. Lat. SY.—"A man, when angry, is beside himself."

Homo homini lupus. Lat. ERASMUS.—"Man is a wolf to man."—The human race have been preying on each other, ever since the creation.

Homo homini aut Deus aut lupus. Lat. ERASMUS. "Man is to man either a god or a wolf."—Nothing can be more contrasted than the human character.

Homo multarum literarum. Lat.—"A man of many letters."—A person endowed with various learning.

Homo solus aut Deus aut dæmon. Lat.—"Man alone is either a God or a devil."—There is no other being in existence which is capable of such violent extremes.

Homo sum, et humani a me nil alienum puto. Lat. TERENCE.—"I am a man, and nothing which relates to man can be foreign to my bosom.—This is the strong phrase of a philanthropist, which, it is to be feared, is less frequently felt than it is quoted.

Honesta mors turpi vitâ potior. Lat. TACITUS. "An honourable death is preferable to a degraded life."—Our revealed religion forbids the act of suicide; but amongst the ancients, it was a prevalent maxim, that a self-inflicted death was preferable to a life of disgrace.

Honesta quædam scelera successus facit. Lat. SEN. —"Success makes some species of wickedness appear honourable."—This can not better be illustrated than by the English epigram,

"Treason does never prosper; what's the reason?
"Why, if it prospers, none dare call it treason."

Honesta quam splendida! Lat.—"How splendid are things honourably obtained!"

Honestum non est semper quod licet. Lat.—"An act is not always honourable because it is lawful."

Honi soit qui mal y pense. Old French.—"Evil be to him that evil thinks."—The motto of the kings of Great Britain.

Honor virtutis prœmium. Lat.—"Honour is the reward of virtue."

Honos alit artes. Lat.—"Honour supports the arts."

Hora e sempre. Ital.—"It is always time."

Horæ
Momento, cita mors venit, aut victoria læta.
Lat. HORACE.

"In one short hour comes either death, or joyful victory."—Spoken of a military life in which the suspense, however painful, is seldom protracted.

Horrea formicæ tendunt ad inania nunquam;
Nullus ad amissas ibit amicus opes. Lat. OVID.

"As the ant does not bend his way to empty barns; so no friend will be found to haunt the place of departed wealth."—This maxim is explained by the kindred proverb; "*ubi mel, ibi apes.*" Where the honey is, there the bees will be.

Hors de combat. Fr.—"Out of condition to fight."—Applied to a discomfited army.

Hortus siccus. Lat.—Literally, "A dry garden."—A collection of the leaves of different plants preserved in a dried state. "The *Hortus siccus* of dissent."—BURKE.—The opinions of dissenters in all their varieties.

Hostis humani generis. Lat.—"An enemy of the human race."—A pirate.

Hotel Dieu. Fr.—"The house of God."—A common name in France for an hospital.

Huic versatile ingenium sic pariter ad omnia fuit, ut natum ad id unum diceres, quodcunque ageret. Lat. LIVY.—"This man's parts were so convertible to all uses, that you would pronounce him to be born for whatever he undertook.—This is the character of the elder CATO.

Humani nihil alienum. Lat.—"Nothing is foreign to me which relates to man."

Humanum est errare. Lat.—"It is the lot of humanity to err."

Hunc tu caveto. Lat.—"Beware of him."

Ὕστερον πρότερον. Gr. *Hysteron proteron.*—"The last put first."—The positions or arguments inverted from their natural order: or, as we familiarly say, "The cart put before the horse."

I

Ibidem.—Ibid. Lat—"In the same place."—A note of reference.

Ibit eo quo vis, qui zonam perdidit. Lat. HORACE. "He will go where you will, who has lost his purse."—Poverty incites men to the most desperate actions.

Ich dien. Germ.—"I serve."—Motto of the Prince of Wales.

Id cinerem, aut manes credis curare sepultos?
Lat. VIRGIL.
"Do you think that this can affect the shade or ashes of the buried dead?"—Do you suppose that mortal cares can disturb the tranquillity of the grave?

Idem velle et idem nolle, ea demum firma amicitia est. Lat. Sallust.—"To wish for and reject things with similar feelings, is the only foundation of friendship."—True friendship can only spring from perfect sympathy.

I demens! et sævas curre per Alpes,
Ut pueris placeas, et declamatio fias. Lat. Juv. "Go, madman! rush over the wildest Alps, that you may please children, and be made the subject of declamation."—Go, desperate man, and encounter the severest hazards, to be rewarded only by the most trivial consolations.

I. E. an abbreviation of *id est.* Lat.—"That is."

Id facere laus est quod decet, non quod licet. Lat. Seneca.—"The man is deserving of praise who considers not what he *may* do, but what it is becoming him to do."

Id genus omne. Lat. Hor.—"All the persons of that description."—A phrase of contempt, as loan-jobbers, contractors, and *id genus omne,*—the rest of that rabble.

Id maximè quemque decet, quod est cujusque suum maximè. Lat. Cic.—"That best becomes every man, which is more particularly his own," or in other and coarser words, which he is "*best at.*"

Idoneus homo. Lat.—"A fit man."—A man of known ability.

Ignavissimus quisque, et ut res docuit, in periculo non ausurus, nimiò verbis et linguâ ferox. Lat. Tacitus.—"Every recreant who proved his timidity in the hour of danger, was afterwards the most talkative and bold in his discourse."

Igneus est ollis vigor, et cælestis origo. Lat.—"They possess a fiery ardour, and evince their celestial origin."

Ignis fatuus. Lat.—"A foolish fire."—The meteor, or ignited vapour, commonly known by the name of "Will o' the Wisp."—It is applied metaphorically to a discourse or treatise, which, whilst it affects to enlighten, tends only to confound and mislead

Ignoramus. Lat.—"We are ignorant."—This is the term used when the grand jury, empaneled on the inquisition of criminal causes, reject the evidence as too weak to make good the presentment or indictment, brought against a person, so as to bring him on his trial by a petty jury. This word, in that case, is endorsed on the back of the indictment, and all further proceedings against the party are stopped. An *ignoramus* sometimes implies an uninformed blockhead.

Ignorantia facti excusat. Lat. Law Maxim.—"Ignorance of the fact excuses."—"As, if an illiterate man seals a deed which is read to him falsely, the same shall be void.

Ignorantia non excusat legem. Law Lat.—"The ignorance of the individual does not prevent the operation of the law."—Every man is subject to the penalty of laws, which perhaps have never been duly promulgated.

Ignoscito sæpe alteri, nunquam tibi. Lat.—Of the same purport with the following quotation—

Ignoscas aliis multa, nil tibi. Lat. AUSON.—"You should forgive many things in others, but nothing in yourself."

Ignoti nulla cupido. Lat.—"No desire is felt for that which is unknown."—The African or American savage does not feel the want of European luxuries.

Ignotum per ignotius. Lat.—"That which is unknown by something more unknown."—He has explained the matter—*ignotum per ignotius*—he has offered as an illustration, that which tends to involve the matter in deeper obscurity.

I. H. S.—an abbreviation of *Jesus Hominum Salvator.*—"Jesus the Saviour of mankind."

Il aboye à toute le monde. Fr. Prov.—"He snarls at every body."

Il a la mer à boire. Fr.—"He has to drink up the sea."—He has entered on a prodigious enterprise.

Il a de l'esprit comme quatre. Fr. Prov.—"He has

as much wit as four men."—A vulgar mode of describing a superior genius.

Il a le diable au corps. Fr.—"The devil is in him."

Il a le vin mauvais Fr.—"He is quarrelsome when in his cups."

Il a semé des fleurs sur un terrain aride. Fr.—"He has planted flowers on a barren soil."

Il conduit bien sa barque. Fr. Prov.—"He steers his boat well."—He knows how to make his way through the world.

Il coute peu à amasser beaucoup de richesses, et beaucoup à en amasser peu. Fr.—"It requires but little effort to amass a great deal of riches, but it requires much effort to collect a little."—The man of property can easily enlarge his wealth; but the man who has nothing, has to maintain a hard struggle in his weak beginnings.

Il croit qu'il trompe, parce qu'il mente. Fr.—"He thinks he deceives, because he lies."

Il en fait ses choux gras. Fr. Prov.—"He thereby makes his cabbage fat."—He feathers his nest by it.

Il est comme l'oiseau sur la branche. Fr. Prov.—"He is like the bird on the branch."—His disposition is too wavering.

Il est plus aisé d'être sage pour les autres, que pour soimême. Fr. Rochefoucault.—"It is more easy to be wise for other persons than for ourselves."

Il est plus honteux de se defier de ses amis, que d'en être trompé. Fr. Rochefoucault.—"It is more digraceful to suspect our friends, than to be deceived by them."

Il faut attendre le boiteux. Fr. Prov.—"It is necessary to wait for the lame man."—This news is doubtful, we must wait for the truth which comes haltingly behind.

Il faut de l'argent. Fr.—"Money is wanted—or must be had."

Il faut des plus grands vertus pour soutenir la bonne fortune que la mauvaise. Fr.—"It requires a greater share of virtue to sustain a situation of prosperity, than to support one of adversity."

Iliacos intra muros peccatur et extra. Lat. Hor.—"They sin both within, and without the walls of Troy."—There are faults to be found on both sides.

Illa dolet verè, quæ sine teste dolet. Lat. Mart. "She grieves sincerely who grieves unseen."—Before company her grief may partake of affectation.

Ille crucem, sceleris pretium tulit, hic diadema. Lat. Juv.—"One man meets an infamous punishment for that crime, which confers a diadem upon anther."

Ille igitur nunquam direxit brachia contra
Torrentem; nec civis erat, qui libera posset
Verba animi proferre, et vitam impendere vero.
Lat. Juvenal.

"He never was that citizen who would attempt to swim against the torrent; who would freely deliver his opinion, and devote his life for the truth."—This is an admirable description, though in negative terms, of the qualities of a good patriot.

Ille potens sui
Lætùsque degit, cui licet in diem
Dixisse, Vixi. Lat. Horace.

"That man lives happy, and in command of himself, who from day to day can say, *I have lived.*"

Ille sinistrorsùm, hic dextrorsùm abit: unus utrique
Error, sed variis illudit partibus omnes.
Lat. Horace.

"One deviates to the right, another to the left; the error is the same with all, but it deceives them in different ways."

Illi mors gravis incubat, qui, notus nimis omnibus, ignotus moritur sibi. Lat. Seneca.—"Death must press heavily on that man, who being but too well known to others, dies at last in ignorance of himself."—The blackest horrors belong to him, who has passed a life of unreflecting wickedness.

Illium fuit. Lat.—"Troy has existed."— Such things *have* been.

Illæso lumine solem. Lat.—"With sight unhurt to view the sun."—This is the quality ascribed to the eagle.

Illud amicitiæ sanctum ac venerabile nomen
Nunc tibi pro vili, sub pedibusque jacet.
Lat. Ovid.

"The sacred and venerable name of friendship is now, by you, trodden upon and despised."

It n'a pas inventé la poudre. Fr. Prov.—"He was not the inventor of gunpowder."—He is no conjuror.

Il n'appartient qu'aux grands hommes d'avoir des grands défauts. Fr. Rochefoucault.—"It belongs only to great men to possess great defects."—Such defects are palliated at least, where great qualities can be pleaded as a set-off.

Il n'a ni bouche ni éperon. Fr. Prov.—"He has neither mouth nor spur."—He has neither wit nor courage.

Il ne faut pas éveiller le chât qui dort. Fr. Prov.—"It is not right to waken the cat that sleeps."—You should not bring into question a dormant secret or stir a sleeping mischief.

Il n'est sauce que d'appetit. Fr. Prov.—"Hunger is the best sauce."

Il ne sait sur quel pied danser. Fr. Proverb.—"He knows not on which leg to dance."—He is at his wit's ends.

Il n'y a que moi, qui a toujours raison. Fr.—"There is no one who is always in the right but myself."—This is a species of egotism frequently *practised*, though but seldom expressed.

Il n'y a rien de beau, que l'utile. Fr.—"There is nothing but the useful which is beautiful."

Il sabio muda conscio, il nescio no. Spanish Prov.—"A wise man sometimes changes his mind, a fool never."

Il sent de fagot. Fr. Prov.—"He smells of the fagot," which is to burn him as an *heretic.*

Il vaut mieux tâcher d'oublier ses malheurs, que d'en

parler. Fr.—"It is much better for a man to forget his misfortunes than to talk of them."—He who is too querulous not only feeds his own regret, but excites disgust in others.

Il volto sciolto, gli pensieri stretti. Ital. Prov.—"The countenance open, but the thought closely concealed."—This is the difficult maxim so strongly recommended by Lord CHESTERFIELD.

Il y a anguille sous la roche. Fr. Prov.—"There is an eel under the rock."—There is a mystery in the affair.

Il y a bien des gens qu'on estime, parcequ'on ne les connoit point. Fr.—"There are many persons who are esteemed, only because they are not known."

Il y a des gens qui résemblent aux vaudevilles, qu'on ne chante qu'un certain temps. Fr. ROCHEFOUCAULT.—"There are certain men whose fame is like that of a popular ballad, which is sung for a certain time, and then forgotten."

Il y a des gens à qui la vertu sied presque aussi mal que le vice. Fr. BOUHOURS.—"There are some persons on whom virtue sits almost as ungraciously as vice."

Il y a des gens dégoutans avec du mérite, et d'autres qui plaisent avec des défauts. Fr.—"There are people of merit who are disgusting, and there are others who please with all their defects."—So much depends upon manner, suavity and conciliation.

Il y a des reproches qui louent, et des louanges qui médisent. Fr. ROCHEFOUCAULT.—"There are some reproaches which form a commendation, and some praises which are in fact a slander."—There are some persons whose censure is praise, and whose praise is infamy.

Il y a encore de quoi glaner. Fr. Prov.—"There is something yet to be gleaned."—The subject is not wholly exhausted.

Imitatores! servum pecus. Lat. HORACE.—"Ye imitators! a servile herd."—Addressed to servile copy ists, who show at once their meanness and their weakness by living on the borrowed spoils of others.

Impendam et expendar. Lat.—"I will spend and be spent," in this service.

Imperat aut servit collecta pecunia cuique. Lat. HOR.—"Riches either serve or govern their possessor."—They are advantageous or hurtful, according to the uses to which they are turned.

Imperium facile iis artibus retinetur, quibus initio partum est. Lat. SALLUST.—"Power is easily retained by those means which acquired it."—It is generally gained by conciliation, and kept whilst that is continued. It is lost by oppression and intolerance.

Imperium, flagitio acquisitum, nemo unquam bonis artibus exercuit. Lat. TAC.—"The power acquired by guilt is never directed to any good end, or useful purpose."—When command is obtained by crime, the power which is thus usurped is most generally abused.

Imperium in imperio. Lat.—"A government existing within another government."—An establishment existing under, but independent, in a degree, of a superior establishment. This is instanced in each of the states composing the American union, in relation to the Federal or general government.

Impotentia excusat Legem. Lat. Law Max.—"Impotency does away the law."—This maxim relates to the infirmity of certain persons whom the law excuses from doing certain acts, as men in prison, idiots and lunatics, persons blind and dumb, &c.

Imprimatur. Lat.—"Let it be printed."—The phrase of permission to print, in countries where the press is under a vexatious control.—The word is figuratively used to denote any sort of authority.

Improbe amor! quid non mortalia pectora cogis? Lat. VIRG.—"O, cruel love! to what do you not impel the human breast?"

Improbè Neptunum accusat qui naufragium iterum facit. Lat. Prov.—"The man improperly blames the sea, who is a second time shipwrecked."—He should have learned prudence from his first misfortune.

Improbis aliena virtus semper formidolosa est. Lat. SALLUST.—"To the wicked the virtue of other men is ever formidable."—They dread that which lowers them by comparison, and hate the excellence to which they can not aspire.

Impromptu.—"In readiness."—A witticism made out of hand.

In amore hæc omnia insunt vitia; injuriæ,
Suspiciones, inimicitiæ, induciæ,
Bellum, pax rursus. Lat. TERENCE.

"In love there are all those evils,—wrongs, suspicions, enmities, treaties and alternate war and peace."

In articulo mortis. Lat.—"In the article of death."

In capite.—"In the head."—A tenure by which lands are held immediately of the crown.

In causâ facili, cuivis licet esse diserto. Lat. OVID.—"In an easy cause, any man may be eloquent."—The most indifferent orator may assume a triumphant air when he occupies "the vantage ground."

Incedimus per ignes,
Suppositos cineri doloso. Lat. HORACE.

"We tread on fires which are merely covered by deceitful ashes."—We have subdued the obvious peril, but not the lurking danger.

Incidit in Scyllam, qui vult vitare Charybdim. Lat. Prov.—"He falls into *Scylla* in struggling to escape *Charybdis.*"—The one was a rock, and the other a whirlpool, in the sea which divides Italy from Sicily.—When endeavouring to avoid one danger or mistake, we too frequently fall into another.

In civilibus voluntas pro facto reputabitur.—In criminalibus voluntas pro facto non reputabitur. Lat. Law Maxim.—"In civil cases, the will or intention is taken for the act, but in criminal cases it is not."

Inclusio unius est exclusio alterius. Lat. Law Max

"The name of one being included supposes an ex clusion of the other."—This is a maxim frequently used in arguments on testamentary devises. If of two persons of equal affinity, one is especially mentioned, it is supposed that the other was out of the intention of the testator.

In cœlo quies. Lat.—"There is rest in heaven."—A motto usually found on funeral achievements, commonly called hatchments.

Incognito. Lat.—"Unknown."—In disguise.

In commendam.—This phrase of modern Latin is used to denote a person "*commended,*" or recommended, to the care of a living whilst the church is vacant. It is used by a fiction to permit a bishop to retain the profits of a living within or without his own diocese.

Incubus. Lat.—"The night-mare."

In curia. Lat.—"In the court."

Inde iræ. Lat.—"Hence proceed those resentments."

Index expurgatorius. Lat.—"A purging or purifying index."—A list formerly published under the authority of the Roman pontiffs, specifying the books which were prohibited to be read. This was continued until it was found, that the wayward wishes of those who could read, were almost uniformly di rected to the treatises thus forbidden.

Indignante invidia florebit justus. Lat.—"The just man will flourish in despite of envy."

Indocti discant, et ament meminisse periti. Lat.—"Let the ignorant learn, and let the learned im prove their recollection."—This is a motto fre quently prefixed to works of a general and useful tendency.

In dubiis. Lat.—"In matters of doubt."—In cases of uncertainty.

In eâdem re, utilitas et turpitudo esse non possunt Lat. CICERO.—"Usefulness and baseness can not exist in the same thing."—It is in vain to plead the advantages of a proceeding, when those advan tages are to be purchased by the loss of honesty or of honour.

In equilibrio. Lat.—"In an even poise."—As a scale beam, when it has equal weights attached to each end.

Inerat Vitellio simplicitas ac liberalitas; quæ nisi adsit modus, in exitium vertuntur. Lat. TAC.—"There was in *Vitellius*, a simplicity and a liberality; qualities which, unless taken in the degree, are generally ruinous to the possessor."—There are virtues the most amiable in private life, which exercised by a public man, beyond their due bounds, will ever be found dangerous in the extreme.

In esse. Lat.—"In being."—In existence.

In extenso. Lat.—"At large—in full."

Inest sua gratia parvis. Lat.—"Even little things have their peculiar grace."

In favorem vitæ, libertatis et innocentiæ omnia præsumuntur. Lat. Law Maxim.—"Where life, liberty, and the character of a person are at stake, every presumption is to be taken in his favour."

Infelix Dido, nulli bene juncta marito;
Hoc pereunte, fugis; hoc fugiente, peris.
Lat. OVID.

"Unhappy Dido, deprived of both husband and lover—the former by dying, causes thy flight, the latter by flying, causes thy death."

In ferrum pro libertate ruebant. Lat.—"For freedom's sake they rushed upon the sword."

Infinita est velocitas temporis, quæ magis apparet respicientibus. Lat. SENECA.—"The swiftness of time is infinite, as is most evident to those who look back."

In flagranti delicto. Lat.—"In the apparent guilt." – Taken in the very commission of the crime.

In forma pauperis. Lat.—"In the form of a poor man."—According to the statute 11 Henry VII. any man who is too poor to meet the expenses of suing at law or in equity, making oath that he is not worth more than 5*l.* after his debts are paid and producing a certificate from a lawyer that he has just cause of suit, the judge in this case is to admit him to sue *in forma pauperis;* that is, without paying any fees to the counsel, attorney, or clerks.

In foro conscientiæ. Lat.—"Before the tribunal of conscience."—In a man's own conviction of what is equitable.

In futuro. Lat.—"In future."—Henceforth.

Ingenii largitor venter. Lat. PERSIUS.—"The belly is the giver of genius."—Ironically spoken of those whose only *stimulus* to authorship is their poverty.

Ingenio stat sine morte decus. Lat. PROPERT.—"The honours of genius are eternal."—This is the boast of many a poet.

Ingenium cui sit, cui mens divinior, atque os
Magna sonaturum. Lat. HORACE.
"Who is possessed of genius, of a superior mind, and an overpowering eloquence."

Ingenium ingens
Inculto latet hoc sub corpore. Lat. HORACE.
"A powerful mind is concealed within this unpolished body."

Ingenium res adversæ nudare solent, celare secundæ. Lat. HOR.—"In adversity those talents are called forth, which are concealed by prosperity."

Ingenuas didicisse fideliter artes,
Emollit mores, nec sinit esse feros. Lat. OVID.
"To have studied carefully the liberal arts is the surest mode of refining the grossness, and subduing the harshness, of the human mind."

Ingens telum necessitas. Lat. SENECA.—"Necessity is a powerful weapon."—To provoke a needy man is to encounter with desperation.

Ingrato homine terra pejus nil creat. Lat. AUSON. "The earth never produces any thing worse than an ungrateful man."—See the following quotations.

Ingratum si dixeris omnia dicis. Lat.—"If you pronounce a man ungrateful, you say all that can be urged against him."

Ingratus unus miseris omnibus nocet. Lat. SYRUS. —"One ungrateful man does an injury to all who are wretched."—He, by his baseness, has perhaps steeled the heart, which might otherwise have relieved their distresses.

In hoc signo spes mea. Lat.—"In this sign is my hope."

In hoc signo vinces. Lat.—"In this sign thou shalt conquer."—This was the motto assumed by the emperor CONSTANTINE, after having seen a *Cross* in the air, which he considered as the presage of victory.

Iniqua nunquam regna perpetua manent. Lat. SENECA.—"Authority founded on, or maintained by, injustice, is never of long duration."

Iniquissimam pacem justissimo bello antefero. Lat. —"I prefer the most unjust peace to the justest war."—The horrors of war are so numerous and so afflicting, that peace should, at all times, be purchased at any price, *short of national dishonour.*

Initia magistratuum nostrorum meliora firma, finis inclinat. Lat. TACITUS.—"The discharge of our public offices is generally more exemplary in their commencement; its vigour declines towards the conclusion."—Our proverb of "New Brooms," gives of this an apt, though a homely illustration.

In jure, non remota causa, sed proxima, spectatur. Lat. Law Maxim.—"The law does not regard the remote, but the proximate cause."

Injuriarum plerasque non accipit, qui nescit. Lat. SENECA.—"He avoids many inconveniences, who does not appear to notice them."

Injuriarum remedium est oblivio. Lat.—"The best remedy for injuries is to forget them."

In limine. Lat—"In the threshold."—In the outset, or commencement.

In loco. Lat.—"In the place."—In the proper place. —Upon the spot.

In magnis voluisse sat est. Lat. PROP.—"It is laud

able even to attempt a great act," though without success.

In medias res. Lat. HOR.—"Into the midst of things."—Spoken generally of an author who rushes abruptly and without preparation into his subject.

In medio tutissimus ibis. Lat.—"In the middle path you will proceed with the most safety."

In necessariis unitas, in non necessariis libertas, in omnibus charitas. AUGUSTIN.—"In those things which are essential, let there be unity, in non-essentials, liberty, and in all things charity."

In nova fert animus. Lat—"My mind leads me to new matters, or to discuss new topics."—This is an hemistich: the following is the complete line.

In nova fert animus mutatas dicere formas. Lat. OVID.—"I am inclined to speak of bodies changed into new forms."

In nubibus. Lat.—"In the clouds."

Innuendo. Latin Law Term.—"By signifying."—Thereby intimating.—A word much used in declarations of slander and libel, to ascertain the application to a person or thing which was previously named. An oblique hint.

In nullum avarus bonus est, in se pessimus. Lat. Prov.—"The avaricious man is kind to no person, but he is most unkind to himself."

In nullum reipublicæ usum ambitiosâ loquelâ inclaruit. Lat. TACITUS.—"He became celebrated for an affected and ambitious verbosity, attended with no advantage whatever to the state."

In omnibus fere minori ætati succurritur. Lat. Law Maxim.—"In all cases relief is afforded to persons under age."—The law is so careful of persons of this description, that it will not suffer them to alienate, sell, or bind themselves by deed, unless it be for eating, drinking, schooling, physic, or such other matters as are absolutely necessary.

In omnibus quidem, maximè tamen in Jure, Æquitas est. Lat. Law Maxim.—"In all things, but particularly in the law, there is equity."—Equity is said to be a corrective of the law, where the latter is deficient on account of its generality.

Inopem copia fecit. Lat.—"His plenty made him poor."—His copiousness of ideas retarded and embarrassed his language.

In pace leones, in prælio cervi. Lat.—"In peace they are lions, in the battle deer."—They are blusterers and cowards.

In perpetuam rei memoriam. Lat.—"To perpetuate the memory of the thing."—An inscription generally found upon pillars, &c. raised to commemorate any particular incident.

In pertusum ingerimus dicta dolium. Lat. PLAUT. "We fling our sayings into a cask bored through." Our advice is wholly thrown away in that quarter.

In petto. Ital.—"Within the breast."—Held in reserve.

In presenti. Lat.—"At the present time."

In propriâ personâ. Lat.—"In his own person."—In personal attendance.

In puris naturalibus. Lat.—"In a purely natural state."—*i. e.* Stark naked.

Inquinat egregios adjuncta superbia mores. Lat. CLAUD.—"The best manners are stained by the addition of pride."—Even virtue itself is disgusting in a severe and haughty garb.

In quo hoc maximum est, quod neque ante illum, quem ille imitaretur, neque post illum, qui eum imitari posset, inventus est. Lat. PATERCULUS. "Concerning whom this is most worthy of being noted, that neither before him was there found an example for his imitation, nor among his successors one who could imitate him.

In rerum natura. Lat.—"In the nature of things.

Insanire parat certâ ratione modoque. Lat. HOR.—"He is preparing to be mad according to a certain rule and manner."—He has much "method in his madness."

Insanus omnis furere credit cæteros. Lat. Prov.

"Every madman thinks that all the rest of the world is mad."

In sæcula sæculorum. Lat.—"For ages of ages."—Throughout eternity.

In se magna ruunt. Lat. LUCAN.—"Great bodies are apt to rush against each other."—Two great powers are naturally inclined to jealousy, and thence to hostility.

In se totus teres atque rotundus. Lat. HORACE. "Smooth, round, and collected in himself."—This is a brief but excellent description of a man of the world. The metaphor is taken from a bowl, which launched from a firm hand, is not to be diverted from its course by slight obstacles.

Inistâ hominibus libidine alendi de industria rumores. Lat.—"Men having in them a natural desire to propagate reports."

Insitâ hominibus natura violentiæ resistere. Lat. TAC.—"To resist violence is implanted in the nature of man."

In situ. Lat.—"In position."—In its natural situation.

Inspicere, tanquam in speculum, in vitas omnium
Jubeo, atque ex aliis sumere exemplum sibi.
Lat. TERENCE.

"The lives of other men should be regarded as a mirror, from which we may take an example, and a rule of conduct for ourselves."—The accurate observer of human life, in witnessing the follies of others, will thence derive to himself so many lessons of caution and correctness.

Instanter. Lat.—"Instantly."

Instar omnium. Lat.—"Like all the rest."

In statu quo. Lat.—"In the state in which it was."—The condition in which a nation or individual was at a certain anterior time.—See *status quo*, and,

In statu quo ante bellum. Lat.—"In the condition in which it was before the war."

Intaminatis fulget honoribus. Lat. HORACE.—"He shines with unspotted honours."

In te, Domine, speravi. Lat.—"In thee, O Lord, have I put my trust."

Integer vitæ, scelerisque purus,
Non eget Mauri jaculis nec arcu. Lat. Hor.
"The man who is pure in life, and unconscious of guilt, wants not the aid of Moorish bows and darts."—In most situations of life, the consciousness of innocence is our best shield and our firmest security.

Integra mens augustissima possessio. Lat.—"A mind fraught with integrity is the noblest possession."

Integros haurire fontes. Lat.—"To drink from overflowing fountains."—To supply our wants from a plentiful source.

Intentum animum, tanquam arcum, habebat. Lat. Cic.—"He kept his mind bent like a bow."

Intenti expectant signum. Lat. Virg.—"Eager they wait the sign."

In tenui labor; at tenuis non est gloria. Lat. Virg. "The labour was bestowed on a small object, but the fame of the achievement was not the less."—To do little things well, is in some cases highly honourable.

Inter alia. Lat.—"Among other things."

Inter arma leges silent. Lat.—"The laws are silent in the midst of arms."—During the violence of hostility, but little attention is paid to the precepts of justice.

Interdum lachrymæ pondera vocis habent. Lat. Ovid.—"Tears are sometimes equal in weight to words."

Interdum populus recte videt. Lat.—"The people sometimes see aright."—They are occasionally deceived and misled; but they as often can judge, and with sound discretion.

Interdum vulgus recte videt; est ubi peccat. Lat. Hor.—"Sometimes the people decide justly; but they do in some instances form erroneous conclusions."

Intererit multum, Davusne loquatur, an Eros. Lat. HOR.—"There is a great difference when *Davus* is speaking, and when a Hero."—The former is a servant: the rule is addressed to dramatic writers, who should always make their characters speak in appropriate language.

Inter nos. Lat.—"Between ourselves."—This is *inter nos*—to be kept a secret.

Interregnum. Lat.—The interval between the death of one king and the succession of another.

In terrorem. Lat.—"In terror."—As a warning.

Inter se. Lat.—"Between, or among, themselves."

Inter utrumque tene. Lat. Prov.—"Keep between both."—Steer through life a safe and middle course, avoiding equally all extremes.

In toto. Lat.—"In the whole"—altogether—entirely.

In toto et pars continetur. Lat.—"In the whole is contained also the part."

Intra fortunam quisque debet manere suam. Lat. OVID.—"Every man should confine himself within the bounds of his own fortune."

In transitu. Lat.—"On the passage."—Goods, *in transitu*, are goods consigned by one person to another, and which have not yet reached the consignee.

Intus et in cute novi hominem. Lat. PERSIUS.—"I know the man thoroughly."—I have a thorough knowledge of his character.

Intuta quæ indecora. Lat. TACITUS.—"Those things that are unseemly are unsafe."—Men in certain situations should remember, that as much danger frequently arises from forfeiting the respect, as from incurring the resentment of those who are beneath them.

In utroque fidelis. Lat.—"Faithful in both."

In utrumque paratus. Lat.—"Prepared for either event."

Invidia, Siculi non invenere tyranni
Tormentum majus. Lat. JUVENAL

"The Sicilian tyrants never devised a greater punishment than envy is."

Invidus alterius macrescit rebus opimis. Lat. Hor. "The envious man grows lean at the success of his neighbour."

In vino veritas. Lat.—"There is truth in wine."—It extracts secrets from the reserved, and puts the habitual liar off his guard.

Invisa potentia, atque miseranda vita eorum, qui se metui, quam amari, malunt. Lat. Corn. Nep. —"Their power is hateful, and their life miserable, who wish to be feared rather than beloved."

Invisibilia non decipiunt. Lat.—"The things which are unseen do not deceive."

Invitat culpam qui peccatum præterit. Lat. Syrus. "He, who overlooks one crime, invites the commission of another."

Invitum sequitur honos. Lat.—"Honour follows him against his inclination."

Invita Minerva. Lat.—"*Minerva* (the goddess of wisdom) being unwilling."—The work was brought forth, *invita Minerva,* without any aid from genius, or from taste.

In vitium ducit culpæ fuga. Lat. Horace.—"The avoiding of one fault sometimes leads into another."—Thus a writer, in avoiding dull prolixity, often flies into the opposite extreme of obscure brevity.

Ipse dixit. Lat.—"He said it himself."—On his *ipse dixit*—on his mere assertion.

Ipsisima verba. Lat.—"The very words."—The most strict and literal meaning of the expression.

Ipso facto. Lat.—"By the very act."—By the fact when it shall appear.

Ipso jure. Lat.—"By the law itself."—By the law when it shall be pronounced.

Ira furor brevis est. Lat. Hor.—"Anger is a short madness."—All the mischiefs of madness may be produced by a momentary passion.

Iram qui vincit, hostem superat maximum. Lat.—

"He who subdues his anger, conquers his greatest enemy."

Ira quæ tegitur nocet;
Professa perdunt odia vindictæ locum.
Lat. SENECA.
"Concealed resentment alone is dangerous.—Hatred, when manifest, loses its opportunity of revenge."

Iras et verba locant. Lat. MART.—"They let out for hire their passions and their words."—This is the severest sarcasm ever uttered against the gentlemen of the bar; who, it intimates, not only hire out their eloquence, but can also feign a degree of passion proportioned to the magnitude of the fee.

Is maximè divitiis utitur, qui minimè divitiis indiget. Lat. SENECA.—"He makes the best use of riches, who has the smallest share of personal wants."

Is minimo eget mortalis, qui minimum cupit.
Lat. P. SYRUS.
"That man has the fewest wants, who is the least anxious for wealth."

Is mihi demum vivere, et frui animâ videtur, qui aliquo negotio intentus, præclari facinoris, aut artis bonæ, famam quærit. Lat. SALLUST.—"He alone appears to me to live, and to enjoy life, who, being engaged in active scenes, seeks after reputation by some famous action, or some honest art."

Is ordo vitio careto, cæteris specimen esto. Lat.—"Let that order be free from vice, and afford an example to all others."—This was an ordinance contained in the Roman laws of the Twelve Tables, and addressed to the senatorial or patrician order.—The best example should come from the highest place.

Ita lex scripta est. Lat.—"Thus the law is written."—A phrase used in polemics, to refer the adversary to the letter of the text in question.

Ita me Dii ament! ast ubi sim nescio. Lat. TER.—"As God shall judge me, I know not where I am."

—I am so confounded, that I know not what to do or say.

J

Jacta est alea. Lat.—"The die is cast."—I have put every thing to venture, and I now must stand the hazard.

Jactitatio. Lat.—"A boasting."—Jactitation of marriage is cognisable in the ecclesiastical court.

J'ai bonne cause. Fr.—"I have a good cause."

J'ai eu toujours pour principe, de ne faire jamais par autrui, ce que je pouvois faire par moi-méme. Fr. Montesquieu.—"I have ever held it as a maxim, never to do that through another, which it was possible for me to execute myself."

Jamais arrière. Fr.—"Never behind."

Jamais on ne vaincra les Romains, que dans Rome. Fr.—"The Romans can never be conquered but in Rome."

Jamque opus exegi; quod nec Jovis ira, nec ignis,
Nec poterit ferrum, nec edax abolere vetustas.
Lat. Ovid.

"I have now completed a work, which neither the wrath of Jove, nor fire, nor the sword, nor the corroding tooth of time shall be able to destroy."—At present this passage, as well as the *Exegi monumentum*, &c. of Horace, are chiefly used in an ironical sense, and for the purpose of holding some proud boaster up to ridicule.

Januis clausis. Lat.—"The doors being shut."—The matter was debated *januis clausis*—in a secret committee.

Jejunus raro stomachus vulgaria temnit. Lat. Hor.—"The hungry stomach seldom despises coarse fare."—Or, as it may be differently translated—"The stomach which is seldom hungry, holds vulgar fare in contempt."—It is more generally quoted in the former acceptation.

Je le tiens Fr.—"I hold it."

Je ne cherche qu'un. Fr.—"I seek but for one."

Je n'oublierai jamais. Fr.—"I shall never forget."

Je ne sais quoi. Fr.—"I know not what."—Used to express something that will not admit of a description.

Je suis prêt. Fr.—"I am ready."

Jet d'eau. Fr.—"A water spout—an artificial fountain."

Jeu de main, jeu de vilain. Fr.—"Practical tricks belong only to the lowest classes."—No gentleman should deal in horse play, or vulgar roughness.

Jeu de mots. Fr.—"A play on words."—A pun.

Jeu d'esprit. Fr.—"A play of wit."—A witticism.

Jeu de theâtre. Fr.—"Stage-trick, attitude," &c.

Jeune, on conserve pour la vieillesse: vieux, on épargne pour la mort. Fr. La Bruyere.—"When young, men lay up for old age; when aged, they hoard for death."—It is in the nature of parsimony to confirm itself and to increase.

Jetsam, Flotsam, Ligan.—These are three barbarous law terms, or appellations given to goods thrown overboard, or otherwise lost at sea. The first indicates such articles as are thrown out, and sink, and remain under water—the second is when they continue floating on the surface; and *ligan* denotes such as are sunk, but made fast to a cork or buoy, that they may be found again.

Joco di mano, joco villano. Ital. Prov.—This is precisely in its meaning similar to the French proverb quoted above—"*Jeu de main,*" &c.

Jour de ma vie. Fr.—"The day of my life."

Jucunda atque idonea dicere vitæ. Lat. Hor.—"To describe whatever is pleasant and proper in life."—This line well describes the duty of the didactic poet.

Jucundi acti labores. Lat. Cic.—"The labours and difficulties through which we have passed are pleasing to the recollection."

Jucundum et carum sterilis facit uxor amicum. Lat Juvenal.—"A barren wife will always produce a pleasant and engaging friend."—This is spoken in derision of the legacy hunters; a race every where common and despicable, and who pay their court more assiduously, where there is no expectation of an heir.

Judex damnatur cum nocens absolvitur. Lat.—"The judge is found guilty when a criminal is acquitted."—This is to be understood as applying, only where prejudice or corruption has dictated the sentence.

Judicandum est legibus non exemplis. Lat. Law Max.—"The judgment must be pronounced from law, not from precedent."—As no two precedents, in the legal phrase, run together "on four legs," the strict letter of the law must be consulted.

Judicata res pro veritate accipitur. Lat. Law Max. "A thing which has been judged, is considered as a truth."—A decision in one case may be cited, as authority in another which is similar.

Judicis est jus dicere, non dare. Lat. Law Maxim.—"It is the duty of a judge to declare the law, and not to make it."

Judicium Dei. Lat.—"The judgment of God."—This was the name given by our ancestors to the *ordeal, i. e.* walking blindfold over red hot plough shares, &c. which has been long since disused.

Judicium parium, aut leges terræ. Lat.—"The judgment of our peers, or the law of the land."—It is only by these, according to *Magna Charta,* that an Englishman can be condemned.

Jugulare mortuos. Lat.—"To stab the dead."—To exercise superfluous cruelty.

Jugulo hunc suo gladio. Lat. Ter.—"I foil him with his own weapons."—I silence him with his own arguments.

Juncta juvant. Lat.—"These things, when conjoined, mutually aid each other."—Individually considered, they are of little avail; but taken conjunctively, they form a strong body of evidence.

Jure humano. Lat.—"By human law."—By that

law which is founded on the assent of men. It is generally used in opposition to the following:

Jure divino. Lat.—" By divine right."—This is the tenure by which, according to the high-flying tories, the Kings of Great Britain hold their crowns, without any reference to the will of the people.

Juris præcepta sunt hæc; honestè vivere, alterum non lædere, suum cuique tribuere. Lat. JUST. INST.—" The precepts of the law are these; to live correctly, to do an injury to none, and to render to every one his own."

Jus civile. Lat. —" The civil law."—The law of many European nations, and of some of our courts, particularly the Ecclesiastical, founded on the Code of JUSTINIAN.

Jus gentium. Lat.—" The law of nations."

Jus sanguinis, quod in legitimis successionibus spectatur, ipso nativitatis tempore quæsitum est. Lat. Law Maxim.—" The right of blood, which is regarded in all lawful inheritances, is found in the very time of nativity."—It is the *jus primogenituræ*, or right of eldership, that is principally respected; the maxim being, that the next of worthiest blood should always inherit.

Jus summum sæpe summa est malitia. Lat. TER. " Law, enforced to strictness, sometimes becomes the severest injustice."

Justitia liberalitati prior. Lat.—" Justice should precede liberality."—A man should be "*just* before he is *generous.*"

Justitia virtutum regina. Lat.—" Justice is queen of the virtues."

Justitiæ soror fides. Lat.—" Faith is the sister of justice."

Justum et tenacem propositi virum,
Non civium ardor prava jubentium,
Non vultus instantis tyranni,
Mente quatit solidâ. Lat. HORACE

" The man, who is just and firm to his purpose, will not be shaken from his fixed resolution, either by the misdirecting ardor of his fellow-citizens, or by the threats of any imperious tyrant."

Justus propositi tenax. Lat.—"The just man is steady to his purpose."

Juvat in sylvis habitare. Lat.—"It is pleasant to dwell in the woods," or in the country.

Juvenile vitium regere non posse impetum. Lat. SENECA.—"It is the fault of youth that it can not govern its own violence."

K

Καιρον γνωθι. *Kairon gnothi.* Gr.—"Know your opportunity."—This was the advice of PITTACUS, one of the seven Grecian sages. To let slip an occasion is a great proof of imbecility.

Κατ' εξοχην. *Kat' exochen.* Gr.—"By way of excellence," or "of peculiar distinction."

L

La beauté de l'esprit donne de l'admiration, celle de l'âme donne de l'estime, et celle du corps de l'amour. Fr.—"The charms of wit excite admiration, those of the heart impress esteem, and those of the body provoke to love."

La beauté sans vertu est une fleur sans perfum. Fr. Prov.—"Beauty without virtue is like a flower without perfume."—It may retain its colour, but has lost its essence.

Labitur et labetur in omne volubilis ævum. Lat. HOR.—"The stream still flows, and will continue to flow through every age."

La bonne fortune, et la mauvaise sont nécessaires à l'homme, pour le rendre habile. Fr.—"Good and bad fortune are necessary to a man, in order to make him adroit and capable."—Few men are equal to the emergencies of life, who have not experienced some of its vicissitudes.

Labor ipse voluptas. Lat.—"The labour itself is a pleasure."

Labor omnia vincit. Lat. VIRGIL.—"Labour conquers every thing."—There are few difficulties which will not yield to perseverance.

Laborum dulce lenimen. Lat. HOR.—"The sweet solace of our labours."—The appellation is given by the poet to his favourite study

La confiance fournit plus à la conversation que l'esprit. Fr. ROCHEFOUCAULT.—"Confidence is, in general, found to furnish more towards conversation, than wit or talent."

La criaillerie ordinaire fait qu'on s'y accoutume, et que chacun la méprise. Fr.—"A clamorous abuse too often repeated, becomes so familiar to the ear as to lose its effect."—If you scold your servant inordinately for not rinsing a glass, he will scarcely feel your rebuke when you charge him with a robbery.

La critique est aisée, et l'art est difficile. Fr.—"To criticise the productions of art and science is easy, but to create them is difficult."

La decence est le teint naturel de la vertu, et le fard du vice. Fr. Prov.—"Decency is the genuine tint of virtue, and the false colouring of vice."

L'adversité fait l'homme, et le bonheur les monstres. French.—"Adversity makes men, but prosperity makes monsters."

La faim chasse le loup du bois. Fr. Prov.—"Famine drives the wolf from the wood."—According to the English Proverb—Hunger breaks through stone walls."

La faveur met l'homme au-dessus de ses égaux, et sa chute au-dessous. Fr. LA BRUYERE.—"Favour places a man above his equals, and his fall or disgrace, beneath them."

L'affaire s'achemine. Fr.—"The business is going forward."

La foiblesse de l'ennemi fait notre propre force. Fr. "The weakness of the enemy forms a part of our own strength."—This is a maxim in war, where all advantages are fairly to be taken.

La fortune vend ce qu'on croit qu'elle donne. Fr. La Fontaine.—" Fortune *sells* the favours which she seems to lavish."

La grande sagesse de l'homme consiste à connoitre ses folies. Fr.—" The great wisdom of man consists in the knowledge of his follies."

L'aigle d'une maison est un sot dans une autre. Fr. Gresset.—" The eagle of one house is but a fool in another."

Laissez nous faire. Fr.—" Let us act for (or take care of) ourselves."—Let us alone.

La langue des femmes est leur épée, et elles ne la laissent pas rouiller. Fr. Prov.—" The tongue of a woman is her sword, which she seldom suffers to rust."

La libéralité consiste moins à donner beaucoup, qu'à donner à propos. Fr. La Bruyere.—" Liberality does not consist so much in giving a great deal, as in giving seasonably."

L'Allegorie habite un palais diaphane. Fr. Le Mierre.—" Allegory dwells in a transparent palace."—Its only use being to offer truth from the mirror of reflection, it should not be dimmed by obscurity.

La maladie sans maladie. Fr.—" The disease without a disease."—The hypochondriac distemper.

L'âme n'a point de secret que la conduite ne revèle. Fr. Prov.—" The soul has no secret which the conduct does not reveal."—The most practised hypocrite can not, at all times, conceal his secret feelings.

La moitié du monde prend plaisir à médire, et l'autre moitié à croire les médisances Fr. Prov. " One half the world takes a pleasure in detracting, and the other half in believing all that detraction utters."

La moquerie est souvent une indigence d'esprit. Fr. La Bruyere.—" Jesting, in some cases, only proves a want of understanding."

La mort est plus aisée à supporter sans y penser, que

la pensée de la mort sans péril. Fr. PASCAL.—"Death is itself more easy, when it comes without previous reflection, than the thought of death, even without the danger."

L'amour de la justice n'est, en la plûpart des hommes, que la crainte de souffrir l'injustice Fr. ROCHEFOUCAULT.—"The love of justice is in most men nothing more than the fear of suffering injustice."—Our anxiety on this subject may be traced to a motive of selfishness.

L'amour et la fumée ne peuvent se cacher. Fr. Prov. —"Love and smoke are two things which can not be concealed."

L'amour-propre est le plus grand de tous les flatteurs. Fr. ROCHEFOUCAULT.—"Self-love is the greatest of all flatterers."

L'amour soumet la terre, assujettit les cieux—
Les rois sont à ses pieds, il gouverne les dieux.
Fr. CORNEILLE.

"Love rules o'er the earth and controls the heavens —kings are at his feet, and gods are his subjects." This extravagant flight, as it may be supposed, is seldom quoted but in the way of ridicule.

Langage des halles. Fr.—"The language of the markets."—Billingsgate.

La passion fait souvent un fou du plus habile homme, et rend souvent habiles les plus sots. Fr. ROCHEFOUCAULT.—"Love often makes a fool of the cleverest man, and as often gives cleverness to the most foolish."

La patience est amère, mais son fruit est doux. Fr. J. J. ROUSSEAU.—"Patience is bitter, but its fruit is sweet."

La patience est la rémède la plus sûr contre les calomnies: le tems tôt ou tard découvre la vérité. Fr.—"Patience is the surest antidote against calumny. Time, sooner or later, will discover the truth."

La philosophie, qui nous promet de nous rendre heureux, nous trompe. Fr.—"Philosophy, which promises to render us happy, deceives us"

La philosophie triomphe aisément des maux passés et des maux à venir; mais les maux presens triomphent d'elle. Fr. ROCHEFOUCAULT.—" Philosophy can hold an easy triumph over *past* and *future* mifortunes; but those which are *present* triumph over her."

Lapides crescunt; vegetabilia crescunt et vivunt; animalia crescunt, vivunt et sentiunt. Lat.—" Stones grow; vegetables grow and live; animals, grow, live and feel."—This is a general distinctive definition, given by Linnæus, of the three great natural kingdoms.

Lapsus linguæ. Lat.—" A slip of the tongue."

La reputation d'un homme est comme son ombre, qui tantôt le suive, et tantôt le précede; quelquefois elle est plus longue, et quelquefois plus courte que lui. Fr. Prov.—" The reputation of a man is like his shadow; it sometimes follows and sometimes precedes him; it is sometimes longer, and sometimes shorter than his natural size."

L'argent est un bon serviteur, et un méchant maître. Fr. BOUHOURS.—" Money is a good servant, but a bad master."

L'art de vaincre est celui de mépriser la mort. Fr. M. DE SIVRY.—" The art of conquering is that of despising death."

La science du gouvernement n'est qu'une science de combinaisons, d'applications, et d'exceptions, selon les tems, les lieux, les circonstances. Fr. ROUSSEAU.—" The science of government is only a science of combinations, of applications, and of exceptions, according to times, places, and circumstances."

La silence est la vertu de ceux qui ne sont pas sages. Fr. BOUHOURS.—" Silence is the virtue, or the best quality of the foolish."—If it does not remove, it at least conceals, their deficiency.

Lateat scintillula forsan. Lat.—" A small spark may lurk unseen."—This hemistich, alluding to the vital spark, is very happily adopted as the motto of the Humane Society.

Latet anguis in herba. Lat.—"There is a snake concealed in the grass."—There is a lurking danger before you, which you do not immediately perceive.

Latitat. Law Lat.—"He lurks."—A writ of summons issuing from the King's Bench, which, by a fiction, states the defendant to be in a state of concealment.

Laudari a viro laudato. Lat.—"To be praised by a man, himself deserving of praise."—This is certainly the most valuable species of commendation.

Laudato ingentia rura—exiguum colito. Lat. Virg. "Bestow your praise upon large domains, but your preference on a small estate."—The latter, to a contented mind, is likely to produce the greatest share of happiness.

Laudator temporis acti. Lat. Hor.—"A praiser of the times which are past."—An old man who commends nothing but what he has seen in his early days.

Laudum arrecta cupido. Lat. Virg.—"The eager desire of praise."

Laudum immensa cupido. Lat.—"The insatiate thirst for applause or flattery."

La vérité ne fait pas autant de bien dans le monde, que ses apparences y font de mal. Fr.—"Truth does not so much good in the world, as its appearances do mischief."—The deceit and hypocrisy of men are the prime sources of evil in the moral world.

La vertu n'iroit pas si loin, si la vanité ne lui tenoit compagnie. French. Rochefoucault.—"Virtue would not go so far, if vanity did not bear it company."—We are propelled in our best actions by a secret wish to gain the good opinion of others.

Laus Deo. Lat.—"Praise be to God."

Le beau monde. French.—"The gay or fashionable world."

Le bien ne se fait jamais mieux, que lorsqu'il s'opère lentement. Fr. De Moy.—"Good is never effected more happily, than when it is produced slowly." Sudden changes either in the affairs of empires or individuals, are seldom productive of beneficial consequences.

Le bonheur de l'homme en cette vie ne consiste pas à être sans passions: il consiste à en être la maître. Fr.—" The happiness of man in this life does not consist in the absence, but in the mastery, of his passions."

Le bon temps viendra. Fr.—" The good time will come."

Le coût en ôte le goût. Fr. Prov.—" The cost takes away the taste."—I should like the thing, but I dislike the expense.

Le dessous des cartes. Fr.—" The lower side of the cards."—*Il est au dessous des cartes*—he sees the faces of the cards.—He is in the secret.

Le diable est aux vaches. Fr.—" The devil is in the cows."—There is the devil to pay.

Leges legum. Lat.—" The laws of laws."—The original and controlling source of legislation.

Lege totum, si vis scire totum. Lat.—" Read all, if you would know all."

Legis constructio non facit injuriam. Lat. Law Maxim.—" The interpretative construction of the law shall wrong no person."—If a person, for instance, grants away all his goods and chattels, those of which he is possessed as an executor shall not pass; for that would be a wrong to the estate of the testator.

Le grand œuvre. Fr.—" The great work."—That is, the philosopher's stone.

Le jeu est le fils d'avarice, et le père du desespoir. Fr. Prov.—" Gaming is the son of avarice, and the father of despair."

Le jeu n'en vaut pas la chandelle. Fr. Proverb.—" The game is not worth the candles."—The object which you aim at is not worthy of your expense or labour.

L'elévation est au mérite, ce que la parure est aux

belles personnes. Fr.—"Elevation is to merit, what dress is to handsome persons."—It adorns and sets off that excellence, of which it forms no constituent part.

Le mieux est l'ennemi du bien. Fr.—"The best is the enemy of well."—We lose our present advantages, in seeking after those which are unattainable.

Le moineau en la main vaut mieux que l'oie qui vole. Fr. Prov.—"A sparrow in the hand is better than a goose on the wing."—"A bird in the hand," &c.

Le monde est le livre des femmes. Fr. ROUSSEAU.—"The world is the book of women"—They generally profit more from observation than from reading.

Le mot d'énigme. Fr.—"The word of the enigma." —The key of the mystery.

Le moyen le plus sûr de se consoler de tout ce qui peut arriver, c'est d'attendre toujours au pire. Fr.—"The most certain consolation against all that can happen, is always to expect the worst."

L'empire des lettres. Fr.—"The republic of letters."

L'ennui du beau amène le gout du singulier. Fr. Prov.—"A disgust of that which is proper, leads to a taste for singularity."

Leonina societas. Lat.—"A lion's company."—That dangerous association where the whole of the prey is monopolized by the strongest and most powerful.

Le pays du mariage a cela du particulier, que les étrangers ont envie de l'habiter, et les habitans naturels voudroient en être exilés. Fr. MONTAIGNE.—"The land of marriage has this peculiarity, that strangers are desirous of inhabiting it, whilst its actual inhabitants would willingly be banished from thence."

Le plus lent à promettre est toujours le plus fidèle à tenir. Fr. ROUSSEAU.—"The man who is most slow in promising is most sure to keep his word."

Le plus sage est celui qui ne pense point l'être. Fr

Boileau.—" The wisest man, in general, is he who does not think he is so."—The truly wise bear with them a consciousness of their own failings.

Le present est pour ceux qui jouissent; l'avenir pour ceux qui souffrent. Fr.—" The present is for those who enjoy, the future for those who suffer."

Le refus des louanges est souvent un désir d'être loué deux fois. Fr.—" The refusal of praise often intimates nothing more than that the praise is regarded as insufficient;"—and of course that a double portion would be more acceptable.

Le Roi le veut. Fr.—" The King wills it," and,

Le Roi s'avisera. Fr.—" The King will consider."—These are phrases derived from the Normans, by which the King either gives his sanction to an act, or postpones his assent.—The latter is disused in practice.

Les amertumes sont en morale ce que sont les amers en medecine. Fr.—" Misfortunes are in morals what bitters are in medicine."—They are equally disagreeable in the first instance, but act in the same manner as corroborants.

Les cartes sont brouillés. Fr.—" The cards are mixed."—There is a violent misunderstanding.

Les consolations indiscrètes ne font qu'aigrir les violentes afflictions. Fr. Rousseau.—" Consolation, when improperly administered, does but irritate the affliction."

Les esprits médiocres condamnent d'ordinaire tout ce qui passe leur portée. Fr. Rochefoucault.—" Men of limited understandings, in general, find fault with every thing which is beyond their comprehension."

Les extremités se touchent. Fr.—" Extremes touch each other."

Les grands hommes ne se bornent jamais dans leurs desseins. Fr. Bouhours.—" Great men never limit themselves in their plans."—They extend them beyond the reach of ordinary capacities.

Le sage entend à demi mot. Fr.—" The sensible man

understands half a word."—He can take a brief intimation.

Le sage songe, avant que de parler, à ce qu'il doit dire; le fou parle, et ensuite songe à ce qu'il a dit. Fr. Prov.—"A wise man thinks before he speaks; but a fool speaks, and then thinks of what he has been saying."

Le savoir faire. Fr.—"The knowledge how to act." —Address, subtlety.

Le savoir vivre. Fr.—"The knowledge how to live." —An acquaintance with life and manners.

Les doux yeux. Fr.—"Soft or amorous glances."

Le secret d'ennuyer est celui de tout dire. Fr. Voltaire.—"The secret of tiring and disgusting is to say all that can be said."

Les eaux sont basses chez lui. Fr.—"The waters are low with him."—His resources are exhausted.

Les femmes pouvent tout, parcequ'elles gouvernent les personnes qui gouvernent tout. Fr. Prov.— —"Women can do every thing, because they rule those who command every thing."

Les fous font des festins, et les sages les mangent. Fr. Prov.—"Fools make feasts, and wise men eat them."

Les hommes sont la cause que les femmes ne s'aiment point. Fr. La Bruyere.—"It is the men that cause the women to dislike each other."

Le silence est le parti le plus sûr de celui qui se défie de soi-même. Fr. Rochefoucault.—"To be silent is the safest choice for the man who distrusts his powers."

Les jeunes gens disent ce qu'ils font, les vieillards ce qu'ils ont fait, et les sots ce qu'ils ont envie de faire. Fr.—"Young folks tell what they do, old ones what they have done, and fools what they wish to do."

Les malheureux, qui ont de l'esprit, trouvent des ressources en eux-memes. Fr. Bouhours.—"The unfortunate men of genius find resources in themselves."—They have that within, which tends to console them for the neglect of the world.

Les Mœurs. Fr.—"Manners or morals."—Neither of these English words, however, convey the idea of the original. "Manners" comprehending too little, and "Morals" too much. The ingenious author of "The World" defines it thus: "A genteel exterior, decency, fitness, and propriety of conduct, in the common intercourse of life."

Les murailles ont des oreilles. Fr.—"Walls have ears."—Be cautious how you speak.

Le soleil ni la mort ne peuvent se regarder fixement. Fr. ROCHEFOUCAULT.—"Neither the sun nor death can be looked upon with fixed attention."

L'espérance est le songe d'un homme éveillé. Fr. Prov.—"Hope is the dream of a man awake."

L'esprit est toujours la dupe du cœur. Fr. ROCHEFOUCAULT.—"The understanding is ever the dupe of the heart."—Our feelings are, in general, sure to get the better of our reason.

L'esprit qu'on veut avoir gate celui qu'on a. Fr GRESSET.—"Extravagant pretensions to wit or wisdom depreciate the value of either, in the hands of their actual possessor."

Les vertus se perdent dans l'intéret, comme les fleuves se perdent dans la mer. Fr. ROCHEFOUCAULT.—"Our virtues lose themselves in our interest, as the rivers lose themselves in the ocean."

Le temps présent est gros de l'avenir. Fr. LEIBNITZ. "The present time is big with the future."—Great events are in the womb of time.

Le travail éloigne de nous trois grands maux, l'ennui, le vice, et le besoin. Fr. VOLTAIRE.—"Labour rids us of three great evils—irksomeness, vice, and poverty."

Lettre de cachet. Fr.—"A sealed letter."—An arbitrary order privately issued by a monarch, for the banishment or imprisonment of any person.

Levari facias. Law Lat.—"Cause a levy to be made." A judicial writ directed to a sheriff, requiring him to seize and take in execution, the property therein mentioned.

Le vent du bureau est bon. Fr.—"The official wind is good."—Things take a favourable turn.

Leve fit quod benè fertur onus. Lat. OVID.—"That load becomes light which is cheerfully borne."—If the spirits are buoyant, they diminish in a great degree the weight of suffering.

Levis est dolor qui capere consilium potest. Lat. SENECA.—"That grief is light which can take counsel."—On excessive grief all advice is thrown away.

Levius fit patientia,
Quicquid corrigere est nefas. Lat. HORACE.
"Patience makes that more tolerable, which it is impossible to prevent or remove."—In the homely language of our proverb—"What can't be cured, must be endured."

Levius solet timere qui propiùs timet. Lat. SEN.—"He fears less who fears more nearly."—Our apprehensions in general diminish with the approach of the object we dread.

Le vrai mérite ne depend point du tems ni de la mode. Fr. Prov.—"True merit depends not on the time nor on the fashion."

Le vrai moyen d'être trompé, c'est de se croire plus fin que les autres. Fr. ROCHEFOUCAULT.—"The sure mode of being deceived, is to believe ourselves to be more cunning than the rest of the world."

Lex loci. Law Lat.—"The law, or custom of the place."

Lex neminem cogit ad impossibilia. Lat. Law Max.—"The law compels no man to impossibilities." Thus the condition of a bond to go to Boston or New Orleans in a few hours, would be void from its impossibility.

Lex neminem cogit ostendere quod nescire præsumitur. Lat. Law Maxim.—"The law will oblige no man to declare that of which he is presumed to be ignorant."

Lex non scripta. Lat.—"The unwritten law."—The Common Law of England; and,

Lex scripta. Lat.—"The written or Statute Law."—The former, though not originally set down in writing, is paramount to all modern enactments, in clearness, brevity, and authority.

Lex talionis. Lat.—"The law of retaliation."—The law of requital in kind—as alluded to in the scriptures, of "an eye for an eye, a tooth, for a tooth" &c.

Lex terræ. Lat.—"The law of the land."—Taken generally in contradistinction to the civil law, or code of JUSTINIAN.

L'homme n'est jamais moins misérable, que quand il paroit dépourvû de tout. Fr. ROUSSEAU.—"Man is never less miserable than when he appears to be deprived of every thing."

L'hypocrisie est un hommage que le vice rend à la vertu. Fr. ROCHEFOUCAULT.—"Hypocrisy is an homage, which vice renders to virtue."

Libertas et natale solum. Lat.—"Liberty, and my native soil."—This was the motto, which, when assumed by a new made Irish peer, gave birth to the rhyming line of SWIFT,

"Fine words, I wonder where he stole 'em.

Libertas est potestas faciendi id quod jure liceat. Lat. CICERO.—"Liberty consists in the power of doing that which is permitted by the law."—This is certainly a just definition. There can not be rational freedom, where there are *arbitrary* restraints.

Libertas ultima mundi,
Quo steterit, ferienda loco. Lat. LUCAN.
'The remaining liberty of the world, in that precise place, was to be smitten and destroyed."—This is the sentiment attributed by the poet to Cæsar. It has been used in many a subsequent struggle for freedom, which it has been said, "if there subdued, could never revive."—Factions, however, are temporary, but principles are everlasting.

Liberté toute entière. Fr.—"Liberty complete."

Licet superbus ambules pecuniâ,
Fortuna non mutat genus. Lat. HORACE.
"Though you strut proud of your money, yet fortune has not changed your birth."—Addressed to a wealthy upstart.

Licuit, semperque licebit
Parcere personis, dicere de vitiis. Lat.
"It has been, and ever will be, lawful to attack vice, sparing at the same time the individual."

Ligan. See *Jetsam.*

Limæ labor ac mora. Lat.—"The labour and delay of the file."—The slow process of polishing a literary production.

L'imagination galope, le jugement ne va que le pas. Fr.—"The imagination gallops, the judgment only goes a foot-pace."—The former anticipates the conclusion, which the latter awaits in sober leisure.

L'industrie des hommes s'épuise à briguer les charges; il ne leur en reste plus pour en remplir les devoirs. Fr. D'ALEMBERT.—"The industry of men is now so far exhausted in canvassing for places, that none is left for fulfilling the duties of them."

Lingua mali pars pessima servi. Lat. JUVENAL.—"The tongue is the worst part of a bad servant." Their calumny surpasses all their other faults.

Litem lite resolvere. Lat.—"To remove one difficulty by introducing another."

Litera scripta manet. Lat.—"The written letter remains."—Words may pass away and be forgotten, but that which is committed to writing, will remain as evidence.

Literatim. Lat.—"Letter by letter."

Littus ama, altum alii teneant. Lat. VIRG.—"Do you keep close to the shore, let others venture on the deep."—Consult your own safety, and let others indulge in the spirit of adventure.

Livre rouge. Fr.—"The red book"—The increased and increasing history of pensions.

Locum tenens. Lat.—"One who holds the place of another."—A deputy; a substitute.

Locus sigilli. Lat.—"The place of the seal."—Denoted by L. S. on all diplomatic papers.

L'on espère de vieillir, et l'on craint la vieillesse. c'est à dire, on aime la vie, et on fuit la mort. Fr. La Bruyere.—"We hope to get old, and yet are afraid of age;—in other words, we are in love with life, and wish to fly from the thoughts of mortality."

Longa est injuria, longæ
Ambages. Lat. Virgil.
"The account of this injury is rather long, and the particulars tedious."—Used as an apology in recounting one's own wrongs.

Longum iter est per præcepta, breve et efficax per exempla. Lat. Sen.—"Even the wisest counsels make their way but slowly: the effect of good example is more immediate and effectual."
"Example serves where precept fails."

L'on ne vaut dans ce monde, que ce que l'on veut valoir. Fr. La Bruyere.—"Every man is valued in this world, as he shows by his conduct that he wishes to be valued."

L'oreille est le chemin du cœur. Fr.—"The ear is the road to the heart."—This maxim is easily explained.

L'orgueil ne veut pas devoir, et l'amour-propre ne veut pas payer. Fr. Rochefoucault.—"Pride wishes not to *owe*, and self-love is unwilling to *pay.*"

Louer les princes des vertus qu'ils n'ont pas, c'est leur dire impunement des injures. Fr. Rochefoucault.—"To praise princes for virtues which they have not, is to reproach them with impunity."

Loyal devoir. Fr.—"Loyal duty."

Loyal je serai durant ma vie. Fr.—"I shall be loyal during my life."

Loyauté m'oblige. Fr.—"Loyalty binds me."

Loyauté n'a honte. Fr.—"Loyalty has no shame."

Lubricum linguæ non facile in pænam est trahendum. Lat. Law Max.—"A light expression (or as it is familiarly called, 'a slip of the tongue,') is not easily punishable."—Words of heat, as to call a man rogue, knave, &c, will bear no action at law, unless they are specifically applied, as,—in such an affair—to a certain person, &c.

Lucina sine concubitu. Lat.—"Child-birth without sexual intercourse."—The possibility of such an occurrence was, at one time, stoutly but absurdly maintained. The phrase is now used only in a ludicrous sense, to mark the birth of a child, unprefaced by the rites of matrimony.

Lucri bonus est odor ex re quâlibet. Lat.—"The smell of gain is good, from whatever it proceeds." This was the answer of VESPASIAN to his son TITUS, when the latter reproached him with having laid a tax on urine.

Lucus à non lucendo. Lat.—The word "*lucus*," a *grove*, is derived from "*lucere*," to shine, because the rays of the sun are supposed rarely to penetrate through its foliage. The phrase is generally used to mark an absurd or discordant etymology.

Ludere cum sacris. Lat.—"To trifle with sacred things." To jest profanely on consecrated matters.

Ludit in humanis divina potentia rebus,
Et certam præsens vix habet hora fidem.
Lat. OVID.

"The powers above seem to sport with human affairs, so that we can scarcely be assured of the hour which is passing."

Lugete Veneres, Cupidinesque. Lat. CATULLUS.
"Weep all ye Venuses and Cupids."—Mourn all ye Loves and Graces. This quotation is generally used in an ironical sense.

L'une des marques de la médiocrité de l'esprit est de toujours conter. Fr. LA BRUYERE.—"One of the marks of mediocrity of understanding, is to be fond of telling long stories."

Lupus pilum mutat non mentem. Lat. Prov.—"The wolf changes his coat, but not his disposition."—No change of appearance can alter that which is radically perverse.

Lusisti satis, edisti, atque bibisti.
Tempus abire tibi est. Lat. HORACE.
"Thou hast sported, eaten, and drunk enough. It is time for thee to depart."—These lines were addressed to a worn-out debauchee, still clinging to life.

Lusus animo debent aliquando dari,
Ad cogitandum melior ut redeat sibi.
Lat. PHÆDRUS.
"The mind ought sometimes to be amused, that it may the better return to thought, and to itself."

Lusus naturæ. Lat.—"A play or freak of nature."—Any anomalous or deformed production, as an animal born with two heads, &c. &c.

M

Macte virtute. Lat. VIRG.—"Proceed in virtue."—In general used ironically, as we sneeringly say, "Go on and prosper."

Magister artis ingeniique largitor,
Venter. Lat. PERSIUS.
"The belly is the teacher of arts, and the bestower of genius."—Hunger or necessity is the mother of invention.

Magistratus indicat virum. Lat.—"The magistrate shows the man."

Magna Charta. Lat.—"The great Charter."—The charter of English liberties obtained from King JOHN, by the Barons of England—*Ann.* 1215.

Magna civitas, magna solitudo. Lat.—"A great city is a great desert."—It is possible to live secluded from the world, even in the midst of a great city.

Magna est veritas, et prævalebit. Lat.—"Truth is most powerful, and will ultimately prevail."

Magna servitus est magna fortuna. Lat. SEN.—"A great fortune is a great slavery."—It brings with it many peculiar burdens and inconveniences.

Magnas inter opes, inops. Lat. HORACE.—"Poor, in the midst of the greatest wealth."—A jus description of a rich miser.

Magni est ingenii revocare mentem à sensibus, et cogitationem à consuetudine abducere. CICERO. *Tusc. Disp.*—"It is a proof of great talents to be able to recall the mind from the senses, and to separate thought from habit."

Magni nominis umbra. Lat. LUCAN.—"The shadow of a mighty name."—Applied to a man who inherits the name or title of a great ancestor, but without any indication of greatness in himself.

Magni refert quibuscum vixeris. Lat. Prov.—"It is a matter of importance to know with whom you live."

Magno conatu, magnas nugas. Lat. TERENCE.—"By great efforts to obtain great trifles." To waste much labour on inadequate objects.

Magnos homines virtute metimur, non fortunâ. Lat. CORN. NEP.—"We estimate great men by their virtue (or valour) and not by their success."—This is unhappily the philosophic, but not the worldly admeasurement.

Magnum est argumentum in utroque fuisse moderatum. Lat.—"It is a great argument in favour of a man, that when placed in different situations, he displayed in each, the same spirit of moderation."

Magnum est vectigal parsimonia. Lat. CICERO.—"Economy is of itself a great revenue."—Many men get rich by their savings, rather than by their gains.

Maintien le droit. Fr.—"Maintain the right."

Maison de campagne. Fr.—"A country seat."

Maison de ville. Fr.—"The town-house."—The place where municipal justice is distributed.

Maîtres des hautes œuvres. Fr.—"The master of the high works."—The hangman.

Maître des basses œuvres. Fr.—"The master of the low works."—The nightman, the gold finder.

Major domo. Ital.—The master of the house, or he who for the time, officiates as such—a steward, or chief servant.

Major è longinquo reverentia. Lat.—"Respect is

greater when coming from a distance."—The persons and objects with which we are familiar, seldom excite a high degree of reverence. No man, it has been well observed, was ever a hero in the view of his *valet de chambre.*

Major famæ sitis est quam
Virtutis; quis enim virtutem amplectitur ipsam,
Præmia si tollas? Lat. JUVENAL.
"The thirst of fame is greater than that of virtue; for who would embrace virtue itself, if you take away its rewards?"—More are in love with the character of virtue, than with virtue itself.

Major hæreditas venit unicuique nostrum a jure et legibus, quam a parentibus. Lat. CICERO.—"A greater inheritance comes to each of us from our rights and laws, than from our parents."

Major privato visus, dum privatus fuit, et omnium consensu capax imperii, nisi imperasset. Lat. TACITUS.—"He was regarded as greater than a private man whilst he remained in privacy, and would have been deemed worthy of governing, if he had never governed."—A political maxim of very general application.

Majus est delictum seipsum interficere quam alium. Lat. Law Maxim.—"Suicide is a greater crime than murder."

Mala fide. Lat.—"In bad faith."—With a design to deceive.

Mala grammatica non vitiat chartam. Lat. Law Max.—"Bad grammar does not vitiate the deed." An error in the language is not to be regarded, if it does not involve some ambiguity.

Malè cuncta ministrat
Impetus. Lat.
"Anger manages every thing badly."—We seldom act rightly when under the dominion of passion.

Maeldicus à malefico non distat nisi occasione. Lat. QUINTILIAN.—"An evil sayer differs from an evil doer, only in the want of opportunity."—The difference is but slight between a calumniator and an assassin

Malè imperando summum imperium amittitur. Lat SYRUS.—"The greatest empire may be lost by the misrule of governors."

Malè parta, malè dilabuntur. Latin PLAUTUS.—"Things ill acquired, are as badly expended."—"What's got over the devil's back," &c.

Malè verum examinat omnis
Corruptus judex. Lat. HORACE
"A corrupt judge is not qualified to inquire into the truth."

Mali exempli. Lat.—In the nature "of a bad example," or precedent.

Malim inquietam libertatem, quam quietum servitium. Lat.—"I would rather have a disturbed liberty, than a quiet slavery."—The ferment of a free, is preferable to the torpor of a despotic, government.

Malitia supplet ætatem. Law Max.—"Malice supplies the defect of age."

Malo indisertam prudentiam, quam loquacem stultitiam. Lat. CICERO.—"I prefer silent prudence to loquacious folly."

Malo mihi malè quam mollitur esse. Lat. SENECA.—"I would rather be sick than idle."—The evil of a slight indisposition is transient; the mischiefs of idleness, once rooted, are incurable.

Malo mori quam fœdari. Lat.—"I had rather die than be debased."

Malum consilium consultori pessimum. VER. FLACCUS.—"Bad advice is often most fatal to the adviser."

Malum in se. Lat.—"A thing evil in itself."—*Malum prohibitum*·—"A thing evil, because forbidden."—To illustrate the legal distinction between those two species of evil, it is only necessary to observe that *murder* is "an evil in itself."—The exportation of wool, commonly called "owning," was not punishable as an *evil* until it was prohibited by the law.

Malum nascens facilè opprimitur; inveteratum fit

robustius. Lat. CICERO.—" An evil, at its birth, is easily crushed, but it grows and strengthens by endurance."

Malum, quo communius, eo pejus. Lat.—" The more generally an evil prevails the more injurious are the consequences"—and the more speedily should it be suppressed.

Malum vas non frangitur. Lat. Prov.—" A bad vessel is seldom broken."—Things which are held most cheaply, are in general the most secure from danger.

Malus pudor. Lat.—" False shame."—Whence the French *mauvaise honte.*

Malus usus abolendus est. Lat. Law Max.—" A bad custom is to be abolished."—A custom in local jurisdictions, existing from time immemorial, has the force of a law; but if that custom be proven to be a bad one, such proof will set it aside.

Mandamus. Law Lat.—" We order."—A writ which issues to a corporation, commanding them to restore, or admit a person to an office, &c.

Manebant vestigia morientis libertatis. Lat. TAC. —" There still remained the traces of expiring liberty."

Manet altâ mente repôstum. Lat. VIRGIL.—" It remains deeply fixed in the mind."—This phrase, by which the poet describes the inveterate resentment of JUNO, is now frequently used to denote a long embosomed sense of injury.

Mania. Gr.—" Madness."—A rage for any object or pursuit—as *Bibliomania,* an eagerness in collecting books.

Mania à potu.—" Madness caused by drunkenness."

Manibus pedibusque. Lat.—" With hands and feet." It was a struggle *manibus pedibusque,* or, as we should express it in English, " With tooth and nail."

Manu forti. Lat.—" With a brave arm."

Manus desunt poscentibus arvis. Lat.—" More labourers are required by the fields."—Or, in the language of scripture—"The harvest is great, but the labourers are few."

Manus hæc inimica tyrannis. Lat.—"This hand is hostile to tyrants."

Manus justa nardus. Lat.—"The just hand is as precious ointment."

Manus manum fricat. Lat. Prov.—"One hand rubs the other."—Applied to two persons who gratify the vanity, or forward the views, of each other by mutual adulation.

Marchandise qui plait est à demi vendûe. Fr. Prov. —"The goods which please are already half sold." —We have a corresponding proverb in English— "Please the eye and pick the purse."

Marchand qui perd, ne peut rire. Fr.—"The man who is on the losing side feels no inclination to laugh."

Mare clausum. Lat.—"A closed sea."—A large bay, or portion of the sea surrounded by the territory of any one nation, and which, therefore, can only be navigated by vessels of other nations, *by permis sion,* is called a *mare clausum.*

Marie ton fils quand tu voudras, mais ta fille quand tu pourras. Fr. Prov.—"Marry your son when you will, and your daughter when you can."—Get rid of the latter precarious charge as soon as possible.

Marqué au bon coin. Fr.—"Marked with a good stamp."—Possessed of superior qualities.

Mars gravior sub pace latet. Lat. CLAUDIAN.—"A severer war lurks under the show of peace."

Materfamiliâs. Lat.—"The mother of a family."

Materiam superabat opus. Lat. OVID.—"The work manship excelled the materials."

Matre pulchrâ filia pulchrior. Lat. HORACE.—"A daughter surpassing in beauty her beautiful mother."

Maturè fias senex. Lat.—"May you early prove an old man."—May you learn the wisdom of age long before you are depressed with its infirmities

Mauvaise honte. Fr.—" False shame."—Excessive bashfulness or timidity.

Maxima illecebra est peccandi impunitate spes Lat. CICERO.—" The greatest incitement to guilt is the hope of sinning with impunity."

Maximas virtutes jacere omnes necesse est, voluptate dominante. Lat. CICERO.—" Where pleasure is eagerly pursued, the greatest virtues will lose their power."

Maximum. Lat.—" The greatest possible."

Maximus in minimis. Lat.—" Very great in very little things."—A studious attention to petty objects is the sure sign of a narrow mind. When Cardinal CHIGI told another member of the *corps diplomatique* that the same pen had served him for three years, he was instantly and properly set down, as a man whose mind was not framed for any enlarged or liberal discussion.

Medio tutissimus ibis. Lat. OVID.—"You will advance most safely in the middle."—To consult your safety, you should through life avoid all extremes.

Mediocra firma. Lat.—" The middle station is the safest."

Mediocribus esse poetis,
Non Dii, non homines, non concessēre columnæ.
Lat. HORACE.

" Mediocrity is not allowed to poets, either by the gods, or men, or the pillars which sustain the booksellers' shops."—By this whimsical periphrase, the poet means simply to say, that *mediocrity*, which in other pursuits is respectable, in that of poetry is generally contemned.

Μεγα βιβλιον, μεγα κακον. Gr. *Mega biblion, mega kakon.*—" A great book is a great evil."—This is a charge which your voluminous authors are perpetually shifting to the shoulders of their neighbours.

Meglio è un megro accordo, che un grassa sentenza. Ital. Prov.—" A lean assent is better than a fat sentence."—A simple grant of the favour requested, is better than an eloquent refusal.

Me judice. Lat.—"I being judge."—In my opinion.

Μελετη το παν. Gr. *Melete to pan.*—"Care and industry effect every thing."—This was the saying of Periander, one of the seven sages of Greece.

Mel in ore, verba lactis,
Fel in corde, fraus in factis. Lat.
"Honey in his mouth, words of milk,
"Gall in his heart, and fraud in his acts."
These are monkish rhymes, in which a mischievous hypocrite is not ill described.

Mellitum venenum, blanda oratio. Lat.—"A smooth speech is honied poison."

Melior est conditio possidentis. Law Lat.—"The condition of him, who is in possession, is the best."

Melius est cavere semper, quam pati semel. Lat. Prov. —"It is better to be always on our guard, than to suffer once."

Melius non tangere, clamo. Lat. Hor.—"I cry out, it is better not to touch me."—This is the language of the Satirist, who has his quiver full of defence.

Melius sentire quam scire. Lat.—Something which it is "more easy to feel than to define,"—or, which may be translated in the words of the philosopher when asked for a definition of a difficult subject, "If you ask me, I do not know; if you do not ask me, I well know."

Memento mori. Lat.—"Remember death."—He is a mere *memento mori*—he serves for nothing but to remind us of our mortality.

Meminerunt omnia amantes. Lat Ovid.—"Lovers remember every thing."

Memorabilia, or *memoranda.* Lat.—"Things to be remembered."—Matters deserving of record.

Memoriâ in æternâ. Lat.—"In eternal remembrance."

Mendici, mimi, balatrones. Lat. Hor.—"Beggars, players, and varlets," of every description.—A crowd or group of contemptible persons.

Mene huic confidere monstro? Lat.—"Shall I trust such a depraved wretch?"

Mene salis placidi vultum, fluctusque quietos
Ignorare jubes? mene huic confidere monstro?
Lat. VIRGIL.
"Do you desire that I should not distrust the appearance of the placid sea, and of the waves which are now quiet? do you wish that I should confide in such a monster?"

Μηνιν αειδε θεα. Gr. *Menin aeide thea.*—"Sing, goddess, the anger."—The first words of *Homer's* Iliad, which are sometimes quoted to ridicule the affectation of scholarship.

Mens conscia recti. Lat.—"A mind conscious of rectitude."

Mens invicta manet. Lat.—"The mind remains unconquered."

Mens pati durum sustinet ægra nihil. Lat. OVID.—"The sick mind can not bear any thing which is harsh."—The mind of affliction is so sensitive, as to shrink from the slightest touch of offence.

Mens sana in corpore sano. Lat. HOR.—"A sound mind in a healthy body."—The first and best wish which can present itself to a rational mind.

Mens sibi conscia recti. Lat. HOR.—"A mind which is conscious to itself of rectitude."

Mensuraque juris
Vis erat. Lat. LUCAN.
"And power was the only measure of right."—This well describes a state of anarchy, where every man feels that what he can do, he may do.

Mentiri nescio, librum,
Si malus est, nequeo laudare. Lat. JUVENAL.
"I can not lie—if your book is badly written (or of an evil tendency) I can not commend it."

Meo periculo. Lat.—"At my own peril, or risk."

Meo sum pauper in ære. Lat. HOR.—"I am poor, but only in debt to myself."—If I have abridged my own comforts, my consolation is that I owe nothing to others.

Merum sal. Lat.—"Pure salt."—Genuine Attic wit.

Mettre les points sur les i. Fr.—"To dot every i"—To be scrupulously exact.

Metu coactus. Lat.—"Impelled by fear."

Meum et tuum. Lat.—"Mine and yours."—It is a question of *meum et tuum.*—The dispute is respecting the distinct rights of property.

Meus mihi, suus cuique carus. Lat. PLAUTUS.—"Mine is dear to me, and dear is his, to every man."—Every one has his own prepossessions and predilections.

Mezzo termine. Ital.—"A middle line or middle course of conduct."

Mieux vaut "un tiens," que deux "tu l'auras." Fr. Prov.—"One 'take this' is better than two 'thou shalt have it.'"

Mihi cura futuri. Lat.—"My care is for the future life."

Mihi turpe relinqui est. Lat.—"It is disgraceful for me to be left behind."

Minimum. Lat.—"The smallest possible."

Minor est quam servus, dominus qui servos timet. Lat. Prov.—"That master is lower than a servant, who is in dread of his servants."

Minus in parvos fortuna furit,
Leviusque ferit leviora Deus. Lat. SENECA.
"The rage of fortune is less directed against the humble, and Providence strikes more lightly on the low."

Minuti
Semper et infirmi est animi exiguique voluptas
Ultio. Lat. JUVENAL.
"Revenge is always the pleasure of a little, weak, and narrow mind."—No man of an enlarged understanding indulges in so dark a passion.

Minutiæ. Lat.—"Trifles."—To enter into *minutiæ*—To discuss the most minute and trifling parts of the business.

Mirabile dictu! Lat.—"Wonderful to tell!"

Mirabile visu! Lat.—"Wonderful to behold!"

Miramur ex intervallo fallentia. Lat.—"We admire at a distance the things that deceive us.—Our sight is apt to misrepresent remote objects, but the deception vanishes on a nearer approach.

Mirantur taciti, et dubio pro fulmine pendent. Lat. Statius.—"They stand in silent astonishment, and wait for the fall of the yet doubtful thunderbolt."—Used to describe a general apprehension and consternation.

Mirum! Lat.—"Wonderful!"

Mirum in modum. Lat.—"In a wonderful manner."

Misce stultitiam consiliis brevem. Lat. Hor.—"Mix short follies with wise counsels."—Let your moments of dissipation bear no proportion to those of sober reflection.

Misera est magni custodia censûs. Lat. Juvenal.—"The care of a large estate is an unpleasant thing." Even wealth itself brings with it its cares and inconveniences.

Misera est servitus, ubi jus est aut vagum aut incognitum. Lat. Law Maxim.—"The servitude is there miserable, where the law is either vague or unknown."—In every good government, the laws should be precisely defined, and generally promulgated.

Miserabile vulgus. Lat.—"A wretched crew."

Miseram pacem vel bello bene mutari. Lat. Tac.—"A peace may be so degrading as not to be ill-exchanged for war."

Miseris succurrere disco. Lat. Virgil.—"I learn to relieve the wretched."

Miserrima fortuna est quæ inimico caret. Lat.—"That is a most wretched fortune which is without an enemy."—His condition must be low indeed, who possesses not any thing for which he can be envied.

Miserum est aliorum incumbere famæ. Lat. Juv.—"It is despicable to live on the fame of others."

Misnomer. Law Fr.—The mistake of a name; or the using of one name for another.

Misprision. Law Fr.—The concealment of treason or felony.

Mittimus. Law Lat.—"We send."—The writ by which a magistrate commits an offender to prison.

Mobilitate viget, viresque acquirit eundo. Lat. VIRG. —"It flourishes in its quickness of motion, and gains new strength in its progress."—The poet speaks of Fame or Common Report, which gathers strength as it proceeds, and swells, like the snow-ball, as it rolls along.

Moderata durant. Lat. SENECA.—"Moderate things last, or continue."—Power, health, and faculties, are all exhausted by excess.

Modo me Thebis, modo ponit Athenis. Lat. HOR.— "He now places me at *Thebes*, and now at *Athens.*"—This it used as a compliment to a great dramatic poet who can change his scene, and lose sight of the unities of time and place, without diminishing the interest which he has once excited.

Modus operandi. Lat.—"The method or manner of operating."

Moins on pense, plus on parle. Fr.—"The less a man thinks, the more he talks."

Mole ruit sua. Lat.—"It is crushed by its own weight."

Mollia tempora fandi. Lat. HOR.—"The favourable occasions for speaking."—These, the poet intimates, are to be sought for with great men. That request may succeed at one time, which, at another, may be considered as an importunity.

Moliter manus imposuit. Lat. Law Term.—"He but gently laid hands."—This phrase is used in a defence set up against an action or indictment for an assault. "He but gently laid hands" on the prosecutor, for the purpose of expelling him, as he had a right to do, from the premises.

Moniti meliora sequamur. Lat. VIRG.—"Being admonished, let us follow better things."—Having had the lessons of experience, let our future prudence attest their effects.

Monstrum horrendum, informe, ingens, cui lumen ademptum. Lat. VIRGIL
"A horrid monster, huge, shapeless, and deprived of his sight."—This is the description given by VIRGIL of the giant POLYPHEMUS, when his one eye had been bored out by Ulysses.—It is sometimes applied to an absurd proposition, conceived in ignorance and brought forth by presumption.

More majorum. Lat.—"According to the customs of our ancestors."

Moribus antiquis stat Roma. Lat.—"Rome stands by her ancient morals."—She has preserved her stability by refusing to give way to innovation.

Mors omnibus communis. Lat.—"Death is common to all men."

Mors sola fatetur,
Quantula sint hominum corpuscula. Lat. JUV.
"Death alone confesses how weak and feeble is the body of man."—It rests with death, to show the weakness of ambition, and the inanity of pride.

Mors ultima linea rerum est. Lat. HOR.—"Death is the last boundary of human affairs."

Mortalitate relicta, vivit immortalitate indutus. Lat.—"Having put off this mortal frame, he lives clothed with immortality."

Mortuo leoni et lepores insultant. Lat.—"Even hares can insult a dead lion."—The mightiest of the dead may be insulted by the weakest of the living.

Mos pro lege. Lat. Law Maxim.—"Custom for law." —Long established usage, as in the case of a fixed *modus* for tythes, shall stand in the place of law.

Mot du guet. Fr.—"A watch-word."

Mots d'usage. Fr.—"Words of usage."—Phrases in common use.

Moveo et propitior. Lat.—"I rise and am appeased."

Movet cornicula risum,
Furtivis nudata coloribus. Lat. HORACE
"The crow, when stripped of her borrowed plumes excites our laughter."

Mugitus labyrinthi. Lat.—"The bellowing of the labyrinth."—This was a favourite topic with the Roman poetasters. It is therefore put for any com mon-place topic of ordinary poets or writers.

Mulier, amissa pudicitia, haud alia abnuerit. Lat. "When a woman has lost her chastity, she will not refuse any thing else."

Mulier quæ sola cogitat, male cogitat. Lat. Prov. "A woman, when thinking by herself, is always thinking of mischief."—One of the common-place railleries directed against the sex.

Multa cadunt inter calicem supremaque labra. Lat. LABERIUS. "Many things fall between the cup and the lip."

Multa docet fames. Lat. Proverb.—"Hunger teaches many things."—Necessity is the mother of invention.

Multa ferunt anni venientes commoda secum;
Multa recedentes adimunt. Lat. HORACE

"The coming years bring many advantages with them—when retreating, they take away as many." There is a tide in the affairs of men.—What we gain by the influx, we miserably lose by the reflux of that tide.

Multa gemens. Lat.—"Mourning deeply."—He complied *multa gemens*, with every expression of grief.

Multa non vetat lex quæ tamen tacite damnat. Lat. Law Maxim.—"There are many acts, not positively prohibited by the law, which it nevertheless condemns."

Multa petentibus desunt multa. Lat. HORACE. "Those who covet many things, are in want of many."—Our wants are limited or extended, in proportion to our desires.

Multa renascentur quæ jam cecidere. Lat. HORACE. "Many things shall revive which have fallen into decay."—Taste and fashion are ever reverting and fluctuating.

Multi adorantur in arâ, qui cremantur in igni

St. Austin.—"Many are worshipped on the altars, who are burning in the flames of hell."

Multi multa sciunt, sed nemo omnia. Lat.—"Many men are well versed in many subjects, but no one can be perfect in all."

Multis ille bonis flebilis occidit,
Nulli flebilior quam mihi. Lat. Horace.
"He died lamented by many good men, but by none lamented more than by me."

Multis terribilis, caveto multos. Lat. Auson.—"If thou art terrible to many, then beware of many."

Multi te oderint, si teipsum ames. Lat.—"Many will hate you, if you love yourself."

Multos ingratos invenimus, plures facimus. Lat.—"We find many ungrateful men, and we make more."—Ingratitude is but too frequent, yet it is sometimes provoked by the arrogance of the benefactor.

Multos in summa pericula misit
Venturi timor ipse mali. Lat. Lucan.
"The mere apprehension of evil has put many into a situation of the utmost danger."—Our alarms frequently lead us into perils more fearful even than those which we at first apprehended.

Multum abludit imago. Lat. Hor.—"The picture is by no means like."—You perhaps intended a likeness, but *multum abludit imago;* you have given a caricature, not a resemblance.

Multum in parvo, Lat.—"Much in little."—A great deal said in a few words. A compendium of knowledge.

Multum mentitur, qui multum vidit. Lat.—"He who has seen much of the world, is very prone to exaggeration"—or, "Great travellers are often great liars."

Mundus universus exercet histrioniam. Lat. Petronius Arbiter.—"All the world practises the art of acting."—"All the world's a stage."

Munus Apolline dignum. Lat. Hor.—"An offering worthy of Apollo."—Spoken of an excellent poem.

Murus æneus conscientia sana. Lat.—"A sound conscience is a brazen wall of defence."

Mus in pice. Lat. Prov.—"A mouse in a pitch barrel."—Applied to a man who is always perplexing himself in useless disquisitions and inquiries.

Mutare vel timere sperno. Lat.—"I scorn to change or fear."

Mutatâ formâ, interimitur propè substantia rei. Lat. Law Max.—"The form being changed, the substance of the thing is destroyed."—Thus, if trees are improperly cut down, and laid as beams in a house, their nature is so far altered, that they can not be seized in that shape; but the owner is to bring his action for the damage.

Mutatis mutandis. Lat. Law.—"After making the necessary changes."—Thus, what was law for A. and B., shall apply to C. and D., only altering terms according to the circumstances.

Mutato nomine, de te
Fabula narratur. Lat. HORACE.
"Change but the name, the tale is told of you."—You smile at the satire whilst you suppose it leveled at another; yet if the name were altered, you would find it reach to "your own business and bosom."

N

Nam dives fieri qui vult,
Et cito vult fieri. Lat. JUVENAL.
"For he who desires to become rich, also wishes that desire to be soon accomplished."—There is a natural alliance between avarice and rapacity.

Nam ego illum periise duco, cui quidem periit pudor. Lat. PLAUTUS.—"I regard that man as lost, who has lost his sense of shame."

Nam genus et proavos, et quæ non fecimus ipsi,
Vix ea nostra voco. Lat. OVID.
"For birth and ancestry, and that which we have not ourselves achieved, we can scarcely call our own"—The man, who prides himself, not on his

personal conduct, but on a long line of ancestry, has been ludicrously, but justly, compared to the potato-plant, the best part of which is under ground

Nam pro jucundis aptissima quæque dabunt Dii,
Carior est illis homo quam sibi. Lat. JUVENAL.
"For the gods, instead of what is most pleasing, will give what is most proper. Man is more dear to them, than he is to himself."

Nam scelus intra se tacitum qui cogitat ullum,
Facti crimen habet. Lat. JUVENAL.
"For he who silently intends a crime, has all the guilt of the deed."—There are cases in which, to resolve upon, and to commit a guilty act, are equal in point of criminality.

Nam vitiis nemo sine nascitur, optimus ille est
Qui minimis urgetur. Lat. HORACE.
"For as no man is born without faults, the best is he who has the fewest."

Natura beatis
Omnibus esse dedit, si quis cognoverit uti.
Lat. CLAUDIAN.
"Nature has granted to all to be happy, if we did but know how to use her benefits."

Naturâ ipsâ valere, et mentis viribus excitari, et quasi quodam divino spiritu afflari.
Lat. CICERO.
"To be strong from nature; to be excited by the powers of the mind; and to be inspired, as it were, by a divine spirit."—Such is the definition of genius, given by this great orator.

Natura lo fece, e poi ruppa la stampa. Ital. ARIOSTO.
"Nature, after making him, broke the mould."

Natura! quam te colimus, inviti quoque! Lat. SEN.
"Oh! Nature, how we worship thee, however unwilling!"—How potent are thy dictates, and how resistless are thy laws!

Naturam expellas furcâ, tamen usque recurret. Lat. HOR.—"You may turn nature out of doors with violence, but she will still return."—Nature will continue to plead and enforce her rights, in despite of every temporary restraint.

Ne cede malis,
Sed contra audentior ito. Lat. VIRGIL.
"Do not yield to misfortunes, but advance to mee. them with greater fortitude."

Ne cede malis. Lat.—"Do not yield to misfortunes.'

Nec cupias nec metuas. Lat.—"Neither desire nor fear."

Nec deus intersit, nisi dignus vindice nodus. Lat. HORACE.—"Nor let a god interfere, unless the difficulty be worthy of such intervention."—The poet is advising play-wrights.—Do not introduce an extraordinary or supernatural appearance, unless on an occasion of the highest importance.

Necessse est cum insanientibus furere, nisi solus relinqueris. Lat. PETRONIUS.—"It is necessary to be mad with the insane, unless you would be left quite alone."—Even the wise man will bend and accommodate himself in some degree, to the follies and prejudices of those around him, in order to avoid the reproach of singularity.

Necesse est facere sumptum, qui quærit lucrum. Lat. PLAUTUS.—"It is necessary that he who looks for gain, should incur expense."

Necesse est ut multos timeat, quem multi timent. Lat. SYRUS.—"He that is feared by many, must be in fear of many."—The tyrant who governs others by terror, has cause to be himself the most terrified.

Necessitas non habet legem. Lat. Law Max.—"Necessity has no law."—Any man may justify, for instance, the pulling down the house of another, if it be done to prevent the spreading of a dangerous fire.

Nec lex est æquior ulla,
Quam necis artificem arte perire sua. Lat. OVID.
"Nor is there any law more just, than that the contriver of destruction should perish by his own arts."

Nec lusisse pudet, sed non incidere ludum. Lat. HOR.—"The shame is not in having sported, but in not having broken off the sport."

"Once to be wild is not a foul disgrace,
The blame is to pursue the frantic race."

Nec malè notus eques. Lat.—"A horseman or patrician well known."

Nec me pudet, ut istos, fateri nescire quod nesciam. Lat. CICERO.—"I am not ashamed, as some men are, to confess my ignorance of that which I do not know."

Nec mora, nec requies. Lat. VIRG.—"There was no rest or repose."—The affair was prosecuted without the smallest intermission.

Nec placidâ contentus quiete est. Lat.—"Nor is he contented with soft repose," or inglorious ease.

Nec pluribus impar. Lat.—"Not an unequal match for numbers."—This was the vain-glorious motto adopted by Louis XIV, when he formed his chimerical project of universal empire.

Nec prece nec pretio. Lat.—"Neither by bribe nor entreaty."

Nec quærere nec spernere honorem. Lat.—"Neither to seek nor despise honours."

Nec satis est pulchra esse poemata, dulcia sunto. Lat. HORACE.—"It is not enough that poetry should be so finished as to satisfy the judgment; it should appeal to our feeling and imagination."

Nec scire fas est omnia. Lat. HORACE.—"It is not permitted to know all things."

Nec semper feriet quodcunque minabitur arcus. Lat.—"The arrow will not always hit the object which it threatens."—The best aims are often fruitless.

Nec sibi, sed toto genitum se credere mundo. Lat. LUCAN.—"To think that he was born, not for himself, but for the world."—This is the rare character of an enlarged and philosophic mind.

Nec temere nec timidè. Lat.—"Neither rashly or fearfully."

Nec tibi quid liceat, sed quid fecisse decebit,
Occurrat. Lat. CLAUDIAN.
"Do not consider what you may do, but what it

will become you to have done."—This is a most admirable epitome of ethics.

Nec timeo, nec sperno. Lat.—"I neither fear nor despise."

Nec cui de te plusquam tibi credas. Lat.—"Do not believe any man more than yourself, when he speaks of you."—When a man flatters you, you should correct his assertions by your own consciousness.

Nec quies gentium sine armis, nec arma sine stipendiis, nec stipendia sine tributis. Lat. TAC —"The tranquillity of nations is not to be preserved without arms, troops can not be maintained without pay, and their pay can not be made good without taxes."

Nec tamen, hoc tribuens, dederim quoque cætera
Lat. HORACE.
"Nor do I, because I concede *this* point, give up all the rest."

Nec tecum possum vivere, nec sine te. Lat.—"I can not live with you, nor yet without you."

Nec verbum verbo curabis reddere, fidus
Interpres. Lat. HORACE.
"Nor should the translator aim at rendering the original, word for word."—In this servility of translation, the spirit of the original will certainly evaporate.

Nec vixit malè qui natus moriensque fefellit. Lat. HORACE.—"Nor has he spent his life badly, who has passed it from his birth to his burial in privacy." The man is fortunate, who escapes completely from the cares of public life.

Ne exeat. Lat.—"Let him not go out."—A judicial writ prohibiting a person from leaving the state or country.

Nefas nocere, vel malo fratri, puta. Lat. SENECA.—"You should esteem it a crime to hurt even a bad brother."—You should enlighten, admonish, and, if possible, reform him, but abstain from injury or violence.

Negatas artifex sequi voces. Lat. PERSIUS.—"He attempts to express himself in a language which nature has denied him."

Ne in crastinum, quod possis hodie. Lat.—"Defer not, until to-morrow what you can do to day."

Nem. con. Abbrev. for *nemine contradicente*, and,

Nem. diss. Abbrev. for *nemine dissentiente.*—"No person opposing, or disagreeing."—These two phrases are in fact synonymous. The latter, however, is exclusively used in the English house of Peers.

Neminem id agere, ut ex alterius prædetur nescitiâ. Lat. CICERO.—"No man should act so as to take advantage of another's folly."—This is a precept, which those must admire in theory, who outrage in practice.

Neminem oportet esse sapientiorem legibus. Law Lat.—"It does not become any man to make himself wiser than the law."

Nemo, allegans suam turpitudinem, audiendus est. Lat. Law Maxim.—"No man, alleging his own baseness, is to be heard."—The evidence of spies, informers, and of every man who does not come into court with clean hands, is to be listened to with distrust.

Nemo bis punitur pro eodem delicto. Lat. Law Max. —"No man can be twice punished for the same crime."

Nemo est supra leges. Lat. Law Max.—"No one is above, or beyond the control of, the law."

Nemo est hæres viventis. Lat.—"No one is heir to a living person."—He can only be an expectant.

Nemo in sese tentat descendere: Nemo! Lat. PERS. —"What! no man attempts to descend into his own bosom?"—and examine his faults.

Nemo læditur nisi seipso. Lat. PETRARCH.—"No man is injured except by himself."—Our troubles and misfortunes may generally be traced to some imprudence or neglect of our own.

Nemo me impunè lacessit. Lat.—"No man provokes me with impunity."—The motto of the order of the *Thistle*, to the rough nature of which plant it has a reference.

Nemo mortalium omnibus horis sapit. Lat. PLINY —"No man is wise at all times."—The wisest of mankind have their lapses of indiscretion.

Nemo plus juris in alium transferre potest, quam ipse habet. Law Maxim.—"No man can transfer to others, rights more extensive than those which he possesses."

Nemo punitur pro alieno delicto. Lat. Law Max.—"No man is to be punished for the crime of another."—It is to be observed that this is a *Law*, and not a *State* Maxim. The people in every state are punished for the sins of those who administer the government.

Nemo repentè fuit turpissimus. Lat. JUVENAL.—"No man ever became in an instant the most base." The progress from virtue towards vice is gradual and insensible.

Nemo sic impar sibi. Lat.—"No man was ever so unlike himself."—Applied to one of those unequal, but not uncommon characters, who can show signs of greatness in one hour, and of weakness in the next.

Nemo tenetur seipsum accusare. Lat. Law Max.—"No man is obliged to accuse himself."

Nemo sine vitiis nascitur. Lat.—"No man is born without faults."

Nemo solus sapit. Lat. PLAUTUS.—"No man is wise alone."—No man should so confident in his own opinion, as to reject all advice.

Ne plus ultra. Lat.—"Nothing more beyond."—He was arrived at his "*ne plus ultra*"—his utmost efforts could not carry him any further.

Né pour la digestion. Fr. LA BRUYERE.—"Born merely for the purpose of digestion."—A man fit only "to keep bread from moulding."

Ne puero gladium. Lat. Prov.—"Do not trust a boy with a sword."—Do not commit a strong measure into inconsiderate hands.

Neque cæcum ducem neque amentem consultorem. Lat. *from* ARISTOPH.—"Do not take either a blind guide, or a weak adviser."—The former is not more dangerous than the latter.

Neque culpa, neque lauda teipsum. Lat.—"Neither blame nor applaud thyself."

Neque enim quies gentium sine armis, neque arma sine stipendiis, neque stipendia sine tributis. Lat TACITUS.—"The quiet of nations can not be main tained without arms: armies can not be supported without pay; nor can that pay be made good with out taxes."

Neque, extra necessitates belli, præcipuum odium gero. Lat.—"I bear no particular hatred beyond the necessity of war."—I feel no resentment beyond that which is justified by the occasion.

Neque fœmina, amissâ pudicitia, alia abnuerit. Lat. TAC.—"When a woman has lost her chastity, she will not shrink from any other crime."

Neque mala vel bona, quæ vulgus putet. Lat. TAC. —"Things are not always good or bad, which are deemed so by the multitude."

Nequeo monstrare, et sentio tantum. Lat. JUV. "What I can only feel, but can not express."—An indefinable sensation.

Neque semper arcum tendit Apollo. Lat.—"Nor does Apollo always bend his bow."—This phrase is generally used as an apology for those, who, being engaged in grave pursuits, indulge themselves in occasional relaxation; but sometimes, in a different sense, that men of talent, who were supposed to be under the special protection of Apollo, do not at all times, reach by their exertion, to the level of their usual merits.

Nequicquam sapit, qui sibi non sapit. Lat.—"He is wise to no purpose, who is not wise to himself." —The first use of wisdom is to correct our own faults.

Ne quid detrimenti Respublica capiat. Lat.—"That the commonwealth shall receive no injury."—This was the injunction given by the Roman Republic, on investing a Dictator with supreme powers. This attention to domestic security, in contradistinction to foreign conquest, is often intimated to the statesman at the helm of affairs, as forming his first and most important duty.

Ne quid falsi dicere audeat, ne quid veri non audeat. Lat. Cicero.—"Let him not presume to utter any falsehood, or suppress any truth."

Ne quid nimis. Lat. Terence.—"Do not take too much of any thing,"—or pursue an object too far. "There may be too much, even of a good thing."

Ne remettez pas à démain, ce que vous pouvez faire aujourd'hui. Fr. Prov.—"Do not defer until to-morrow, that which you have it in your power to do to-day."

Nervis alienis mobile lignum. Lat.—"A puppet moved by wires in the hands of others."—Applied to politicians of a certain class, whose motions are dictated, and whose proceedings are regulated, by persons unseen, or by what is called an interior cabinet.

Nescia mens hominum fati sortisque futuræ,
Et servare modum, rebus sublata secundis.
Lat. Virgil.

"The mind of man is ignorant of fate and future destiny, and of keeping within due bounds when elated by prosperity."

Nescio quâ natale solum dulcedine cunctos
Ducit, et immemores non sinit esse sui.
Lat. Ovid.

"I know not by what charm our native soil still attracts all, and implants itself in our recollection." Neither time nor distance can eradicate the attachment which every man feels for the spot which gave him birth.

Nescio quid curtæ semper abest rei. Lat. Horace.—"Something is always wanting to our imperfect fortune."—Our desires are never fully gratified.

Nescit vox missa reverti. Lat. Horace.—"The word

which has once escaped can never be recalled"—We should be careful of what we say. The impression made by an indiscreet word is scarcely ever to be erased.

Ne scuticâ dignum horribili sectere flagello. Lat. HORACE. "Do not pursue him, who deserves a slight whip, with the weightier scourge."—Let the punishment be proportionate to the crime.

Ne sutor ultra crepidam. Lat.—"Let not the shoemaker go beyond his last"—These were the words of Apelles to a *Crispin,* who properly found fault with an ill-painted slipper in one of his pictures, but ascending to other parts, betrayed the grossest ignorance. No man should pass his opinion in a province of art, where he is without a qualification.

Ne tentes aut perfice. Lat.—"Attempt not, or accomplish."

Ne vile fano. Lat.—"Bring nothing base to the temple."

Ne vile velis. Lat.—"Incline to nothing base.'

Neutiquam officium liberi esse hominis puto,
Cum is nihil promereat, postulare id gratiæ apponi sibi. Lat. TERENCE.
"A man of liberal sentiments will not stoop to ask that as a favour, which he can not claim as a reward."

Nihil cupientium nudus castra peto. Lat. HORACE. "Naked I repair to the camp of those who desire nothing."—Though not rich, I am not dissatisfied, because I have limited my desires.

Nihil dictum quod non dictum prius. Lat.—"Nothing can now be said, which has not been said before."

Nihil est, ab omni parte, beatum. Lat. HORACE.—"Nothing is blessed or perfect on every side."—There is no state or condition of life without its disadvantages.

Nihil est tam volucre quam maledictum; nihil facilius emittitur, nihil citius excipitur, nihil la tius dissipatur. Lat. CICERO.—"Nothing is so swift in its progress as calumny; nothing more easily escapes us, and nothing is more readily received; and nothing can be more widely spread abroad."

Nihil est tam utile, quod in transitu prosit. Lat. SENECA.—"No book can be so good, as to be profitable when negligently read."

Nihil infelicius illo, cui nihil infelix contigit. Lat. —"He is the most wretched of men who has never experienced adversity."

Nihil magis consentaneum est, quam ut iisdem modis res dissolvatur, quibus constituitur. Lat. Law Maxim.—"Nothing is more equitable, than that every thing should be dissolved by the same means as it was first constituted."—A deed under hand and seal can only be released by a similar deed. An obligation in writing can not be discharged by a verbal agreement.

Nihil potest Rex quam quod de jure potest. Lat. Law Maxim.—"The King can do nothing but what he can do by law."—He can not, for instance, order a man to prison, without the writs and processes of law.

Nihil quod tetigit non ornavit. Lat.—"He touched nothing without adorning it."—He embellished and illustrated every subject which he attempted to discuss.

Nihil scriptum miraculi causa. Lat. TAC.—"Nothing composed for the sake of exhibiting prodigies, or exciting wonder."—Applied to a history which narrates simple facts in plain terms.

Nihil tam absurdum, quod non dictum sit ab aliquo philosophorum. Lat. CICERO.—"There is not any thing so absurd, as not to have been said at some time, by some one of the philosophers."

Nihil tam firmum est, cui periculum non fit etiam ab invalido. Lat. QUINT. CURT.—"There is nothing so secure as to be out of the reach of injury, even from an apparently weak cause."

Nil actum reputans, si quid superesset agendum.
Lat. LUCAN.

"Thinking that nothing was done, if any thing remained to do."—This is the character of a man of talent and enterprise.

Nil admirari, prope est res una, Numici,
Solaque, quæ possit facere et servare beatum.
Lat. HORACE.

"Not to be lost in idle admiration (of men or things,) is the only sure means of making, and of preserving happiness."

Nil agit exemplum, litem quod lite resolvit. Lat. HOR.—That example does nothing which, in removing one difficulty, introduces another."—That arbitration is of no avail, which leaves behind it, as great a difficulty as is found in the first instance.

Nil conscire sibi, nullâ pallescere culpâ. Lat. HOR.—"To be conscious of no guilt, and to turn pale at no charge."

Nil debet. Lat. Law Term.—"He owes nothing."—The usual plea in an action of debt.

Nil desperandum Teucro duce, et auspice Teucro.
Lat. HORACE.

"We should not despair of any thing, Teucer being our guide, and we marching under his auspices."—A compliment often applied to the talents and good fortune of a popular general, or leader.

Nil dicit. Lat. Law Term.—"He says nothing."—This plea intimates a failure in the defendant, in not putting in his answer to the plaintiff's declaration.

Nil dictu fœdum, visuque, hæc limina tangat,
Intra quæ puer est. Lat. JUVENAL.

"Let nothing foul either to the eye or to the ear, be seen or heard within those doors which enclose a boy."—Nothing indecent or criminal should be mentioned within the early and eager hearing of children.

Nil ego contulerim jucundo sanus amico. Lat. HOR "Whilst in sound mind, I should never deem any thing preferable to a pleasant friend."

Nil enim prodest, quod lædere non possit idem. Lat. Ovid.—"Nothing can be of advantage which is not also convertible to purposes of injury."—This broad maxim applies to every kind of physical and moral agency. Thus, fire, which is so necessary, may be rendered most mischievous: and that eloquence, which sometimes saves the innocent, may be made the instrument of rescuing the guilty.

Nil falsi audeat, nil veri non audeat dicere. Lat. Cicero.—"That he should not dare to tell a falsehood, or to leave a truth untold."—This is the brief but just character of an honest historian.

Nil habet infelix paupertas durius in se,
Quam quod ridiculos homines facit.
Lat. J. venal.
"The greatest hardship of poverty is, th at it tends to make men ridiculous."

Nil intra est oleam, nil extra est in nuce duri. Lat. Hor.—If this be not true, "There is no kernel in the olive, nor has the nut any shell." –There is no trusting even to physical evidence.

Nil non laudandum, aut sensit, aut dixit, aut fecit. Lat.—"He never thought, spoke, or acted, but in a manner worthy of praise."

Nil oriturum aliàs, nil ortum tale fatentes. Lat. Horace.—"Confessing that nothing of the same kind had arisen, or was likely to arise in future times."—Admitting the existence of an *unique*, a thing not to be equalled.

Nil proprium ducas, quod mutari potest. Lat. Syrus.—"Never deem that your own, which can be transferred."—All worldly possessions are precarious.

Nil similius insano quam ebrius. Lat. Proverb— "Nothing is more like a madman, than a man who is drunk."

Nil sine magno
Vita labore dedit mortalibus. Lat. Horace
"In this life, nothing is given to men without great labour."

Nil tam difficile, quod non solertia vincat. Lat. Prov.—"Nothing is so difficult, but that by diligence and practice it may be overcome."

Ni l'un ni l'autre. Fr.—"Neither the one nor the other."

Nimia illa licentia
Profecto evadet in aliquod magnum malum.
Lat. TERENCE.

"This excessive licentiousness will most certainly terminate in some mischief of magnitude."—This is a maxim often resorted to in political discussions.

Nimirùm insanus paucis videatur, eo quod
Maxima pars hominum morbo jactatur eodem.
Lat. HORACE.

"He appears mad indeed but to a few, because the majority is infected with the same disease."

Nimium altercando veritas amittitur. Lat. Prov.—"In excessive altercation truth is lost."—In protracted disputes, men forget both themselves and the subject.

Nimium risûs pretium est, si probitatis impendio constat. Lat. QUINTIL.—"That laughter costs too much, which is purchased by the sacrifice of decency or propriety."

Nimius in veritate, et similitudinis quam pulchritudinis amantior. Lat. QUINTILIAN.—"Too exact, and rather studious of similitude than of beauty."—In the fine arts, even nature may be too closely copied.

Nisi dominus, frustra. Lat.—"Unless the Lord be with you, all your efforts are in vain."—This, which is the motto of the city of Edinburgh, has been thus whimsically translated:—"You can do nothing here unless you are a lord!"

Nisi prius. Law Lat.—"Unless before."—A judicial writ by which the sheriff is to bring a jury to Westminster Hall on a certain day.—"Unless before" that day the Lords Justices of the King go into his county to take the assizes. They there dispose of the cause, and thus save expense and trouble to the parties, jury, and witnesses.—*Nisi prius* is the appellation given to a Court held in the city and county of Philadelphia, by *one* of the judges of the Supreme court, for the trial of issues.

Nisi utile quod facias, stulta est gloria. Lat. PHÆD. —" Unless what occupies your mind be useful, the pride you derive from thence is foolish."

Nitimur in vetitum semper, cupimusque negata. Lat. OVID. " We always struggle for the things which are forbidden, and covet those denied to us."

Nitor in adversum. Lat.—" I strive against it."

Nobilitas sola est atque unica virtus. Lat. JUV. " Virtue is the only and true nobility."—The pride of birth, and the sound of titles, disappear before the intrinsic dignity of virtue.

Nobilitatis virtus non stemma character. Lat.—" Virtue, not pedigree, should characterize nobility."

Nobis non licet esse tam disertis,
Qui Musas colimus severiores. Lat. MARTIAL. " We who cultivate the muses of a graver spirit, can not indulge ourselves in such license or extravagance."—The nature of our pursuit is such as to exclude those licentious freedoms.

Nocet differre paratis. Lat.—" Those who are prepared, should never delay."—When your preparations are complete, it is injudicious to grant a further time to your adversary.

Nocet empta dolore voluptas. Lat. HORACE.—" That pleasure is injurious which is bought at the price of pain."—We should carefully look to the perils which await certain enjoyments.

Nocturnâ versate manu, versate diurnâ. Lat. HOR. —" Be these your studies by day and by night." Let those objects be never out of your contemplation.

Nolens, volens. Lat.—" Unwilling or willing."

Noli me tangere. Lat.—" Do not touch me."—A name given to a very tender complaint in the nose; or, ironically, to a person who is over-sensitive.

Nolle prosequi. Law Lat.—" To be unwilling to

proceed."—This is used in law when a plaintiff, having commenced an action, declines to proceed therein.—It is also entered officially by the Attorney-general, to stay any further proceedings in certain criminal cases.

Nolo episcopari. Lat.—"I do not wish to be made a bishop."—This is a phrase of form put into the mouth of the person appointed to this high office. It is now applied ironically to those who affectedly disclaim that which is the secret and sole object of their ambition.

Nom de guerre. Fr.—"A war-name."—An assumed or travelling title.—Your "Captain" is excellent as a *nom de guerre.*

Nomenque erit indelebile nostrum. Lat. Ovid. "And my reputation shall be immortal."—This boast of the Latin poet is seldom used but in an ironical sense.

Nomen tantum virtutis usurpas; quid ipsa valeat, ignoras. Lat. Cicero.—"You make much use of the *name* of virtue, but you are ignorant of its value."

Non alia bibam mercede. Lat. Hor.—"I will not drink upon any other conditions."

"On these terms only will I dine,
However excellent your wine."

Non amo argutias in theologia. Lat. Tillotson.—"I do not approve of subtleties in divinity."

Non amo te, Zabidi, nec possum dicere quare;
Hoc solum scio, non amo te, Zabidi. Lat. Mart.
"I do not love you, I can not assign a reason, but this I know, that I do not love you."—Such an unaccountable prejudice finds its way at times, into every human breast. The epigram has been thus pleasantly translated:

"I do not love you Dr. Fell,
The reason why I can not tell;
But this at least I know full well,
I do not love you Dr. Fell."

Non ampliter sed munditer convivium;—Plus salis

quam sumptûs. Lat. CORN. NEPOS.—"The entertainment was more neat than ample; there was more of relish than of cost."

Non assumpsit. Law Lat.—"He did not assume," or take to himself.—A plea in personal actions, when the defendant denies that any promise was made.

Non bene conveniunt, nec in una sede morantur Majestas et amor. Lat. OVID. "Dignity and love do not blend well, or continue long together."

Nonchalance. Fr.—"Carelessness, supineness, indifference."

Non compos mentis. Lat.—"Not of sound mind."—In a delirium of lunacy.

Non conscire sibi. Lat.—"Conscious of no fault."

Non constat. Law Lat.—"It does not appear."—It is not before the court in evidence.

Non cuivis homini contingit adire Corinthum. Lat. HORACE

"It does not happen to every man to go to *Corinth.*"—All men can not possess the same opportunities, or recur to the same sources of information.

Non deficiente crumena. Lat.—"Not with an empty purse."

Non doctior, sed meliore imbutus doctrina. Lat.—"Not more learned, but imbued with a better kind of knowledge."

Non eadem est ætas, non mens. Lat. HOR.—"I am not now of the same age, or disposition, as I was formerly."—I am not inclined to engage actively in the contest for which I feel myself disqualified.

Non ego mordaci distrinxi carmine quenquam, Nulla venenato est litera mista joco. Lat. OVID "I have not attacked any one with biting verse, nor does any impoisoned jest lurk beneath, in what I have written."—I always meant to be rather playful than satirical.

Non ego ventosæ venor suffragia plebis. Lat. HOR.—

"I do not hunt for, or court the votes of the light and veering rabble."

Non enim gazæ, neque consularis
Summovet lictor miseros tumultus
Mentis, et curas laqueata circum
Tecta volantes. Lat. HORACE

"It is not in the power of wealth, or of the consul's lictor (*i. e.* of any of the appendages of greatness,) to subdue the conflicts of a wretched mind, or to remove the cares which hover about the fretted dome."

Non enim tam auctoritatis in disputando, quam rationis momenta quærenda sunt. Lat. CICERO. "In every disputation, we should hope more from the moments of reason, than from the weight of authorities."

Non equidem invidio, miror magis. Lat. VIRG.—"In fact I do not envy, yet still I wonder" how it has come to pass.

Non est ad astra mollis à terris via. Lat. SENECA.—"There is no easy way from the earth to the stars."—It is not by common efforts that men can attain to immortality.

Non est inventus. Lat. Law Term.—"He has not been found."—The return made by the sheriff when the defendant is not to be found in his bailiwick.—It is sometimes used in the way of pleasantry, to mark a sudden disappearance.

Non est jocus esse malignus. Lat. HOR.—"There is no joke in being malignant."

Non est vivere, sed valere, vita. Lat.—"Life is not life, but with the enjoyment of health."—The invalid can scarcely be said to live, when the faculties either of the mind or body are seriously impaired.

Non exercitus, neque thesauri, præsidia regni sunt, verum amici. Lat. SALLUST.—"The safety of a kingdom does not depend so much upon its armies, or its treasures, as on its alliances.

Non expedit omnia videre, omnia audire. Lat. SEN. —"It is not expedient to see or to hear all that is done or said."—It often conduces to our peace of mind, to appear not to notice what we see or hear.

Non fidatevi al alchemista povero, ô al medico ammalato. Ital. Prov.—"Do not trust to a poor alchymist, or a sick physician."—Do not take the advice of those who have not been able to act properly for themselves.

Non fumum ex fulgore, sed ex fumo dare lucem. Lat. HORACE.—"Not to bring smoke from light, but out of darkness to produce splendour."—This is the difference, as stated by the satirist, between a bad poet and a good one.—The former exhausts himself in the glare of his opening, and loses himself in smoke. The latter proceeds from a more modest opening, to disclose all the radiance of poetry.

Non generant aquilæ columbas. Lat.—"Eagles do not bring forth pigeons."

Non hæc in fœdera. Lat. VIRGIL.—"Not into such leagues or alliances as these."

Non id videndum, conjugum ut bonis bona,
At ut ingenium congruat, et mores moribus;
Probitas, pudorque virgini dos optima est.
Lat. TERENCE.

"In marriage the relative proportion of property is not so much to be considered, as the union of mind, and the identity of manner and disposition. Chastity and modesty form the best portion which a virgin can bring to her husband."

Non ignara mali, miseris succurrere disco. Lat. VIRGIL.—"Not being myself a stranger to suffering, I have learned to relieve the calamities of others."

Non ignoro quæ bona sint, fieri meliora posse doctrinâ, et quæ non optima, aliquo modo acui tamen, et corrigi posse. Lat. CICERO.—"I am conscious that those (pieces of composition,) which are good, may be improved by art, and that those which are even excellent, are yet susceptible of a further polish and correction."

Non ille pro charis amicis,
Aut patriâ, timidus perire. Lat. HORACE
"He dares for his country or his friends to die."—This is a flower frequently strewn over the tomb of a hero.

Non inferiora secutus. Lat.—"Not having followed meaner pursuits."

Non libet. Lat.—"It does not please me."—I do not assent.

Non licet in bello bis peccare. Lat.—"It is not permitted in war to err twice."—At other games, a blot may be got over, but at this most dangerous game, a mistake is generally to be considered as irretrievable.

Non magni pendis, quia contigit. Lat. HORACE. "You do not value it highly, because it came incidentally."—The *wind-falls* of fortune are less valued than the *product* of our own industry.

Non missura cutem, nisi plena cruoris hirudo. Lat. HORACE.—"Like a leech, which does not quit the skin, until it is full of blood."—Used to mark a pertinacious claimant or applicant, who can not be induced to retire, until he has obtained his purpose.

Non morbus plerumque, sed curatio neglecta, interficit. Lat.—"It is not the disease, but neglect of the remedy, which generally destroys life."

Non nobis solum. Lat.—"Not merely for ourselves."

Non nobis solum, sed toto mundo nati. Lat.—"Not born for ourselves alone, but for the whole world."

Non nostrum tantas componere lites. Lat.—"It is not for us to adjust such grave disputes."—Ironically quoted, in general, and when the contest is of a trivial nature.

Non numero hæc judicantur, sed pondere. Lat. CIC. "These things are not judged of by their number, but by their weight."

Non nunc agitur de vectigalibus, non de sociorum injuriis: libertas et anima nostra in dubio est. Lat. CICERO.—"The question is not now respecting our revenues, or the injuries done to our allies, our liberties and lives are all at stake."

Non obstante. Lat.—"Notwithstanding."—A phrase used in patents, to intimate a dispensing power.

Non omne molitor quæ fluit undâ videt. Lat.—"The miller does not see every thing that floats by his mill."—Metaphorically—the statesman does not notice all the minor circumstances which may either forward, or embarrass his most favourite measures.

Non omnes eadem mirantur amentque. Lat. Hor.—"All men do not admire and wish for the same objects."—Our pursuits are various.

Non omnia possumus omnes. Lat. Virgil.—"We can not, all of us, do every thing."—The human faculties are generally confined to a narrow line of operation.

Non omnis error stultitia est dicenda. Lat.—"Every error is not to be called a folly."—Fatuity is not to be inferred from a single circumstance of mistake.

Non posse bene geri rempublicam multorum imperiis. Lat. Corn. Nepos.—"A commonwealth can not be well conducted under the command of many."—There must be a *unity* of will in the executive power of any state, to produce a due effect.

Non propter vitam, faciunt patrimonia quidam,
Sed vitio cæci, propter patrimonia vivunt.
Lat. Juvenal.
"Some men do not get estates for the purpose of enjoying life, but blinded with error, they live only for their estates!"

Non quo, sed quomodo. Lat.—"Not by whom, but in what manner," the business is done.

Non revertar inultus. Lat.—"I will not return unrevenged."

Non satis est pulchra esse poemata, dulcia sunto. Lat. Hor.—"It is not enough that poetry should be decorated; it should also be interesting."

Non scribit ille, cujus carmina nemo legit. Lat.

MART.—"That man does not write, whose verses no man reads."—They are as much unknown as if they had perished in *embryo*.

Non sequitur. Lat.—"It does not follow."—It is a *non sequitur*—it is a conclusion not warranted by the premises.

Non sibi, sed omnibus. Lat.—"Not for itself, but for all."—The motto of an institution intended to pro mote the public *weal*.

Non sibi, sed patriæ. Lat.—"Not for himself, but for his country."

Non sibi, sed toto genitum se credere mundo. Lat. LUCAN of CATO. "Believing himself to be born, not for himself, but for the whole world."

Non, si male nunc, et olim sic erit. Lat. HORACE "If matters go on badly at present, they may take better turn hereafter."—One of the usual phrases f encouragement under misfortune.

Non sum qualis eram. Lat. HORACE. "I am not now what I have been."—I feel the natural decay of my vigour and of my faculties.

Non tali auxilio, nec defensoribus istis
Tempus eget. Lat. VIRGIL.
"The cause does not require such aid, or such defenders."

Nonumque prematur in annum. Lat. HORACE.—"Let your piece be kept nine years."—This is a precept, which our dramatic poets are too much "pressed by hunger, and request of friends," to comply with.

Non ut diu vivamus curandum est, sed ut satis. Lat. SENECA.—"Our care should not be so much to live long, as to have lived enough."

Non vi, sed sæpe cadendo. Lat.—"Not by force, but by often falling."—Every thing may be effected by incessant efforts. The idea is taken from drops of water, which unremittingly falling, will hollow out a stone.

Non vis esse iracundus? ne sis curiosus. Lat SEN -

"Would you avoid being offended? be not inquisitive."—Be not too eager to learn the opinions of others respecting you.

Non vultus, non color. Lat.—"There is neither the countenance nor the colour."—This quotation is differently used. It is employed to repel a testimony where there is no verisimilitude, or to rebut the imputation of writings to an author, which bear not the features of his style, or the complexion of his sentiments.

Nosce teipsum. Lat.—"Know thyself."—Form a just estimate of your talents and defects.—The importance of self-examination is great, and must be acknowledged by every reflecting mind.

Noscitur à sociis. Lat. Prov.—"He is known by his companions."—"Tell me," says the *Spanish* proverb, "what company you keep, and I'll tell you who you are."

Nos patriæ fines, et dulcia linquimus arva. Lat. VIRGIL.—"We leave our country, we quit our delightful plains."—We feel all the horrors of migrating from our native soil.

Nosse hæc omnia salus est adolescentulis. Lat. TER. "It is salutary for young men to be informed of all these things."

Nostalgia. Lat.—"Home-sickness," or, pain caused by absence from, or longing for home. It is called by the Germans and Swiss, who are particularly subject to it, *heimweh.*

Nota bene. Lat.—"Mark well."—Used in referring to some remarkable object or circumstance.

Notre défiance justifie la tromperie d'autrui. Fr. ROCHEFOUCAULT.—"Our mistrust justifies the deceit of another."—Men are neither happy nor safe, but in mutual confidence.

Notre mal s'empoisonne
Du secours qu'on lui donne. Fr. Prov
"Our disease is aggravated by the remedies which are administered."

Nous aurions souvent honte de nos plus belles ac

tions, si le monde voyoit tous les motifs qui les produisent. Fr. ROCHEFOUCAULT.—"We should often be ashamed of our brightest actions, were the world but to see the motives by which they were produced."

Nous avons tous assez de force pour supporter les maux d'autrui. Fr. ROCHEFOUCAULT.—"We have all of us sufficient strength to bear the misfortunes of others."

Nous désirerions peu de choses avec ardeur, si nous connoisions parfaitement ce que nous désirons. Fr. ROCHEFOUCAULT.—"We should wish for few things with eagerness, if we perfectly knew the nature of that which was the object of our desire."

Nous ne savons ce que c'est que bonheur ou malheur absolû. Fr. ROUSSEAU.—"We do not know what is absolutely good or bad fortune."

Nous ne trouvons guère de gens de bon sens, que ceux qui sont de notre avis. Fr. ROCHEFOUCAULT.—"We seldom find any persons of good sense, but such as are of our opinion."—Our self-love, on such occasions, induces us to pass a favourable judgment.

Novi ingenium mulierum;
Nolunt ubi velis, ubi nolis capiunt ultro.
Lat. TERENCE.
"I know the nature of women. When you request, they refuse; when you forbid, they are sure to do it."

Novos amicos dum paras, veteres cole. Lat. HERMES. "Whilst you seek new friendships, take care to cultivate the old."—Do not lose sight of old attachments for the sake of making new connexions.

Novus homo. Lat.—"A new man."—This is used by Sallust to denote a man who, without the advantage of birth and fortune, has risen by his own exertions, to influence in the nation.

Nucleus. Lat.—"The kernel."—Any thing about which matter is gathered or conglobated.

Nudum pactum. Lat.—"A naked agreement."—A promise unconfirmed by any written obligation.—A void contract.

Nugæ canoræ. Lat.—" Melodious trifles."—Mere sing-song without meaning.

Nugis addere pondus. Lat.—" To give weight to trifles."—To lend a consequence to matters of slight moment.

Nugis armatus. Lat.—" Armed with trifles."

Nulla aconita bibuntur
Fictilibus. Lat. JUVENAL.
" No wolfsbane is drunk out of earthenware."—The danger of poison is reserved for those who drink out of vessels of plate.

Nulla bona. Law Lat.—" No goods."—A return made by a sheriff to an execution, where he can find no property belonging to the defendant.

Nulla est sincera voluptas,
Sollicitumque aliquid lætis advenit. Lat. OVID.
" No joy comes unmixed, and something of anxiety attends every pleasure."

Nulla falsa doctrina est, quæ non permisceat aliquid veritatis. Lat.—" There is no doctrine so false, but that it may be intermixed with some truth." Even amidst the wild follies of the *Alcoran*, there are some few precepts, which would not disgrace the purity of the *Christian* code.

Nulla ferè causa est, in quâ non fæmina litem
Moverit. Lat. JUVENAL.
" There are few disputes in life, which may not, when traced, be found to originate with a woman."

Nulla fides regni sociis, omnisque potestas
Impatiens consortis erit. Lat. LUCAN.
" There will be no common faith between those who share in power, and each man will be jealous of his associate."—This is a strong description of the jealous and distracting councils of a nation on the eve of ruin.

Nullâ pallescere culpâ. Lat. HORACE.—" Not to turn pale on any imputation of guilt."

Nulla venenato litera mista joco est. Lat. OVID.
" My writings are free from any envenomed jest."

Nulli jactantius mærent quam qui maxime lætan-

tur. Lat. Tacitus.—"None mourn with more affectation of sorrow, than those who are inwardly rejoiced."

Nulli negabimus, nulli differemus Justitiam. Lat
"We will not refuse or postpone the justice which is due to any man."—This emphatic phrase is in *magna charta*—the "great charter of English rights."

Nullis amor est medicabilis herbis. Lat. Ovid
"Love is not to be cured by any medicinal herbs."

Nullis defunctum malis affici. Lat. Seneca.
"The dead man is affected by no evils."—He is now insensible to the cares and pains which before beset him.

Nullius addictus jurare in verba magistri. Lat. Horace.—"Not bound to swear, or speak, according to the dictates of any master."—This quotation is fairly used by a writer professing to give, and using only his own free, honest, and independent opinions.

Nullum est jam dictum, quod non dictum prius. Lat. Terence.—"Nothing can be now said, which has not been said before."—The meaning is, that in these latter days, it is difficult to arrive at novelty.

Nullum imperium tutum, nisi benevolentia munitum. Lat. Corn. Nep.—"No government is safe, unless it be fortified by good will.'

Nullum iniquum in jure præsumendum est. Lat. Law Maxim.—"Nothing unjust is to be presumed in the law."—All things are taken to be lawfully done until proof is adduced to the contrary: Fraud shall never be intended, or presumed, or adduced by the law, unless it be expressly averred.

Nullum magnum ingenium sine mixturâ dementiæ. Lat. Seneca.—"There never was a great genius without some tincture of madness," or, as Dryden has it,

"Great wit to madness sure is near allied."

Nullum magnum malum quod extremum est. Lat.

NEPOS.—"That evil can never be great which is the last."—A man can undergo almost any suffer ing under the persuasion that it is the last which he shall endure. This quotation is, however, generally employed against the fear of death, which terminates all our sufferings,

Nullum numen abest, si sit prudentia. Lat. JUV "No protecting power is wanting, if prudence be but employed."—If men in general acted with prudence, they need not be under the necessity of in voking any other aid.

Nullum simile est idem. Lat. Law Max.—"Those things which are *similar* are not the *same.*"

Nullum tempus occurrit regi. Lat. Law Max.—"No time impedes the King."—The rights of the crown are indefeasible by any lapse of time.

Nullum vitæ genus est improbrius, quam eorum qui sine causæ respectu, mercede conducti, militant. Lat. GROTIUS.—"No calling in life is more vile than that of those who, without any regard to the justice of the cause, hire themselves to fight for pay."

Nullus commodum capere potest de injuriâ suâ propriâ. Lat. Law Maxim.—"No man can take advantage of his own wrong."—If a lessor and lessee of lands for years, join in the cutting down of timber, the lessor shall not afterwards punish the lessee for waste, as this would be to take advantage of his own wrong.

Nullus tantus quæstus, quam quod habes parcere. Lat. Prov.—"There is no gain so certain as that which arises from sparing what you have."—There is no road to wealth more certain than that of economy.

Nul n'aura de l'esprit,
Hors nous et nos amis. Fr. MOLIERE
"No person shall be allowed to have wit, out of our circle, and that of our friends."—This alludes to the little *juntos* of witlings to be found in al most every town, who associate to be-praise and be-puff each other, with a view of excluding the

pretensions of those who are not of the party of these monopolists.

Nul tiel record. Law French."—There is no such record."—The return of a sheriff to a *Certiorari*, when there is no declaration or writ, between the parties named, in his custody.

Numerisque fertur lege solutis. Lat. HOR.—"He is borne along in numbers free from law."—His verses are licentious, or unrestrained by any of the existing rules.

Numerus certus pro incerto ponitur. Lat.—"A certain is put for an uncertain number."—As we say a thousand, or a million, to express a large number, but without meaning to ascertain the precise amount."

Numini et patriæ asto. Lat.—"I stand to God and my country."

Nunc aut nunquam. Lat.—"Now or never."

Nunc omnis ager, nunc omnis parturit arbor;
Nunc frondent sylvæ, nunc formosissimus annus. Lat. VIRGIL.

"Now every field and every tree is in bloom; the woods are now in full leaf, and the year is in its highest beauty."—Used, generally, to introduce a poetical description of summer.

Nunc patimur longæ pacis mala; sævior armis,
Luxuria incubuit, victumque ulciscitur orbem. Lat. JUVENAL.

"Now we suffer the mischiefs of a long peace.—Luxury, more destructive than war, has enervated us, and avenges the vanquished world."—This is a fine description of Rome in its decline; it exhibits what Shakspeare calls

"The cankers of a calm world, and a long peace."

Nunc te offer melioribus. Lat. HORACE.—"Now prepare yourself for better things,"—or, for more worthy pursuits.

Nunquam ad liquidum Fama perducitur. Lat.—"Fame never reports things in their true light."

Nunquam aliud natura, aliud sapientia dicit. Lat.

Juvenal.—"Nature never says one thing, and wisdom another."—Their dictates are always in complete accordance.

Nunquam libertas gratior extat,
Quam sub rege pio. Lat. Claudian.
"Liberty never existed in a more gracious form, than under a pious king."—Monarchy is not unfavourable to liberty, *if* (a *very rare* occurrence!) the monarch adheres to the obligations which exist between him and the people.

Nunquam minùs solus, quam cum solus. Lat.—"Never less alone than when alone."—This was the saying of the ancient philosopher, who found his greatest luxury in solitary reflection.

Nunquam nimis dicitur, quod nunquam satis discitur. Lat. Seneca.—"That never is too often said, which is never sufficiently learned."—There are some maxims of so grave and important a nature, that they can never be too often repeated, or too deeply impressed.

Nunquam non paratus. Lat.—"Never unprepared."

Nunquam periclitatur religio, nisi inter reverendissimas. Lat. Luther.—"The cause of religion is never so much endangered, as by (the disputations of) its reverend teachers."

Nunquam potest non esse virtuti locus. Lat. Sen.
"There must ever be a place for virtue."—A wise and good man can never be without a proper scope for his exertions.

Nunquam sunt grati qui nocuêre sales. Lat.—"Those witticisms are never agreeable, which wound the feelings of any."

Nusquam tuta fides. Lat. Virg.—"Our confidence is no where safe."—This is spoken of a period of civil war, in which, more particularly, every social tie is unhappily dissolved.

O

Obiter dictum. Law Lat.—"A thing said by the way."—An opinion given in passing, and which not applying judicially to the case, is not to be resorted to as an authority.

Obruat illud male partum, male retentum, male gestum imperium. Lat. CICERO.—"Perish that power which has been obtained by evil means, retained by similar practices, and which is administered as badly as it was acquired."

Obscuris vera involvens. Lat.—"Involving the truth in obscure terms"

Obscurum per obscurius. Lat.—To explain what was "obscure by something more obscure."—This phrase occurs, and frequently with justice, in polemic argument, when the opponent professing to explain, involves himself in a cloud of words, and thus renders more dark, what was sufficiently dark before.

Obsecro, tuum est? Vetus credideram. Lat.—"Pray is it yours? I had thought it an old invention."

Obsequium amicos, veritas odium parit. Lat. TER. "Obsequiousness procures friends, but truth begets hatred."

Obstupui, steteruntque comæ et vox faucibus hæsit. Lat. VIRGIL.
"I was astonished, my hair stood at end, and my voice lingered in my throat."—Used to describe an extreme degree of consternation.

Obtrectatio ac livor pronis auribus accipiuntur; quippe adulationi fædum crimen servitutis, malignitati falsa species libertatis inest. Lat. TACITUS.—"Spleen and calumny are devoured with a greedy ear.—Flattery wears the badge of servitude, whilst malignity speaks the tone of independence," and is therefore well received.

O cæca nocentum
Consilia! O semper timidum scelus! Lat. STAT. "Oh, the blind counsels of the guilty! Oh, how ever cowardly is wickedness!"—It has been often remarked that Providence seems to darken the understandings, and to depress the spirits of great criminals.

Occupet extremum scabies. Lat. Prov.—"Let the itch

infect the last."—*Anglice*, "the devil take the hindmost."

Occurrent nubes. Lat.—"Clouds will intervene."

O! cives, cives, quærenda pecunia primùm;
Virtus post nummos Lat. HORACE.
"Oh! my fellow citizens, we must first amass wealth, and afterwards seek for virtue."

O! curas hominum, O quantum est in rebus inane. Lat. PERSIUS.
"Oh! how vain are the cares of men, and how unsatisfying are their enjoyments!"

Oderint dum metuant. Lat. CIC.—"Let them hate, provided they fear."—This is the sentiment of a tyrant towards his subjects.

Oderunt hilarem tristes, tristemque jocosi. Lat. HORACE.—"The grave dislike the cheerful, and the gay hate the grave."—There can be no pleasurable association between people of different temperaments.

Oderunt peccare boni, virtutis amore. Lat. HOR.—"Good men forbear to sin, merely from their love of virtue."—Those who love virtue for herself, will act solely from her impulses, and without any regard to extrinsic circumstances.

Odia in longum jaciens, quæ reconderet, auctaque promeret. Lat. TACITUS.
"A man who lays his resentment aside, but stores it up, to bring it forward with additional acrimony."—This, as JUNIUS observes, is a description of the very worst of characters.

Odia qui nimium timet, regnare nescit. Lat. SEN. "He who is too fearfully alive to hatred, is ignorant of the art of reigning."—The sovereign who aims at the general good of his people, should learn to contemn the resentments of individuals.

Odimus accipitrem, quia semper vivit in armis. Lat. Prov.—"We hate the hawk, because she always lives in arms."—All men must detest that power, which is in a state of eternal hostility.

Odi profanum vulgus et arceo. Lat. HORACE.—"I

hate and repel from me the profane vulgar."—This is the exordium of the poet to a religious hymn; and on a subject of which the common people were supposed to be wholly ignorant.

Odium theologicum. Lat.—"A theological hatred." —The hatred of divines.

O faciles dare summa deos, eademque tueri
Difficiles. Lat. LUCAN
"Oh! how gracious are the gods in giving high situations, and how reluctant are they to insure them when given!"

O fortunatos nimium, sua si bona nôrint,
Agricolas, quibus ipsa procul discordibus armis,
Fundit humo facilem victum justissima tellus.
Lat. VIRGIL.
"Oh! more than happy, if you knew your own advantages, husbandmen, to whom, remote from clashing arms, the grateful earth pours forth an easy sustenance."—An eulogy often quoted on the condition of agriculturists. The first line is sometimes taken apart, and applied to those who either rightly or causelessly urge any motives of political discontent.

Ogni medaglia ha il suo reverso. Ital. Proverb.—"Every medal has its reverse."—There are two sides to every statement.

Ohe! jam satis. Lat. HOR.—"Oh! there is now more than enough."—A phrase used to denote satiety and disgust.

O! Imitatores! servum pecus! Lat. HOR.—"Oh! ye imitators, what a servile herd ye are."—How much does the servile copyist sink below the originality of genius!

Οι πλειονες κακοι. Gr. *Oi pleiones kakoi.*—"The greater part of mankind are bad."—This was the observation of Bias, one of the seven sages of Greece. It is the maxim of cold prudence to regard all men as vicious, until the contrary appears in proof.

Olent illa supercilia malitiam. Lat. CIC.—"That superciliousness savours strongly of malice."

Olim meminisse juvabit. Lat. VIRGIL.—"The future recollection will be pleasing."—There is a melancholy consolation in the retrospect of past misfortunes.

O l'utile secret que de mentir àpropos. Fr. Prov.—"Oh! what a useful secret it is to be able to lie to the purpose."—In the world of politics, all morality being out of the question, nothing is more useful than a well-coined lie.

O major, tandem parcas, insane, minori. Lat. HOR. "Oh! thou who art greatly mad, deign to spare me the lesser madman."—A phrase often used ironically in a paper warfare.

O! miseras hominum mentes, O! pectora cæca!
Lat. LUCRETIUS.
"How wretched are the minds of men, and how blind their understandings?"—A quotation frequently and well applied, in a moment of popular delusion.

Omne actum ab agentis intentione est judicandum. Lat. Law Maxim.—"Every act is to be judged from the intention of the agent."—In contracts and obligations, the law particularly looks to the intention of the parties. In wills, the intent of the tes tator is to be religiously regarded.

Omne animi vitium tanto conspectius in se
Crimen habet, quanto major, qui peccat, habetur. Lat. JUVENAL.
"Every fault of the mind becomes more conspicu ous and more guilty, in proportion to the rank of the offender."—Persons in high station are not only answerable for their own conduct, but for the example which they may hold out to others. Th.s, joined to their advantages of education, aggravates their vices, and loads them with a greater share of responsibility.

Omne capax movet urna nomen. Lat. HOR.—"In the capacious urn of death every name is shaken."—With respect to mortality all are subject to the same lot.

Omne ignotum pro magnifico. Lat.—"Every thing

unknown is taken for magnificent."—We are apt to annex the idea of greatness to that which is mysterious or remote.

Omne in præcipiti vitium stetit. Lat. Juv.—"Every kind of vice has reached its summit."—There remains nothing for posterity to add.

Omnem crede diem tibi diluxisse supremum. Lat. Hor.—"Believe that each day is the last to shine upon thee."—Always suppose that your death is near, and when it comes you will be found better prepared.

Omne nimium vertitur in vitium. Lat. Prov.—"Every excess becomes a vice."—Even our virtues are changed into vices, when pushed to an extreme.

Omne principium tarde. Lat.—"Every work progresses slowly in the beginning."

Omnes amicos habere operosum est; satis est inimicos non habere. Lat. Seneca.—"It is a thing, almost impracticable, to have all men as your friends: it is enough, if you have no enemies."

Omnes eodem cogimur; omnium
Versatur urna, seriùs, ocyùs,
Sors exitura. Lat. Horace.

"We are all compelled to follow the same course. The urn of death is shaken for all, and sooner or later, the lot must come forth."—The duration of life depends on so many chances, that we should always be prepared for the worst.

Omne solum forti patria est. Lat. Ovid.—"To a brave man, every soil forms his country."—He will find his country in every clime.

Omnes, quibus res sunt minus secundæ, magis sunt, nescio quomodo,
Suspiciosi; ad contumeliam omnia accipiunt magis;
Propter suam impotentiam, se credunt negligi.
Lat. Terence.

"All those persons, whose affairs are not prosperous, are in a certain degree suspicious. They take every matter as an affront, and from their conscious weakness, they presume that they are neglected and despised."

Omnes sibi malle melius esse quam alteri. Lat. Ter It is in the nature of man that "every individual should wish for his own advantage, in preference to that of others."

Omnes stultos insanire. Lat. Horace.—"That all fools are mad."—A favourite doctrine of *Damasippus* the Stoic.—Mr. Locke has an acute disputation on this subject. He states the difference to be, that fools draw false conclusions from just principles, whilst madmen draw just conclusions from false principles.

Omne supervacuum pleno de pectore manat. Lat Horace.—"Every thing that is superfluous escapes from the full bosom."—The poet who means to interest, should not overload his subject with unnecessary description, or improbable aggravation.

Omne tulit punctum, qui miscuit utile dulci.
Lat. Horace,
"He has carried every point, who has mixed the useful with the agreeable."—It is the highest praise of a writer, to entertain whilst he instructs, and to interest the heart, whilst he informs the mind.

Omnia bona bonis. Lat.—"All things are good with good men."

Omnia cum amico delibera, sed de teipso priùs. Lat. Seneca.—"Consult with your friend on every thing, but particularly on that which respects yourself."—He may be able to direct in cases, where otherwise, your self-love may mislead.

Omnia fert ætas, animum quoque. Lat. Virgil.—"Age bears away with it all things, even the powers of the mind."—This is a reflection too strikingly true, to be enforced by any comment.

Omnia Græcè!
Cum sit turpe magis nostris nescire Latinè.
Lat. Juvenal
"Every thing is affectedly Greek, when it is more shameful for our Romans to be ignorant of Latin."—This is used as a sarcasm on those who devote

themselves to the study of other languages, without having previously attained to the mastery of their own.

Omnia inconsulti impetûs cœpta, initiis valida, spatio languescunt. Lat. TAC.—"All matters commenced with hasty violence, are strenuous in the beginning, but languish in the end."—That fervour which seeks no aid from wisdom, soon evaporates: the means are therefore exhausted before the end can be attained.

Omnia mala exempla bonis principiis orta sunt. Lat.—"All bad precedents have had their rise in good principles."—A daring offence may give birth to a stretch of power; and, the punishment, being just in the first instance, gains a sanction from those who do not foresee or dread the extent or abuse of the precedent.

Omnia mea mecum porto. Lat.—"All that is mine I carry with me."—All my property, it has been waggishly translated, is *personal.*

Omnia non pariter rerum sunt omnibus apta.
Lat. PROPERTIUS

"All things are not alike for all men fit."

Omnia orta occidunt, et orta senescunt. Lat. SALLUST.—"All things rise but to fall, and flourish to decay."

Omnia priùs verbis experiri, quam armis, sapientem decet. Lat. TER.—"It is becoming wisdom to try all that can be done by negotiation, before recourse is had to arms."

Omnia quæ nunc vetustissima creduntur, nova fuere: et quod hodie exemplis tuemur, inter exempla erit. Lat. TAC.—"All that we now deem ancient, at one time was new; and what we now defend by examples, on a future day will stand as precedents."

Omnia suspendens naso. Lat.—"One who turns up his nose at every thing."—An eternal joker or sneerer.

Omnia tuta timens. Lat. VIRGIL.—"Fearing all

things, even those which are safe."—A mind long harassed with dangers, can not look with confidence to any quarter for security or repose.

Omnia vincit amor, et nos cedamus amori. Lat. VIRGIL.—"Love conquers all things, and let us yield to love."—His power is so despotic, that nothing is left to mortals but submission.

Omnibus hoc vitium est. Lat.—"All have this vice or fault."—It is a common failing.

Omnibus hostes
Reddite nos populis—Civile avertite Bellum.
Lat. LUCAN.

"Lead us into hostility against every people upon earth; but at all hazards prevent a civil war."—If blood must be shed—be it so—but let it not be the blood of countrymen fighting against each other.

Omnibus invideas, Zoile, nemo tibi. Lat. MARTIAL. "Thou mayest envy all men, Zoilus, but no man envies thee."

Omni exceptione major. Lat.—"Superior to all exception."—Applied in the first instance, to the competence and credibility of a legal witness; or, more generally, to the character of a man, which is to be considered as unimpeachable.

Omnis enim res,
Virtus, fama decus, divina humanaque, pulchris
Divitiis parent. Lat. HORACE.

"For all divine and human affairs, virtue, fame, and honour, now obey the alluring influence of riches."—It was said in the days of this poet, "that at *Rome*, all things were venal."

Omnis fors ferendo superanda est. Lat.—"Every chance is to be overcome by enduring."—By patience and perseverance, a man can subdue the worst vicissitude of fortune.

Omnis pœna corporalis, quamvis minima, major est omni pœnâ pecuniariâ, quamvis maximâ. Lat. Law Maxim.—"The smallest corporal punishment falls with more weight, than the largest pecuniary penalty."

Omnium. Lat.—"Of all."—A term applied to public funds, and denoting that fund, which was composed of all the others then extant.—Also, the different stocks given by government, for any particular loan.

Omnium consensu capax imperii, nisi imperâsset. Lat. TACITUS.—"In the opinion of all men, he would have been regarded as capable of governing, if he had never governed."—This was the language of this great historian respecting the emperor GALBA. It is now frequently applied to others, who exhibit something like a show of talent, but which, when brought to the test, proves to be nothing more than a glittering superficiality.

On commence par être dupe; on finit par être fripon. Fr. Mad. DESHOUILIERES.—"They begin by being fools, and end in being knaves."

On dit. Fr.—"It is said."—It is an *on dit.*—It is a loose report.

On fait souvent tort à la vérité, par la manière dont on se sert pour la defendre. Fr.—"An injury is frequently done to the cause of truth, by the manner in which some men attempt to defend it."

On n'a jamais bon marché de mauvaise marchandise. Fr. Prov.—"You can not make a good bargain in the purchase of bad articles."—The best is always the cheapest.

On n'auroit guère de plaisir, si l'on ne se flattoit point. Fr.—"A man would have but little pleasure, if he did not sometimes flatter himself."

On ne cherche point à prouver la lumière. Fr. Prov. "There is no necessity for proving the existence of light."—It is idle to adduce proofs of that which is self-evident.

On ne donne rien si libéralement que ses conseils. Fr. ROCHEFOUCAULT.—"Men give away nothing so liberally as their advice."

On ne loue d'ordinaire que pour etre loué. Fr. ROCHEFOUCAULT.—"Praise is generally given only that it may be returned."

On ne se blâme, que pour etre loué. Fr. ROCHEFOUCAULT.—"Men only blame themselves for the purpose of being praised."

On n'est jamais si heureux ni si malheureux, qu'on se l'imagine. Fr. ROCHEFOUCAULT.—"People are never so fortunate, nor so unfortunate, as they suppose themselves to be."—In either case, the feeling is exaggerated. We are ever too much elated, or too much depressed.

On n'est jamais si ridicule par les qualités que l'on à, que par celles que l'on affecte d'avoir. Fr. ROCHEFOUCAULT.—"Men are never so ridiculous from the qualities which really belong to them, as from those which they pretend to have."—Affectation is even more contemptible than weakness.

On ne trouve guère d'ingrats, tant qu'on est en état de faire du bien. Fr. ROCHEFOUCAULT.—"We find but few people ungrateful, whilst we are still in a condition to confer benefits."—Expectation, in this case, sustains the office of gratitude.

On ne vaut point dans ce monde, que ce qu'on veut valoir. Fr. BRUYERE.—"A man of the world must seem to be what he wishes to be."

On parle peu quand la vanité ne fait pas parler. Fr. ROCHEFOUCAULT.—"Men speak but little when vanity does not induce them to speak."

On perd tout le temps qu'on peut mieux employer. Fr. ROUSSEAU.—"All that time is lost which might be better employed."

On peut attirer les cœurs par les qualités qu'on montre, mais on ne les fixe que par celles qu'on a. Fr. DE MOY.—"Hearts may be attracted by assumed qualities, but the affections are only to be fixed by those which are real."

On peut etre utile, sans atteindre à la perfection. Fr. DE SAUSSURE.—"A man may become useful (in an art), without attaining to perfection."

On prend le peuple par les oreilles, comme on prend un pot par les anses. Fr. PROV.—"The people are to be taken by the ears, as a pot is by the handl s."

Onus probandi. Lat.—"The burden of proving."—The *onus probandi* should lie on the person making the charge."—He is bound to prove what he asserts.

Opera illius mea sunt. Lat.—"His works are mine."

Operæ pretium est. Lat.—"It is worth while" to hear or to attend.—If *non* be placed before *est*, the meaning is reversed.—It *is not* worth while.

Opere in longo fas est obrepere somnum. Lat. Hor. "In a long work, it is allowable that sleep should sometimes creep on a writer."—A lapse is pardonable in a poem of great length.

Opinionum commenta delet dies, naturæ judicia confirmat. Lat. Cic.—"Time effaces the comments of opinion, but it confirms the judgment of Nature."—Speculative opinions pass away, whilst inferences drawn from nature and truth remain permanently on record.

Opprobrium medicorum. Lat.—"The disgrace of the physicians."—A name given to a disorder like the Cancer, which is generally considered as incurable.

Optat ephippia bos; piger optat arare caballus. Lat. Horace. "The ox wishes for horse-trappings; and the lazy steed wishes to plough."—It is the same in human nature.—Every man wishes to exchange his situation; and frequently to adopt one which is unsuited to his powers.

Optima interpres legum consuetudo. Lat. Law Max. "Custom is the best interpreter of the laws."

Optimates. Lat.—"Of the first rank or quality."—The chiefs in any state—among the Romans it denoted the Patrician party.

Optimum obsonium labor. Lat. Prov.—"Labour is the best sauce."—Labour, like hunger, can give a relish to the homeliest food.

Optimus, atque interpres legum sanctissimus. Lat. Juv.—"A most wise and upright expounder of the law."

Opum furiata cupida. Lat. Ovid.—"The ungov

ernable passion for wealth."—An avarice which knows no bounds.

O, qui complexus, et guadia quanta fuerunt! Lat. HORACE

"Oh! what embraces, and what transports of joy there were!" on that occasion.—The poet speaks of his meeting with some of his literary friends, in his journey to Brundusium.

Ora et labora. Lat.—"Pray and labour."

Orandum est ut sit mens sana in corpore sano. Lat. JUVENAL.

"Our prayers should be for a sound mind in a healthy body,"—as the first great requisites to human happiness.

Ore tenus. Lat.—"From the mouth."—The testimony was *ore tenus—i. e.* parole, in contradistinction to written, evidence.

Ornari res ipsa negat, contenta doceri. Lat.—"The subject is not, in its nature, susceptible of ornament, but aims only at being instructive."

Ortus a quercu, non a salice. Lat.—"A bough from an oak, not from a willow."—A man of unbending firmness, not a pliant sycophant.

Os homini sublime dedit, cœlumque tueri. Lat. Ov. "To man, he (God) gave an upright countenance, and to survey the heavens."—Other animals move in a horizontal posture.

O! si sic omnia. Lat.—"Oh! had he thus conducted himself in every respect."—This quotation is applied to an inconsistent character, who is as meritorious in one great instance, as he is censurable in other points of his conduct.

Os rotundum. Lat.—"A round mouth."—Metaphorically, a flowing and eloquent delivery.

O tempora! O mores! Lat. CIC.—"Oh the times and the manners."—How the former are changed, and the latter debased.

Otia si tollas, periere Cupidinis arcus. Lat. OVID "Remove but the temptations of leisure, and the bow of Cupid shall lose its effect."—It is indolence that gives force to our passions.

Otium cum dignitate. Lat.—"Leisure with respect." —He enjoys his *otium cum dignitate.*—He is withdrawn from business, and honoured in his retreat.

Otium sine dignitate. Lat.—"Leisure without dignity."—A character precisely the reverse of the preceding.

Otium sine literis mors est, et vivi hominis sepultura. Lat. SENECA.—"Leisure without literature is death—is the tomb of the living man."

Oublier je ne puis. Fr.—"I can never forget."

Ου γνωσις αλλα πραξις. Gr. *Ou gnosis alla praxis.*—"Not the theory, but the practice."—The former, without the latter, is generally found deficient in the day of trial.

Oui et Non sont bien courts à dire, mais avant que de les dire, il y faut penser long-tems. Fr. GRACIAN.—"Yes and no are very easily said, but before they are said, it is necessary to think a long time."—In matters of consequence, it is most necessary to deliberate before we give a precipitate assent, or an hasty negative.

Ouvrage de longue haleine. Fr.—"A long-winded business."—A work too tediously spun out.

P

Pabulum Acherontis. Lat. PLAUTUS.—"Food for *Acheron*,"—a fabled river in the infernal regions. —An old person just ready to drop into the grave.

Pacta conventa. Lat.—"Conditions agreed upon."—A diplomatic phrase used to describe certain articles, which are to be observed,—until one of the parties finds a convenience in their violation.

Palladium. A Trojan statue of Pallas, or Minerva, on which the fate of the city of Troy was supposed to depend—whence, it has acquired its modern meaning of a bulwark, or sure defence.

Pallida mors æquo pulsat pede
Pauperum tabernas, regumque turres.
Lat. HORACE.
"Pale death approaches with an equal step, and knocks indiscriminately at the door of the cottage and the portals of the palace."—Peasants and princes are alike subjected to the immutable law of mortality.

Palmam qui meruit ferat. Lat.—"Let him who has won it, bear the palm."—This was the motto of Lord NELSON.

Palma non sine pulvere. Lat.—"I have gained the palm, but not without labour."

Panacea. From the Greek.—"A remedy for all diseases."

Papier maché. Fr.—"Chewed paper."—That mashed substance of which snuff-boxes and other articles are made.

Pantheon. From the Greek.—An ancient temple at Rome, dedicated to all the heathen deities.

Par accés. Fr.—"By snatches, or starts."

Parcere personis, dicere de vitiis. Lat.—"To be sparing of persons, and to lash their crimes."—This is a precept of which the honest satirist should never lose sight. It is his duty to lash the vice in general terms; if he descends to personalities, the world will attribute it to spleen against the individual, or perhaps to some motive even less honourable.

Parcere subjectis, et debellare superbos. Lat. VIRG. "To spare the lowly, and subdue the proud."

Par excellence. Fr.—"By way of eminence."

Pari passu. Lat.—"With an equal pace."—By a similar gradation.

Paritur pax bello. Lat. CORN. NEP.—"Peace is produced by war."—The party desirous of peace is often compelled to make a greater show of hostile preparation, in order to bring about the return of that inestimable blessing.

Par le droit du plus fort. Fr. Prov.—"By the right

of the strongest."—This is a right more frequently acted upon, than pleaded.

Par les mêmes voies on ne va pas toujours aux mêmes fins. Fr. St. Real.—"By the same means we do not always arrive at the same ends."—Though acting from the best experience, our plans may be deranged by unforeseen occurrences.

Parlez du loup, et vous verrez sa queue. Fr. Prov.—"Speak of the wolf, and you will see his tail."—Mention but a person's name, and he instantly makes his appearance. Or, as the English proverb has it, "Talk of the Devil," &c.

Parlez peu et bien, si vous voulez qu'on vous regarde comme un homme de mérite. Fr.—"Speak but little and well, if you would be esteemed as a man of merit."

Par manière d'acquit. Fr.—"By way of discharge."—Carelessly.

Par negotiis, neque supra. Lat. Tac.—"Neither above nor below his business."—Used to describe a man, whose abilities are exactly fitted to his station.

Par nobile fratrum. Lat.—"A noble pair of brothers."—Used ironically, to denote two associates exactly suited to each other.

Par oneri. Lat.—' Equal to the burthen."—Competent to the undertaking.

Par pari refero. Lat.—"I return like for like."—I have recourse only to means similar to those which were previously employed by my adversary.

Pars beneficii est, quod petitur si cito neges. Lat. Syrus.—"It is something like kindness, immediately to refuse, what it is intended to deny."

Pars hominum gaudet vitiis constanter, et urget
Propositum; pars multa natat, modo recta capessens,
Interdum pravis obnoxia. Lat. Horace.

"Some men exult in their vices, and constantly pursue their vicious objects—but the greater part are fluctuating, sometimes undertaking what is right, and sometimes yielding to that which is wrong."

Pars minima sui. Lat.—" The smallest part of the man, or of the thing."—The poor shadowy remains of the man—or the frittered remnant of the subject.

Pars sanitatis, velle sanari, fuit. Lat. Seneca.—" The wish to be cured is, of itself, an advance to health."—Metaphorically: to be conscious of one's own folly is a negative advance to amendment.

Par signe de mepris. Fr.—" As a token of contempt."

Parthenon. A temple at Athens, sacred to Minerva; on the front of which were minutely represented in bas relief, all the circumstances that related to the birth of that goddess.

Particeps criminis. Lat.—" A partaker in the crime —an accessary."

Parturiunt montes; nascitur ridiculus mus. Lat. Hor.—" The mountain is in labour, and a ridiculous mouse is brought forth."—Applied to an author or orator, whose laboured openings produce nothing in the end, but abortion or imbecility.

Partus sequitur ventrem. Law Lat.—" The offspring follows the condition of the mother."—Thus, a child is born a *slave*, or *free*, according to the state of the *mother*, without any reference to that of the father.

Parum claris lucem dare. Lat. Hor.—" To throw light upon an obscure subject."

Parva leves capiunt animos. Lat. Ovid.—" Little minds are caught with trifles."

Parvum parva decent. Lat. Hor.—" Little things befit the humble man."—The man in a low station never makes himself ridiculous, but when his efforts exceed his means.

Pas à pas on va bien loin. Fr.—" Step by step one goes very far."—To advance by degrees is, in general, the most secure, as well as most successful mode of proceeding.

Pascitur in vivis livor, post fata quiescit,
Tunc suus, ex merito, quemque tuetur honor.
Lat. OVID.
"Envy is nourished against the living. It ceases when the object is dead—his deserved honours then will defend him against calumny."

Passe-partout. Fr.—The name given to a key or instrument calculated to open any lock.—"A master key."

Passato il pericolo, gabbato il santo. Italian Prov.—"When the danger is past, the saint (whose aid was before invoked) is mocked."—In Catholic countries, in every case of danger and difficulty, prayers are eagerly offered to some peculiar saint. If the peril be avoided, the patron saint relapses into cold neglect, until he is elevated into respect, by the approach of new danger. It applies to cases of friendship exerted, or protection extended, which are too often forgotten with the occasion.

Passim. Lat.—"Every where."—In various places.

Pater est quem nuptiæ demonstrant. Lat. Law Max. "He is (in law) the father of the child, who is the husband to its mother, at the time of its birth."

Paterfamiliâs. Lat.—"The father of a family."

Pater ipse colendi
Haud facilem esse viam voluit, primusque per [*artem,*
Movit agros, curis acuens mortalia corda.
Lat. VIRGIL.
"The father himself of tillage did not wish the way to be easy: he was the first to turn the soil by art, inciting the human heart by anxiety."—Providence has put care and labour in our way, as blessings too easily enjoyed are soon neglected, if not despised.

Pater noster. "Our father."—The two first words of the Lord's Prayer, in Latin, by which it is frequently designated.

Pater patriæ. Lat.—"The father of his country."

Patience passe science. Lat.—"Patience surpasses knowledge."

Patientia læsa fit furor. Lat.—"Patience abused becomes fury."

Patitur qui vincit. Lat.—"He who conquers, suffers."

Patriæ fumus, igne alieno, luculentior. Lat.—"The smoke of one's own country appears brighter than any foreign fire."—Every man must love his natal soil, in spite of all its comparative disadvantages.

Patria cara, carior libertas. Lat.—"My country is dear, but liberty is dearer."

Patriâ quis exul se quoque fugit? Lat. HORACE. "What exile from his country is able to escape from himself?"—Guilt vainly seeks for refuge, in foreign climes, from its own consciousness.

Patriæ infelici fidelis. Lat.—"Faithful to my unhappy country."

Patriis virtutibus. Lat.—"By hereditary virtue."

Pauci dignoscere possunt
Vera bona, atque illis multum diversa.
Lat. JUVENAL.
"Few men can distinguish between that which is really good, and that which is directly the opposite."—There are many who are incapable of choosing that course, which is likely to prove advantageous to themselves.

Paucis carior est fides quam pecunia. Lat. SALLUST. "There are few who do not set a higher value on their money, than on their good faith."

Paulum sepultæ distat inertiæ
Celata virtus. Lat. HORACE.
"Virtue or energy, when concealed, differs but little from buried inertness."—If a man can serve his country or his friend, and withholds his exertions he is as liable to blame for his indolence, as another for his incapacity.

Pauper enim non est, cui rerum suppetit usus.
Lat. HORACE.
"That man is not poor, who has the use of necessary things."—The wise man, when the wants of life are supplied, can smile at those who are running after its luxuries and superfluities.

Paupertas fugitur, totoque arcessitur oroe. Lat LUCAN.—"Poverty is shunned, and persecuted all over the globe."

Pauvres gens, je les plains; car on a, pour les fous,
Plus de pitié que de courroux. Fr. BOILEAU. "Poor gentlemen, I pity them:—for one always entertains for fools more pity than anger."—A sarcasm addressed to a class of diappointed authors.

Pax in bello. Lat.—"Peace in war."—A relaxed or incompetent system of hostility.

Pax potior bello. Lat.—"Peace is preferable to war."

Peccavi. Lat.—"I have sinned."—To make one cry *peccavi*—to compel him to acknowledge his transgression.

Pectus est quod disertum facit. Lat. QUINTIL.—"The breast is the fountain of eloquence."—The faithful transcript of *cordial feeling* must always produce a high degree of eloquence.

Pecuniam in loco negligere maximum est lucrum. Lat. TERENCE.—"To despise money on some occasions leads to the greatest gain."—There are circumstances where nothing is to be expected, but from a liberal expenditure.

Pedibus timor addit alas. Lat.—"Fear gives wings to his feet."—Terror urges him on more rapidly.

Peine forte et dure. Fr.—"A harsh and severe pain."—This was applied in the old law to the punishment of placing under heavy weights, and feeding only with bread and kennel water, the culprit, who refused to plead on his arraignment.

Penchant. Fr.—"Propensity, inclination, desire."

Pendente lite. Lat.—"Whilst the suit or contest is ciding."

Peninsula. Lat.—"Almost an island."

Penumbra. Lat.—"A faint or partial shadow."

Per acuta belli. Lat.—"Through perils of war."

Per angusta ad augusta. Lat.—"Through difficulties to grandeur."

Per annum—Per diem. Lat.—"By the year By the day."

Per ardua liberi. Lat.—" Freedom through difficulty.

Per centum. Lat.—" By the hundred."

Percunctatorem fugito, nam garrulus idem est. Lat. HORACE.—" Shun the inquisitive person, for he is also a talker."—Those who inquire much into the affairs of others, are seldom capable of retaining the secrets which they learn.

" Fly the inquisitive—*they'll talk again.*"

Pereant amici, dum una inimici intercidant. Lat. CICERO.—" Let our friends perish, provided that our enemies fall at the same time."—This is quoted by the orator, only to be marked by his reprobation.

Pereant qui ante nos nostra dixerunt. Lat.—" May they perish who said our good things before us." This was an humorous exclamation used even by the ancients, when charged with having borrowed from their predecessors. They acknowledged thereby the truth of the adage, *Nil dictum quod non dictum prius.*—" Nothing can be said, which has not been said before;"—or, in the words of the English adage, " that there is nothing new under the sun!"

Per fas et nefas. Lat.—" Through right and wrong." He pursued his purpose, *per fas et nefas.* He left no possible means untried.

Periculosæ plenum opus aleæ. Lat.—" A work full of dangerous hazard."—A business pregnant with danger.

Periēre mores, jus, decus, pietas, fides,
Et qui redire nescit, cum perit, pudor. Lat. SEN. " We have lost all morals, justice, honour, piety, and faith; and with these, that modest sense of shame, which, once extinguished, never can be restored."—This is one of the complaints, frequently, and at all times repeated, of the dissoluteness of the present age.

Periissem ni periissem. Lat.—" I had perished unless I had perished."

Per il suo contrario. Italian.—" By its reverse or opposite."

Perjurii pœna divina exitium, humana dedecus. Lat.—"The crime of perjury is punished by Heaven with perdition, and by man with disgrace." This, which was one of the laws of the Romans, called the laws of the Twelve Tables, is sometimes quoted as a maxim by modern judges and lawyers.

Per mare, per terras. Lat.—"Through sea and land."

Permitte divis cætera. Lat. Hor.—"Leave the rest to the gods."—Discharge your duty, and leave the rest to Providence.

Per multum risum, poteris cognoscere stultum. Lat. "By his excessive laughter, you can always distinguish the fool."

Per quod servitium amisit. Lat. Law Term.—"By which he lost her service."—The words are used to describe the injury sustained by the plaintiff, when the defendant has debauched a daughter or apprentice.

Per saltum. Lat.—"By a leap."—He has taken his degrees *per saltum.*—He has attained to high honours, passing over the intermediate degrees.

Per scelera semper sceleribus certum est iter. Lat. Sen.—"The way to wickedness is always through wickedness."—The perpetration of one crime generally leads to the commission of another."

Per se. Lat.—"By itself."—No man likes mustard *per se.* Johnson.

Perseverando. Lat.—"By perseverance."

Per varios casus, per tot discrimina rerum. Latin. Virgil.—"Through various chances, and through so many vicissitudes of affairs."—After such a strange variety of adventures.

Pessimum genus inimicorum laudantes. Lat. Tac "Flatterers are the worst species of enemies."

Petites maisons.—"The little houses."—A French phrase for a mad-house; probably from the narrowness of the cells.

Petit-maitre. Fr.—"A coxcomb—a beau."

Peu de bien, peu de soin. Fr. Prov.—"He who has not much wealth, has not much care."

Peu de gens savent être vieux. Fr. Rochefoucault. "Few persons know how to be old."—When the manners of youth are suffered to accompany old age, they only tend to make it ridiculous.

Phœbe, fave! novus ingreditur tua templa sacerdos. Lat.—"Be propitious, O Phœbus! to a new votary who enters thy temples."—This invocation to Apollo, who was the tutelary god of Physic and Poetry, is chiefly used by young poets.

Philippe, homo es. Lat.—"Philip, thou art but a man."—This memento was, by order of Philip, king of Macedonia, repeated by his servant to him, thrice every morning before he went out, or gave audience.

Philosophia stemma non inspicit. Platonem non accepit nobilem philosophia, sed fecit.
Lat. Seneca.

"Philosophy does not look into pedigrees. She did not receive Plato as noble, but she made him such."—In the eye of true philosophy, all men are equal; distinction is only to be acquired by superior birth and talents.

Phœnomenon, in the plural, *Phœnomena.* From the Greek.—"Any unusual appearance, or occurrence"—An effect of an unknown cause.

Pictoribus atque poetis
Quidlibet audendi semper fuit æqua potestas.
Lat. Horace

"The power to dare every thing always belonged to painters and to poets."—The sister arts are entitled to avail themselves of equal boldness of invention.

Piè poudrè. Law Fr.—"Dusty feet."—The court of—This is the lowest court recognized by the law of England.—The etymology of the name is somewhat doubtful. Sir Edward Coke says that it has its name, because justice is done "as speedily as dust can fall from the foot," whilst others derive it from the "dusty foot" of the suitors

Piger scribendi ferre laborem;
Scribendi recte; nam, ut multum, nil moror.
Lat. HORACE,
"Too indolent to undergo the toil of writing, I mean of writing well; for as to the quantity of his composition, that is wholly out of the question." Applied with propriety to the numerous tribe of careless, dashing writers, who can not endure the labour of revising or correcting their own works.

Pirata communis omnium hostis. Lat. Law Max.—"A pirate is the common enemy of all."

Pis aller.—See *Au pis aller.*

Plerumque gratæ divitibus vices. Lat. HORACE. "Changes are generally agreeable to the opulent." The poet alludes to the love of variety, so generally prevalent in those who can afford to indulge in it.

Ploratur lacrymis amissa pecunia veris. Lat. JUV "The loss of money is deplored with real tears." Whatever may be affected on other subjects, nothing wounds the feelings of most men, so much as their pecuniary losses.

Ploravēre suis non respondere favorem
Speratum meritis. Lat. HORACE.
"They lamented that the encouragement for which they hoped did not await their merits."—This was applied in the first instance to the disappointment of poets; but men of talent in other walks of life, are but too sensible that it will bear a wider range of application.

Plura faciunt homines è consuetudine, quam è ratione. Lat.—"Men do more from custom than from reason."—In our general conduct, we are found to act rather from habit than from reflection.

Plura sunt quæ nos terrent, quam quæ premunt; et sæpius opinione quam re laboramus. Lat. SEN. "Our alarms are much more numerous than our dangers; and we suffer much oftener in apprehension than in reality."—The experience of human life has proved, that imaginary terrors occur more frequently than real dangers.

Plures crapula quam gladius. Lat. Prov.—"Gluttony kills more than the sword."

Pluribus intentus, minor est ad singula, sensus. Lat.—"When the mind is distracted by many pursuits, it derives but little benefit from any of them."

Pluries. Lat. Law Term.—"At several times."—It is a name given to a writ which issues after two former writs have gone out without effect.—The original writ is the *capias*—then follows an *alias*, which failing, the *pluries* issues.

Pluris est oculatus testis unus quam auriti decem. Lat. PLAUTUS.—"One eye-witness is of more weight than ten who give evidence from hearsay."

Plurimum facere, et minimum ipse de se loqui. Lat. TACITUS.—"To do the most, and say the least of himself."—This is the portrait given by the Roman historian, of a great but unostentatious character.

Plus aloës quam mellis habet. Lat.—"He has more of gall than of honey."—Applied to a writer whose *forte* lies chiefly in sarcasm.

Plus apud nos vera ratio valeat, quam vulgi opinio. Lat. CIC.—"Reason shall prevail with me more than popular opinion."—I shall prefer my own judgment to general prejudice.

Plus dolet quam necesse est, qui ante dolet quam necesse est. Lat. SEN.—"He grieves more than is necessary, who grieves before it is necessary."

Plus est quam vita salusque,
Quod perit: in totum mundi prosternimur ævum. Lat. LUCAN.

"More than life and safety is lost in the present conflict; we are laid prostrate for ever."

Plus habet operis quam ostentationis. Lat.—"There is more labour than ostentation in it."—There is more difficulty in the undertaking than is apparent

Plus impetûs, majorem constantiam penes miseros. Lat. TACITUS.—"There is more violence as well as perseverance amongst the lowly and wretched"

A wise government will therefore always be cautious of provoking this description of men to opposition or resistance.

Plus je vis l'étranger, plus j'aimai ma patrie. Fr.—"The more I saw of foreign lands, the more I loved my own."

Plusque exemplo quam peccato nocent. Lat.—"They do more mischief by the example, than from the sin." Spoken of persons in distinguished situations

Plus ratio quam vis cæca valere solet. Lat. Corn Gallus.—"Reason can in general do more than blind force."—That which can not be done by mere strength, is sometimes to be accomplished by address.

Plus sages que les sages. Fr.—"Wiser than the wise."

Plus salis quam sumptûs. Lat. C. Nepos.—"There was more of relish than of cost."—A proper definition of a philosophical entertainment.

Plus valet oculatus testis unus quam auriti decem. Lat. Law Max.—"One eye-witness is of more importance than ten hear-say witnesses."

Plus vident oculi quam oculus. Lat.—"Many eyes see more than one."

Plutôt mourir que changer. Lat.—"Sooner die than change."—This favourite motto is that which was written by a fair one on the sands, when walking by the sea shore. Her lover arrived in time to read it: his joy however was soon dashed by a prophetic wave which instantly erased the inscription.

Pœna ad paucos, metus ad omnes perveniat. Lat. Law Max.—"Punishment should extend to *few*, but the dread of it to *all.*"

Pœna non debet anteire crimen. Lat. Law Maxim.—"The punishment should not anticipate the offence."

Poeta nascitur non fit. Lat. Prov.—"A poet is born, but is not made."—Study can not make a poet, unless the man be possessed of innate genius.

Point d'appui. Fr.—"Point of support,"—fulcrum, or prop.

Point d'argent, point de Suisse. Fr. Prov.—"No more money, no more Swiss."—An allusion to the mercenary services of that nation.

Pol! me occidistis, amici. Lat. Hor.—"By H——n, you have destroyed me, my friends."—Your misplaced zeal has inflicted on me an injury.

Ponamus nimios gemitus; flagrantior æquo
Non debet esse dolor viri, nec vulnere major.
Lat. Juvenal.

"Let us dismiss all excessive sorrow: the grief of a man should not pass the bounds of propriety, or show itself greater than the cause."—A man is debased by that womanish sorrow which knows no bounds, and passes far beyond the occasion.

Pondere non numero. Lat.—"By their weight or force, and not by their numbers."

Pone seram, cohibe; sed quis custodiet ipsos
Custodes? Lat. Juvenal.

"Apply locks and restraint, but who shall watch your own spies?"

Pons assinorum. Lat.—"The asses' bridge."

Ponton. Fr. Military Term.—"A temporary bridge for an army."—*Pontonniers,* men who are employed in the construction of such bridges.

Populus me sibilat; at mihi plaudo
Ipse domi, simul ac nummos contemplor in arcâ.
Lat. Horace.

"The people hiss me, but I applaud myself at home, when I contemplate the money in my chest."—The miser finds, in the view of his hoards, a consolation and refuge from the public contempt.

Poscentes vario multum diversa palato. Lat. Hor. "Requiring, with various tastes, things widely different from each other."—This phrase is used by an author, who found, like many of his less fortunate successors, how difficult it was to please the varying taste of each individual reader.

Posse comitatûs. Lat.—"The power of the county,"

which the sheriff is authorized to call forth, whenever an opposition is made to his writ, or to the execution of justice.

Posse videor. Lat.—" The appearance of being able." He has the *posse videor*—he seems equal to his undertaking.

Possunt quia posse videntur. Lat.—" They are able, because they seem to be able."—The greater energy in all cases of force, will be found on that side, which, from any cause whatever, can be taught to look confidently for success.

Post amicitiam credendum est, ante amicitiam judicandum. Lat. Sen.—" After forming a friendship, you should render implicit belief; before that period, you may exercise your judgment."—In a state of perfect friendship, there should be nothing like hesitation or distrust on either side.

Post bellum auxilium. Lat.—" Aid after the war."—A vain and superfluous succour, offered when the difficulty is passed.

Postea. Law Lat.—" Afterwards."—The name given to the writ by which the proceedings by *nisi prius* are returned after the verdict, into the court of common pleas.

Post equitem seaet atra cura. Lat. Hor.—" Dark care sits behind the horseman."—This is said of the man of guilt, who vainly endeavours to fly from his own reflections.

Post factum, nullum consilium. Lat.—" After the deed is done, there is no use in consultation."

Post obitum. Lat. and, } " After death."
Post mortem. Lat. }

Post mortem, nulla voluptas. Lat.—" After death no pleasure remains."—An Epicurean maxim.

Post prælia præmia. Lat.—" After the battle the rewards" are bestowed.

Post malam segetem serendum est. Lat. Seneca.—" After a bad crop, you should instantly begin to sow."—Instead of sinking under misfortune, we should immediately think of renewing our industry

Post nubila Phœbus. Lat.—"The sun shines forth after the clouds have passed."

Post tenebras lux. Lat.—"After darkness comes light."

Post tot naufragia portum. Lat.—"After so many shipwrecks, there appears a harbour."—After so many dangers, an asylum at length presents itself.

Postulata. Lat.—"Things required."—The admissions demanded from an adversary, before the main argument is entered upon.

Potentiam cautis, quam acribus consiliis, tutius haberi. Lat. TACITUS.—"Power is more safely to be retained by cautious than by severe councils."—Mildness combined with vigilance, as a prop of power, is more to be relied upon than a system of irritating severity.

Potentia non est, nisi ad bonum. Lat. Law Max.—"Power is never conferred, but for sake of the public good."

Potentissimus est qui se habet in potestate. Lat. SENECA.—"He is most powerful, who has himself in his power;"—who is able to command himself.

Potius ignorantia juris litigiosa est, quam scientia. Lat. CIC. DE LEGIBUS.—"Ignorance of the laws is more frequently the cause of litigation, than an acquaintance with them."

Pour comble de bonheur. Fr.—"As the height of happiness."—As an increase of satisfaction.

Pour connoître le prix de l'argent, il faut etre obligé d'en emprunter. Fr.—"In order to know the value of money, a man must be obliged to borrow."—He will then learn its value, from the price which is set upon the obligation.

Pour passer le temps. Fr.—"To pass away the time."

Pour se faire valoir. Fr.—"To give himself a value." To add to his consequence.

Pour s'établir dans le monde, on fait tout ce que l'on peut, pour y paroître établi. Fr. ROCHEFOUCAULT.—"When a man has to establish himself in the world, he makes every effort in his power to exhibit himself as being already established."

Pour y parvenir. Fr.—"To attain the object."

Præferre patriam liberis regem decet. Lat. SENECA "A king should prefer his country to his children." —His duty to his subjects should take place of his family affections.

Præmunire. Law Lat.—(From *Præmonere*, "to forewarn.")—A writ by which offenders in certain cases are put out of the protection of the law.

Præsertim ut nunc sunt mores, adeo res redit,
Si quisquis reddit, magna habenda est gratia.
Lat. TERENCE.

"In the present state of manners, the matter is brought to this point, that if any man pays a debt, the creditor must accept it as a favour."—In every state of life, which is called civilized, it appears that this same payment of debts was always considered as a most awkward, reluctant, and ill-complexioned sort of business.

Præsto et persto. Lat.—"I perform and I persevere."

Prætextu legis injusta agens, duplo puniendus. Lat.—"He who under the cloak of the law acts unjustly, should bear a double punishment."

Præteritorum memoria eventorum. Lat.—"The remembrance of past events.

Pravo vivere naso,
Spectandum nigris oculis, nigroque capillo.
Lat. HORACE.

"With an ugly nose, to be remarkable for fine black eyes and hair."—Beauty consists in the proportion, correspondence and harmony of parts.—A fine eye, the poet hints, will only serve to make an ugly nose the more conspicuous. Thus the value of one qualification is frequently impaired through the want of another.

Précepte commence, exemple acheve. Fr. Prov.—"Precept begins, but example completes.

Preces armatæ. Lat.—"Armed prayers."—Claims

made with feigned submission, but which at the same time are to be sustained by force."

Prend moi tel que je suis. Fr.—" Take me just as I am."

Prendre la lune avec les dents. Fr.—" To seize the moon with one's teeth."—To aim at impossibilities.

Prendre martre pour renard. Fr. Prov.—" To take a marten for a fox."—To catch a Tartar—To take the wrong sow by the ear.

Prêt d'accomplir. Fr.—" Ready to perform."

Prêt pour mon pays. Fr.—" Ready for my country."

Primâ facie. Lat.—" On the first face."—On the first view of an affair; or, in parliamentary phraseology, on the first blush of the business.

Primæ viæ. Lat.—" The first passages" of the human body—the intestinal canal.

Primum mobile. Lat.—" The first cause of motion." —The main spring, or impulse, which puts all the other parts into activity.

Primus inter pares. Lat.—" The first amongst his equals,"—as in a meeting of magistrates, where the senior is called upon of course to preside.

Principia non homines. Latin.—" Principles—not Men."

Principibus placuisse viris non ultima laus est.
Lat. Horace.
" To have pleased great men, is a circumstance which claims not the lowest degree of praise."—This poet was also a courtier.

Principiis obsta. Lat.—" Meet the first beginnings." —Look to the budding mischief, before it has time to ripen into maturity. *See the next article.*

Principiis obsta: sero medicina paratur,
Cum mala per longas convaluere moras.
Lat. Ovid.
" Meet the disorder in its outset. The medicine may be too late, when the disease has gained ground through delay."—This precept is universally just It is at present more frequently applied to political than to animal economy.

Priùsquàm incipias consulto; et ubi consulueris maturè facto opus est. Lat. SALLUST.—"Advise well before you begin; when you have maturely considered, then act with promptitude."

Privatus illis census erat brevis, commune magnum. Lat. HORACE. "Their private fortunes were small, but the wealth of the public was great."—This description was applied to the infancy of the Roman republic, and contrasted with the latter and more corrupt times, when individuals were possessed of enormous wealth, while the public treasury was impoverished.

Pro aris et focis. Lat.—"For our altars and our hearths."—For our religion and our fire-sides.

Probam pauperiem sine dote quæro. Lat.—"I court virtuous poverty without a dowry."—I throw myself into the embraces of poverty, unactuated by any ambitious wishes.

Probitas laudater et alget. Lat. JUV.—"Honesty is praised and freezes."—Acts of probity have too frequently no other reward than a cold commendation.

Probitas, pudorque virgini dos optima est. Lat. TER. "Chastity and modesty are a girl's best dowry."

Probitas verus honor. Lat.—"Probity is true honour."

Pro bono publico. Lat.—"For the public good."

Probum non pænitet. Lat.—"The honest man does not repent."—He may regret the result, but the purity of his intentions precludes remorse.

Procès verbal. Fr.—A written statement in which a person testifies to what he has seen or heard.—"Verbal process."

Prochein amy. Law Fr.—"The nearest friend—or next akin."

Pro Christo et patria. Lat.—"For Christ and my country."

Pro confesso. Lat.—"As if conceded."—To take it *pro confesso*—to take it for granted.

Procul a Jove, procul a fulmine. Lat.—"Being far

from Jupiter, you are also far from his thunder."—Those who feel not the sunshine of court-favour, are exempted, in return, from the dangers of courtly intrigue.

Procul, O! procul este profani,
Conclamat vates, totoque absistite luco.
Lat. VIRGIL.
"Retire! far hence retire, ye profane; and quit entirely the sacred grove."—This was the solemn preface to the *Eleusinian* mysteries. The first line is often quoted in an ironical sense.

Prodesse civibus. Lat.—"To be of advantage to my fellow citizens."—To be employed on a work, the end and aim of which is to be of service to the community to which one belongs.

Prodesse quam conspici. Lat.—"To do good, rather than to be too conspicuous."

Pro et con. Lat.—"For and against."—The reasonings *pro et con*—on both sides of the question.

Pro formâ. Lat.—"For form's sake."—As a formality, or point of etiquette.

Pro hâc vice. Lat.—"For this turn."—A. shall present *pro hâc vice*, when B. has an alternate right of presentation to a living.

Prohibetur ne quis faciat in suo, quod nocere possit in alieno. Lat. Law Maxim.—"It is forbidden that any man should do that on his own property, which may injure another."—If a man does any thing on his ground which offends his neighbour, it is held to be a nuisance, and as such may be abated: Such an offence is the building which darkens the windows of another, erecting a dye-house, forming a tanpit, &c. the smells of which are offensive, and sometimes infectious.

Proh superi! quantum mortalia pectora cæcæ
Noctis habent! Lat. OVID.
"Heavens! what thick darkness pervades the minds of men!"—What infatuation prevails in the world!

Projicit ampullas et sesquipedalia verba. Lat. HOR.—"He throws away his swollen phrases, and his words a foot and a half long."—When reduced to adversity, a man forgets the lofty tone, and supercilious language of prosperity.

Pro libertate patriæ. Lat.—"For the liberty of my country."

Pro patria. Lat.—"For my country."

Promenade. Fr.—"A walk—a fashionable place for walking."

Pro optimo est minimè malus. Lat. Sen.—"That should be considered the best, which has in it the least of evil."—As all human things are imperfect, we can only speak of any good in relative terms.

Propaganda fide. Lat.—"For extending the faith." The name of a missionary society among the Roman Catholics.

Proprium humani ingenii est odisse quem læserit. Lat. Tacitus.—"It is the nature of man to hate those he has injured."

Pro rata. Lat.—"In proportion."

Pro rege et patriâ. Lat.—"For my king and country."

Pro rege, lege, et grege. Lat.—"For the king, the law, and the people."

Pro re natâ. Lat.—"For a special business."—An assembly called *pro re natâ*—for some emergency.

Pro salute animæ. Lat.—"For the health or safety of the soul."—Thus the ecclesiastical court has cognisance in certain cases, *pro salute animæ.*

Prosperum et felix scelus virtus vocatur. Lat. Sen. "Wickedness, when successful and prosperous, is called virtue."

Pro tanto. Lat.—"For so much"—for its value.

Protectio trahit subjectionem, et subjectio protectionem. Lat. Law Maxim.—"Protection implies allegiance, and allegiance should insure protection."—As the subject owes to the sovereign obedience, so the sovereign is bound to defend the laws, the persons, and property of his subjects.

Pro tempore. Lat.—"For the time."—A measure *pro tempore*—a temporary expedient.

Pro virtute felix temeritas. Lat. SEN.—"Instead of valour, there was an happy rashness."—The philosopher speaks of ALEXANDER.

Proximus ardet Ucalegon. Lat. VIRGIL.—"*Ucalegon burns next*"—Your next neighbour's house is on fire.—The danger is so near, that it becomes you to consider your own safety.

Proximus sum egomet mihi. Lat. Law Maxim.—"I am always nearest to myself."—This maxim bears on certain cases, in which a man may, without injustice, take to himself a preference: as an executor may first pay a legacy to himself, or take his own debt, before other debts of an equal degree.

Prudens futuri. Lat.—"Thoughtful of the time to come."

Ψυχης Ιατρειον. Gr. *Psuches Iatreion.*—"Physic for the mind."—Applied to books or reading.

Publicum bonum privato est præferendum. Lat. Law Max.—"The public good is to be preferred before private advantage."—Thus, a woman entitled to a dower, shall not be endowed of a castle of defence, because that is *pro bono publico.*

Pudet hæc opprobria nobis
Et potuisse dici, et non potuisse refelli.
Lat. HORACE.

"It is shameful that such reproaches should be cast upon us, and that we are unable to refute them."

Pudore et liberalitate liberos
Retinere, satius esse credo, quam metu.
Lat. TERENCE

"It is better to keep children to their duty, by a sense of honour, and by kindness, than by fear and punishment."

Pulchrum est accusari ab accusandis. Lat.—"It is an honourable circumstance to be accused by those, who are themselves deserving of accusation."

Pulchrum est benefacere reipublicæ: etiam benedicere haud absurdum est. Lat. SALLUST

"It is commendable to act well for the republic—even to speak well, should not be without its praise."

Pulchrum est, digito monstrari, et dicier hic est. Lat. PERSIUS
"It is pleasant to be pointed at with the finger, and to have it said, 'There goes the man.'"—Applied to those who are fond of intruding themselves upon the public notice.

Pulvis et umbra sumus. Lat.—"We are but dust and fleeting shadows."

Punctum saliens. Lat.—"The leaping or starting point."—The first rudiments of the heart in the formation of the fœtus.

Punica fides. Lat.—"Punic faith."—This phrase was used in an ironical sense by the Romans, to denote the treachery of the Carthaginians—a charge from which they were not themselves to be exempted. It is now used generally to mark the absence of good faith, or the breach of a political engagement.

Punitis ingeniis gliscit auctoritas. Lat. TACITUS. "When men of talents are punished, their authority is strengthened."—When the infliction of the law falls upon the witty or ingenious author of what is termed a libel, it generally serves to give weight and notoriety to that which might have been overlooked in its impunity.

Puras Deus, non plenas, adspicit manus. Lat. SYRUS.—"God looks only to pure, and not to full hands."—The Supreme Judge looks to the innocence, and not to the wealth of the party. It is sometimes otherwise in the courts below.

Q

Quæ amissa, salva. Lat.—"What was lost is safe."

Quæ cura vivos, eadem sequitur tellure repostos. Lat.—"The same cares which agitated them while living, haunt them in the grave."

Quædam virtutes odio sunt. Lat. TACITUS.—"There are some virtues that are hateful,"—as an inflexible severity, and an integrity that admits no favour.

Quæ fuerant vitia, mores sunt. Lat. SENECA.—

"What once were vices, are now the manners of the day."—Such is the general depravity, that what was once imputed as a crime, is now exhibited as a boast.

Quæ fuit durum pati,
Meminisse dulce est. Lat. SENECA.
"That which it was painful to suffer, it is pleasing to remember."—There is something soothing to a man, in the recollection of his past misfortunes.

Quæ lædunt oculos festinas demere: si quid
Est animum, differs curandi tempus in annum.
Lat. HORACE.
"If any thing affects your eye, you hasten to have it removed; but if your mind is disordered, you postpone the term of cure for a year."—Men are infinitely less solicitous about their moral, than their physical state.

Quælibet concessio fortissimè contra donatorem interpretanda est. Lat. Law Max.—"Every man's grant shall be taken most strongly against himself."—Whenever the words of a deed are ambiguous or uncertain, they shall be construed against the grantor. If a man grants an annuity out of land, and has no land at the time of making the grant, it shall charge his person.

Quæ non valerent singula, juncta juvant. Lat.—"Those things which, considered individually, are of no force, may, when taken conjunctively, have great influence."

Quære. Lat.—"Inquire."—A suggestion of doubt, calling for further information.

Quærenda pecunia primùm. Lat.—"Money must first be procured."

Quærit, et inventis miser abstinet, ac timet uti. Lat. HORACE.—"The miser is ever on the search, yet fears to use what he has acquired."

Quæstio fit de legibus, non de personis. Lat. Law Maxim.—"The question must refer to the laws, and not to persons."—In a court of judicature, regard must be had to the letter and meaning of the law, and not to the rank or situation of either of the contending parties.

Quæ supra nos, nihil ad nos. Lat. Proverb.—"The things which are above us, are nothing to us."—A maxim frequently used against astrologers, and sometimes, but falsely, applied to politicians.—Every man who can understand the first principles of government has a right to examine into the conduct of his rulers.

Qualis ab incepto. Lat.—"The same as from the beginning."

Qualis ab incepto processerit, et sibi constet. Latin. HORACE.—"Let him proceed as he began, and be consistent with himself."—This was written as an instruction to the tragic poet. It is now used to recommend an adherence to consistency.

Qualis vita, finis ita. Lat.—"As the life of a man has been, so will be his death."

Quam angusta innocentia est, ad legem bonum esse! Lat. SENECA.—"How narrow is that notion of innocence, which confines it to the *letter* of the law!"

Quamdiu se bene gesserit. Lat.—"As long as he shall conduct himself properly."—A phrase first used in the letters patent granted to the chief baron of the exchequer. All the judges now hold their places by this tenure: they were formerly held, "*Durante bene placito,*" during the king's pleasure.

Quam prope ad crimen, sine crimine? Lat.—"How near may a man approach to guilt, without being guilty?"—This was a favourite question with the Jesuits, who reasoned on the different shades and gradations of criminality, until, if it suited their convenience, they could do away the crime itself.

Quanquam animus meminisse horret, luctuque refugit,
Incipiam. Lat. VIRGIL

"Although my soul shudders at the recollection, and shrinks back with grief, I will begin" my mournful tale.

Quam sæpe fortè temerè
Eveniunt, quæ non audeas optare? Lat. TER

"How often do things occur by mere chance, which we dared not even to hope for?"

Quam seipsum amans sine rivali. Lat. CICERO *de Hertio.*—"How much in love with himself, and that without a rival."—Describing a man absorbed in self-love, and despised by the rest of the world.

Quam temerè in nosmet legem sancimus iniquam. Lat.—"How rashly do we sanction an unjust law against ourselves."—How blindly do the unthinking part of the world lend their aid and approbation to measures, of which, if better instructed, they would perceive that they must ultimately be the victims.

Quand les vices nous quittent, nous nous flattons que c'est nous qui les quittons. Fr.—"When the power of committing vice forsakes us, we flatter ourselves, by assuming the praise of having forsaken the vices."

Quando aliquid prohibetur, prohibetur et omne per quod devenitur ad illud. Lat. Law Maxim.—"When any thing is forbidden to be done, whatever tends or leads to it, as the means of compassing it, is forbidden at the same time."

Quand on ne trouve pas son répos en soi-même, il est inutile de le chercher ailleurs. Fr.—"When a man finds not repose in himself, it is in vain for him to seek it elsewhere."—He can not escape by change of place from the anxiety which is lodged within his bosom.

Quand on parle d'ouvrages d'esprit, il ne s'agit point d'honnêtes gens, mais de gens de bon sens. Fr.—"In speaking of the works of mind, we do not speak of the character of the man, but his fund of wit or sense."

Quandoque bonus dormitut Homerus. Lat. HOR "Sometimes even the good Homer nods."—Superior minds are not at all times exempt from lapses, or from frailty.

Quando ullum inveniemus parem? Lat. HORACE. "When shall we look upon his like again?"—Or, with "*invenient*," when will *they* find any person to equal him?

Quand tout le monde a tort, tout le monde a raison. Fr.—"When all the world is in the wrong, all the world is in the right."—When a community, almost unanimously, agrees upon any subject, their decision is correct, although individuals may impugn it.—Or, according to our proverb, "What every body says must be true."

Quanti est sapere! nunquam accedo ad te, quin abs te abeam doctior. Lat. TER.—"How desirable is wisdom! I never am in your presence without being edified."

Quanto mayor e la fortuna, tanto e menor secura. Spanish Prov.—"The more exalted is the fortune, the less it is secure."

Quanto plura recentium seu veterum revolvo, tanto ludibria rerum mortalium cunctis in negotiis observantur. Lat. TAC.—"The more I revolve in my mind the transactions of the ancients or the moderns, the more of frivolity and absurdity appears to me in all human affairs."

Quanto quisque sibi plura negaverit,
A diis plura feret. Nil cupientium
Nudus castra peto; multa petentibus
Desunt multa. Lat. HORACE.
"The more a man denies himself, the more he shall receive from Heaven. Naked, I seek the camp of those who covet nothing; those who require much, are ever much in want."

Quantum. Lat.—"How much."—The *quantum,* "the due proportion."

Quantum infido scurræ distabit amicus. Lat.—"How much a true friend differs from a faithless sycophant."

Quantum est in rebus inane humanis! Lat. PERS.—"How much folly is there in the affairs of men!"—How senseless and frivolous are the pursuits of men in general.

Quantum libet. Lat.—"As much as you please."

Quantum meruit. Lat.—"As much as he has deserved."—This phrase occurs in an action on the case, for work done without a previous agreement. The law will in this case give the plaintiff "as much as he has fairly earned."

Quantum mutatus ab illo! Lat. VIRGIL.—"How much changed from him!"—How much altered from that figure which we regarded with so much interest.

Quantum quisque suâ nummorum condit in arcâ,
Tantum habet et fidei. Lat. JUVENAL.
"Every man's credit and consequence are proportioned to the sums which he holds in his chest."—It is wealth alone which commands respect.

Quantum Religio potuit suadere malorum! Lat. LUCRETIUS.—"To how many mischiefs does not Religion persuade!"—The poet is speaking of the sacrifice of Iphigenia, enjoined by the priests on her father Agamemnon.—The line is sometimes invidiously used, and in a broader sense.

Quantum sufficit. Lat.—"A sufficient quantity."

Quare facit opium dormire? Quia in eo est virtus dormitiva. Lat.—"Why does opium induce sleep? Because it has in it a sleepy quality."—This question and answer are given by MOLIERE, in ridicule of that pompous ignorance which affects to solve every difficulty, whilst it dwells only in lofty no-meanings; or, as in this instance, only retorts the terms of the original question.

Quare impedit. Law Lat.—"Why does he disturb?" The name of a writ which lies for the patron of a living, against the person who has disturbed his right of advowson.

Quare vitia sua nemo confitetur?
Quia etiam nunc in illis est. Somnum
Narrare vigilantis est. Lat. SENECA.
"Why does no man confess his vices? It is because he is yet in them. It is for a *waking* man to tell his *dreams.*"

Quas aut incuria fudit,
Aut humana parum cavit natura. Lat. HOR

"Faults originating from carelessness, or, of which human nature was not sufficiently aware."—Errors in a literary work either springing from haste, or partaking of the infirmity of nature.

Quas dederis, solus semper habebis opes. Lat. MART. —"The wealth which you give away will ever be your own."—As the poet was ignorant of the Christian precept of "laying up treasures in heaven," he seems to have placed too much reliance on human gratitude.

Quasi. Lat.—"In a manner."—A *quasi* contract,—an implied bargain.

Quemcunque miserum videris, hominem scias, Lat. SEN.—"When you see a man in distress, know him for a fellow-man."—Recollect he is formed of the same materials, with the same feelings as yourself, and then relieve him as you would wish to be relieved.

Quem Deus vult perdere, prius dementat. Lat.—"The man whom God determines to destroy, he previously deprives of his understanding."

Quem pœnitet peccâsse, penè est innocens. Lat. SEN. —"He who is sorry for having sinned, is almost innocent."—His penitence has nearly obliterated his fault.

Quem res plus nimio delectavêre secundæ,
Mutatæ quatient. Lat. HORACE.
"The man who is most fond to revel in prosperity, will most acutely feel the shock of adversity."—He, who is intoxicated by his height, will most severely feel his fall.

Quem semper acerbum,
Semper honoratum (sic Dii voluistis) habebo.
Lat. VIRGIL.
"That day which I shall always recollect with grief, but, as the gods have willed it, with reverence,"—referring to the day on which the speaker had lost a most valued friend.

Quem te Deus esse jussit. Lat.—"What God commanded you to be"

Querelle d'Allemand. Fr—" A German quarrel."—A drunken affray.

Qui ad pauca respiciunt, de facili judicant. Lat.—"Those who bestow but slight attention upon a subject, must form a trivial judgment of it."—The most superficial observers are the most speedy in forming their opinions.

Qui amicus est amat, qui amat non utique amicus est. Itaque amicitia semper prodest; amor etiam aliquando nocet. Lat. SEN.—" He who is a friend must love, but he who loves is not therefore a friend. Thus friendship is always advantageous, whilst love is sometimes injurious."—This is a useful lesson to the fair sex, who should learn to distinguish between that disinterested friendship, which seeks only their happiness, and that selfish love which would destroy their peace for its own gratification.

Qui inquirit quid in se dictum sit, se ipse inquietat. Lat. SENECA.—" He who is anxious to learn what others say of him, destroys his own peace."

Quia te non capio, tu capies me. Lat.—" Because I do not take (or comprehend) thee, thou shalt take me."—This is the language imputed to ARISTOTLE, who is said to have flung himself into the river, because he could not comprehend the fluctuation of the tides!

Qui Bavium non odit, amet tua carmina, Mævi.
Lat. VIRGIL.
" He who does not hate *Bavius*, may be pleased with the verses of *Mævius.*"—These were two of the worst poets of antiquity. He who has so little taste, as to relish one bad performance, can not be disgusted with another equally indifferent.

Qui capit, ille facit. Lat. Prov.—" He who takes it to himself, is the object of the allusion."—Whom the cap fits, let him wear it.

Quicquid agunt homines nostri est farrago libelli. Lat. JUV.—" Our book relates to all the acts and employments of man."—A motto often prefixed to periodical works.

Quicquid erit—superanda omnis fortuna ferendo est. Lat. VIRGIL.
"Whatever the event may be, we must subdue our fortune by bearing it."—The only way to overcome disaster, is by fortitude and perseverance.

Quicquid excessit modum,
Pendet instabili loco. Lat. SENECA.
"Whatever has exceeded its due bounds, is ever in a state of instability." —This is a maxim equally true, whether applied to men or to goverments.

Quicquid præcipies, esto brevis. Lat. HORACE.
"Whatever precepts you give, be short."—All didactic rules should be given with brevity.

Qui cupit optatam cursu contingere metam,
Multa tulit fecitque puer, sudavit et alsit.
Lat. HORACE.
"He who desires to reach with speed the wished-for end (the winning post of the race), must, in his earlier days, have suffered and laboured much, and borne the alternate extremes of heat and cold."—No man ever reached to excellence in any one art or profession, without having passed through the slow and painful process of study and preparation.

Qui Curios simulant, et Bacchanalia vivunt.
Lat. JUVENAL.
"Who affect to be *Curii*, and live like *Bacchanals.*"—Applied to men, whose feigned austerity is nothing more than a mask for their debauchery.

Quid datur a Divis felici optatius horâ? Lat. CATULLUS.—"What is there given by the gods more desirable than a happy hour?"—The *felix hora* of the Romans implied a "lucky occasion," or what our ROWE calls, "a glorious, golden opportunity."

Quid dem? Quid non dem? renuis tu, quod jubet alter. Lat. HORACE.—"What shall I give? what shall I withhold? What you refuse, another imperiously demands."—The poet alludes to what authors in all ages, have complained of, the difference of taste, and the capriciousness of their readers.

Qui de contemnendâ gloriâ libros scribunt, nomen suum inscribunt. Lat.—"Those who write books about despising glory, inscribe their own names." They show a wish for that fame which they affect to contemn.

Quid de quoque viro, et cui dicas, sæpe caveto. Lat. HORACE.
"Take especial care what you say of any man, and to whom it is said."—Nothing in human life requires more caution, than the manner of making our report on the character of others.

Quid dignum tanto feret hic promissor hiatu? Lat. HORACE.—"What will this promiser bring forth worthy of so large a boast?"

Quid domini facient, audent cum talia fures? Lat. VIRG.—"What will their masters do, when low villains can thus presume?"—What are we to expect from the principals, when we are thus insulted by their subalterns?

Quid enim ratione timemus,
Aut cupimus. Lat. JUVENAL.
"For what do we either dread or desire, from a rational motive."

"How void of reason are our hopes and fears!"

Quid est turpius quam senex vivere incipiens? Lat. SENECA.—"What is more scandalous than an old man just beginning to live?"—It is shameful to see a man in advanced life, entering for the first time, on the rudiments of knowledge, or the practice of virtue.

Qui dit docteur, ne dit pas toujours un homme docté, mais un homme qui devroit être docté. Fr. ST. REAL.—"He who speaks of a doctor (or professor) does not always speak of a learned man, but only of a man who *ought* to be learned."—Pompous titles only serve, in some instances, as a cover for ignorance.

Quid leges, sine moribus,
Vanæ proficiunt. Lat. HORACE.
"What can idle laws do without morals?"—If the moral sentiments of a people are completely relaxed

or forgotten, little can be expected from the penalties or restraints to be imposed by the wisest legislature.

Quid munus Reipublicæ majus, meliusve afferre possumus, quam si juventutem docemus, et bene erudimus? Lat. CICERO.—"How can we more essentially benefit our country, than by instructing, and giving a proper direction to, the minds of our youth?"

Quid non ebrietas designat? Operta recludit,
Spes jubet esse ratas, in prælia trudit inermem.
Lat. HORACE.

"To what does inebriety not point? It discloses every secret—it ratifies every hope, and pushes even the unarmed man to battle."—Drunkenness makes men, at the same time, confident and imprudent.

Quid non mortalia pectora cogis,
Auri sacra fames? Lat. VIRGIL.

"Accursed thirst of gold! to what dost not thou compel the human breast?"—To what atrocities can not that mind reach, which is impelled by selfish avarice?

Quid nunc. Lat.—"What now?"—What is the news at present?—Applied in ridicule to a person who makes the acquisition of news his principal pursuit.

Qui docet, discit. Lat.—"He who teaches others, informs himself."

Quid prodest, Pontice, longo
Sanguine censeri, pictosque ostendere vultus
Majorum? Lat. JUVENAL.

"Of what advantage is it to you, Ponticus, to enumerate your remote ancestors, and to exhibit their portraits?"

Quid pro quo. Lat.—"What for what."—A *quid pro quo*, "A mutual consideration."—An equivalent.

Quidquid delirant reges, plectuntur Achivi. Lat HOR.—"Whatever error their kings may commit, the Greeks are punished."— The people always suffer for the crimes or errors of their rulers.

Quidquid in altum fortuna tulit, ruitura levat. Lat. SENECA.
"Whatever fortune has raised to an height, she has raised only that it may fall."—When chance, not merit, has contributed to a man's elevation, his fall may be considered as certain.

Quidquid multis peccatur, inultum est. Lat. LUCAN
"The guilt which is committed by many, must pass unpunished."—Where the offenders are numerous, it is sometimes prudent to overlook the crime.

Quid quisque vitet, nunquam homini satis
Cautum est in horas. Lat. HORACE.
"Man never takes sufficient and hourly care against that which he ought to shun."—Our misfortunes are in general, to be set down to our own want of caution and foresight.

Quid Rides?
Mutato nomine, de te fabula narratur. Lat. HORACE.
"Why do you laugh? Change but the name, and the story is told of yourself."—We smile, as the satirist justly observes, at follies related under feigned names, when we should *smart* if they were linked with our own.

Quid Romæ faciam? Mentiri nescio. Lat. JUVENAL.
"What should I do at Rome? I can not lie."—What should he do in a great capital, who can not adopt its corrupt manners?

Quid sit futurum cras, fuge quærere. Lat. HORACE.
"Avoid all inquiry with respect to what may happen to-morrow."—Look not so anxiously into the future, as to preclude all present enjoyment.

Quid sit pulchrum, quid turpe, quid utile, quid non. Lat. HORACE.—"What is becoming, what is base, what is useful, and what the contrary."—These are stated by the poet as the first aims of every moral enquiry.

Quid tam ridiculum quam appetere mortem, cum vitam tibi inquietam feceris metu mortis. Lat. SENECA.—"What can be so ridiculous as to seek for deatn, when it is merely the fear of death that renders your existence miserable."

Quid te exempta juvat spinis è pluribus una? Lat. JUVENAL.
"What does it avail to you, if one thorn be removed out of many?"—How are you bettered by the removal of a single grievance, if the general pressure is suffered to continue?

Quid terras alio calentes sole mutamus? Lat. HOR. "Why do we change for soils warmed only by another sun?"—*i. e.* for different climates? Of what use is the change of residence, when the mind bears with it its own disease?

Quid times? Cæsarem vehis. Lat.—"Of what are you afraid? You have Cæsar on board."—This was addressed by Cæsar to his boatmen, who were affrighted by a raging tempest.

Quid verum atque decens? Lat.—"What is just and honourable?"

Quid verum atque decens curo et rogo, et omnis in hoc sum. Lat. HOR.—"My cares and my inquiries are directed in search of decency and truth, and in this I am wholly engrossed and occupied."

Quid violentius aure tyranni? Lat. JUV.—"What can be more violent than the ear of a tyrant?"—What more dangerous than the confidence of a despot?

Qui æquitatem petit, æquitatem faciat. Lat.—"Let him who seeks for equity, act equitably himself." Let him "do unto others as he would be done by."

Qui è nuce nucleum esse vult, frangit nucem. Lat. PLAUTUS.—"He who would get at the kernel, must crack the shell."—If we would accomplish any given purpose, we must use the right means.

Qui est plus esclave qu'un courtisan assidu, si ce n'est un courtisan plus assidu? Fr. LA BRUYERE.—"Who can be a greater slave than the assiduous courtier, unless it be the courtier who is more assiduous"

Quieta non movere. Lat.—"Not to disturb things

which are at rest." When a state is tranquil, it should not be unsettled by causeless innovation.

Qui facit per alium, facit per se. Lat. Law Max.—"What a man does by another, he does by or through himself."—Every man must be responsible for that which he empowers or commands another to do. If he orders another to commit a trespass, he is himself a trespasser.

Qui fit, Mæcenas, ut nemo, quam sibi sortem,
Seu ratio dederit, seu fors objecerit, illâ
Contentus vivat: laudet diversa sequentes?
Lat. Horace.

"How comes it, Mæcenas, that no person is contented with his condition in life, whether selected by choice, or thrown in his way by chance, but is always praising those who follow a different pursuit."—Every man, with few exceptions, seems to think that he would have thriven better in any other pursuit, than that which he has adopted.

Qui genus jactat suum, aliena laudat. Lat. Sen.—"He who boasts of his lineage, boasts of that which does not properly belong to him."

Qui hæret in literâ, hæret in cortice. Lat.—"He who clings to the letter, clings to the shell."—In the interpretation of a legal instrument, we may not confine ourselves to the literal meaning alone, but should endeavour to get at the spirit and intention of its maker.

Qui in omni re, atque in omni tempore,
Omni laude vacat, is illaudatus est;
Isque omnium pessimus deterrimusque est. Lat.

"He, who in his every act, and at all times, is undeserving of commendation, is truly unworthy, and is the vilest and worst of men."

Qui inscienter læsit, scienter emendit. Lat. Law Max—"He who ignorantly does an injury, shall knowingly make reparation."

Qui invidet, minor est. Lat.—"He who envies another, admits his own inferiority."

Qui male agit, odit lucem. Lat. Prov.—"He who

commits evil actions, shuns the light."—The worst presumable motives will always be inferred, where the doer of an act seeks to shroud himself in darkness and mystery.

Qui mori didicit, servire dedidicit. Supra omnem potentiam est, certè extra omnem. Lat. SEN.—"He who has learned to die, has learned how to avoid being a slave. Such a man is most certainly beyond the reach of all human power."—The writer, who afterwards suffered himself to bleed to death, when commanded by a tyrant to terminate his existence, seems, when writing this energetic passage, to have had some presentiment of his fate.

Qui n'a point de sens à trente ans, n'en aura jamais. Fr.—"He who has not sense at thirty years of age, will never have any."

Quin corpus onustum [unà,
Hesternis vitiis, animum quoque prægravat
Atque affigit humo divinæ particulam auræ.
Lat. HORACE.

"The body loaded by the excess of yesterday, depresses the mind also, and fixes to the ground this particle of divine breath."

"The body too, with yesterday's excess
"Burden'd and tired, shall the pure soul depress;
"Weigh down this portion of celestial birth,
"The breath of God, and fix it to the earth."
FRANCIS.

Qui nescit dissimulare, nescit vivere. Lat.—"He who knows not how to dissemble, knows not how to live."—The man is little fitted for society, who has not the faculty, on particular occasions, of concealing his feelings, and dissembling for the moment his resentments.

Qui nil molitur ineptè. Lat. HOR.—"Who attempts nothing fruitlessly or absurdly."—Whose means are always suited to his end. Spoken of a wise and provident statesman.

Qui non est hodie, cras minus aptus erit. Lat. MARTIAL.—"He who is not fit for business to-day, will be less fit to-morrow."

Qui non liberè veritatem pronunciat, proditor est veritatis, Lat. 4 Inst. Epil.—"He who does not freely speak the truth, is a betrayer of the truth."

Qui non negat, fatetur. Lat.—"He who does not deny, virtually confesses."—"Silence gives assent."

Qui non obstat cum possit, facere videtur. Lat. Law Max.—"He who does not prevent a crime when he could, is considered as participating in it.

Qui non peccavit, pœnam non feret. Lat.—"He who is innocent of the crime, shall be exempt from the punishment."

Qui non proficît, deficit. Lat.—"He who does not advance, goes backward."—This is a maxim for all ages; the boy at school, who is not gaining, is certainly losing ground.—It will equally apply to the political and military world.

Qui non vetat peccare cum possit, jubet. Lat. Sen. "He orders the commission of a crime, who does not forbid it, when it is in his power.

Qui non vult fieri desidiosus, amet. Lat. Ovid.—"Let him who does not wish to be indolent, fall in love."—That busy passion will call all his faculties into exercise.

Qui pense? Fr.—"Who thinks?"

Qui perd, péche. Fr. Prov.—"He who loses, *sins.*" The man who is unsuccessful, is generally held to be in the wrong.

Qui prægravat artes
Intra se positas, extinctus amabitur idem.
Lat. Horace.

"He whose moral or intellectual excellence causes envy in his life-time, shall be revered when he is dead."

Qui prete à l'ami, perd au double. Fr. Prov.—"He who lends his money to a friend, is sure to lose both."

Qui prior est tempore, potior est jure. Lat. Law Max

"He who is first in point of time, has the advantage in point of law."

Qui proficit in literis et deficit in moribus, non proficit sed deficit. Lat.—"He who acquires his learning at the expense of his morals, is the worse for his education."

Quique sui memores alios fecêre merendo. Lat. VIRG.—"Those who have insured their remembrance by their desert."—Those who have embalmed their memory by benefits conferred upon the human race.

Quis custodiet ipsos custodes? Lat. JUVENAL.—"Who shall guard your own guards?"—What check have you upon the very spies which you have set on this occasion?

Quis desiderio sit pudor, aut modus
Tam chari Capitis? Lat. HORACE.
"What bounds shall we set to our grief, on losing an individual so intimately and justly esteemed?"—This is a common preface to an obituary notice, elegy, or funeral sermon.—By the poet it was originally given as a solemn tribute to the memory of an endeared friend.

Quis enim virtutem amplectitur ipsam,
Præmia si tollas? Lat. JUVENAL.
"For who will embrace even virtue itself, if you take away its rewards?"—What man is wholly disinterested even in the best pursuit?

Quis expedivit psittaco suum χαιρε. Lat. PERSIUS.—"Who taught that parrot his 'how d'ye do.'"—Who instructed that pedant to quote so largely from other languages?

Quis fallere possit amantem? Lat. VIRGIL.—"Who can deceive a lover?"—What can escape a lover's jealousy and penetration?

Qui sentit commodum, sentire debet et onus. Lat. Law Maxim.—"He should endure the burden, who derives the advantage."

Qui se sent galeux, se gratte. Lat. Prov.—"He who feels himself scabby, let him scratch."—Let him who feels the allusion, resent it.

Quis furor, O cives, quæ tanta licentia ferri? Lat. VIRGIL
"What fury, oh citizens, what dreadful outrages of the sword!"—An appeal often and forcibly made in case of popular insurrection.

Qui sibi amicus est, scito hunc amicum omnibus esse. Lat. SENECA.—"He who is his own friend, is a friend to all men."—He who is considerate in his own concerns, will kindly extend his consideration to those of his friends.

Quis iniquæ
Tam patiens urbis, ut teneat se? Lat. JUVENAL.
"Who can have the patience in this wicked city, to restrain his indignation?"

Quisnam hominum est, quem tu contentum videris uno
Flagitio? Lat. JUVENAL.
"Where have you ever found that man who stopped short, after the perpetration of a single crime?"

Quis nam igitur liber? Sapiens qui sibi imperiosus. Lat. HORACE.
"Who then is free? The wise man who can command himself."—No man is less free than the slave to his passion.

Quis novus hic nostris successit sedibus hospes?
Quem sese ore ferens! Lat. VIRGIL.
"What new guest is this that has approached our dwelling, and with so proud a deportment?"

Quis
Peccandi finem imposuit sibi? Quando recepit
Ejectum semel attritâ de fronte ruborem? Lat. JUVENAL.
"What man has ever laid down a boundary to his crimes? Who ever regained the blush of modesty, after repeated transgression had driven it from his cheeks."

Quisque suos patimur manes. Lat. VIRGIL.—"Each man is liable to his peculiar destiny."

Quis talia fando temperet à lachrymis? Lat. VIRG.
"Who, in speaking such things, can abstain from

tears?"—Who can remain unaffected by such a narrative?

Qui statuit aliquid, parte inauditâ alterâ;
Æquum licet statuerit, haud æquus est.
Lat. SENECA.
"If any one decide, upon hearing only one side of the controversy, although such decision prove correct, he has acted unjustly."

Quis tulerit Gracchos de seditione querentes?
Lat. JUVENAL.
"Who could endure the Gracchi complaining of sedition?"—The Gracchi were Roman Tribunes, remarkable for being at the head of every seditious movement. The purport of the question therefore is,—who can bear to hear men complain of faults of which they are themselves particularly guilty?

Qui stultis videri eruditi volunt, stulti eruditis videntur. Lat. QUINCT.—"Those who are anxious to appear wise among the ignorant, usually appear ignorant in the company of the wise."—Or, according to the sarcasm of Lord Chesterfield, "He may be a wit among lords, who is only a lord among wits."

Qui tam. Law Lat.—"Who as well."—An action in the nature of an information on a penal statute.

Qui terret, plus ipse timet. Lat. CLAUDIAN.—"He who awes others, is more in fear himself."—The despot keeps others in dread of his tyranny, whilst he is himself a prey to his own alarms.

Qui timidè rogat, docet negare. Lat. SEN.—"He who asks fearfully, teaches a denial."—The claimant who has the greatest share of confidence is the most likely to succeed.

Qui transtulit sustinet. Lat.—"He who hath brought us hither, preserves and supports us."—Motto of the state of CONNECTICUT.

Qui uti scit, ei bona. Lat.—"That man should be posssessed of wealth, who knows its proper use."

Qui vive! Fr.—"Who goes there?"—He is on the *qui vive*—on the alert.

Qui vult decipi, decipiatur. Lat. Prov.—" If any man wishes to be deceived, let him be deceived." If he will not be advised, let him take the consequences.

Quoad hoc. Lat.—" As far as this."—Or, as relates to this matter.—He is right *quoad hoc,* as to this stage of the business, or point of the argument.

Quo animo? Lat.—" With what mind?"—The *quo animo*—the spirit and intention under which any act was performed.

Quocunque trahunt fata sequamur. Lat. Virgil. " Wherever the Fates direct us, let us follow."—Let us yield to the imperious necessity of circum stances.

Quod ab initio non valet, tractu temporis convalescere non potest. Lat. Law Max.—" That which had no force in the beginning, can gain no strength from the lapse of time."—A claim or title, originally defective, can not derive any additional weight from prescription.

Quod alias bonum et justum est, si per vim aut fraudem petatur, malum et injustum est. Lat. Law Max.—" What otherwise is good and just, if it be attempted by fraud or violence, becomes evil and unjust."—Thus, it is forbidden even to those, who have title of entry, to enter into lands or tenements, otherwise than in a peaceable manner.

Quod avertat Deus! Lat.—" Which God forbid!" —An exclamation frequently used on viewing, or auguring an impending calamity.

Quod caret initio et fine. Lat.—" That which has neither commencement or termination" of existence. This was the reply of Thales, the philosopher of Miletus, to the question " What is God?"

Quod certaminibus ortum ultra metam durat. Lat. Vell. Paterc.—" That which arises from contest often goes beyond the mark."—From all political contentions certain consequences flow, beyond what the actors on the scene had in their immediate contemplation.

Quod cessat ex reditu, frugalitate suppletur. Lat PLIN.—"What is deficient in my income, I sup ply by frugality."

Quodcunque ostendis mihi sic, incredulus odi. Lat. HOR.—"Whatever you show me in such a way, I detest and disbelieve."—This is applied to poets, who deal in nothing but monsters, spectres, and extravaganzas.

Quod dubites, ne feceris. Lat.—"Never do an act, of which you doubt the justice or propriety."

Quod est inconveniens et contra rationem, non est permissum in lege. Lat. Law Maxim.—"Whatever is inconvenient and contrary to reason, is not permitted in the law."—Thus, if a town has customs which can be shown to be unreasonable, they shall be no longer binding.

Quod est violentum, non est durabile. Lat. Prov.—"What is violent, is not durable."

Quod licet ingratum est, quod non licet acriùs urit. Lat. HORACE.
"That which is lawful is less pleasing. Men are more strongly prompted to that which is unlawful."—As they look, for instance, with more desire on other men's goods than to their own.

Quod malè fers, assuesce, feres benè. Lat. SENECA.—"Accustom yourself to that which you bear ill, and you will bear it well."—Patience and resignation will lighten every difficulty.

Quod medicorum est
Promittunt medici; tractant fabrilia fabri. Lat. HORACE.
"Physicians promise that which belongs to physicians; and workmen handle their own tools."—In these cases, no man interferes with another's business.

Quod non potest, vult posse, qui nimium potest. Lat. SENECA.—"He who is too powerful, is still aiming at that degree of power which is unattainable."—It is in the nature of despotism to be insatiable.

Quod nullius est, fit occupantis. Lat. Law Max.—"That which belongs to nobody, becomes the property of the occupier."

Quod optanti divûm promittere nemo
Auserat, volvenda dies, en! attulit ultro.
Lat. VIRGIL.
"Lo! What none of the gods could have promised to your prayer, progressive time has spontaneously supplied."—Spoken of some very unexpected good fortune.

Quod petîit spernit, repetit quod nuper omisit. Lat. HORACE.—"He despises that which he had formerly claimed, and he asks for that which he had at one time rejected."—This is applied to a capricious man who changes his views and intents, not from any change of circumstance, but from the veering and fluctuation of his own opinions.

Quod petis hic est—est Ulubris. Lat. HORACE.—"What you seek is here—it is at *Ulubri.*"—You look for happiness in change of place, when in fact it is every where within your reach, were your search but properly directed.

Quod petis, id sanè invisum est acidumque duobus. Lat. HORACE.—"What you ask is disagreeable and distasteful to two others."—This is the language of an author, labouring under something worse than a dilemma, which has but *two* horns, as not knowing how to please a *trio* of readers!

Quod potui, perfeci. Lat.—"I have done what I could do."

Quod ratio nequiit, sæpe sanavit mora. Lat. SEN.—"That which reason could not avoid, has often been cured by delay."—To forbear and wait for events, is sometimes all that is left to the most consummate prudence.

Quod sapit, nutrit. Lat.—"What pleases the taste, nourishes."—This doctrine has been long since proven not to be of universal application.

Quod satis est cui contingit, nil amplius optet.
Lat HORACE
"He who has enough, should wish for nothing

more."—The man who has a sufficiency, should learn to smile at the artificial wants of others.

Quod sit esse velit, nihilque malit. Lat. MARTIAL.—"Who wishes to be what he is, and sees nothing preferable."—A brief and just definition of a state of contentment.

Quod si deficiant vires, audacia certè
Laus erit; in magnis voluisse sat est.
Lat. PROPERTIUS.
"Even though strength should fail, still boldness shall have its praise: in great attempts it is laudable to dare."—The resolution to attempt a great deed is laudable, even though the attempt should be unsuccessful.

Quod sors feret, feremus æquo animo. Lat. TER.—"Whatever chance shall bring, let us bear it with an equal mind."—As we can not control the vicissitudes of Fortune, let us make sure of a relief and an asylum, in our own fortitude and equanimity.

Quod vide. Lat.—"Which see."—A reference to a subject under its proper head.

Quod volumus bonum; quod placet sanctum. Lat. —"What we wish for, we call good; what pleases us, holy."—Men are rarely at a loss for a justification of, or an excuse for, any of their own actions.

Quod vos jus cogit, id voluntate impetret. Lat. TER. —"What the law insists upon, let your adversary obtain from your own free will."—When the merits of the case are decidedly against a man, it is folly to persist in a vexatious course of litigation.

Quo fata trahunt retrahuntque, sequamur. Lat. VIRGIL.—"Let us follow the fates wherever they may lead or divert our steps."—Let us submit ourselves implicitly to Providence.

Quo jure. Law Lat.—"By what right."—A writ that lies for him who has lands, wherein another challenges common of pasture time out of mind, whereby the party is compelled to show by "what right" he entertains this claim.

Quo me cunque rapit tempestas, deferor hospes. Lat. Horace. "To whatever quarter the storm may blow, it bears me as a willing guest."—I endeavour to accommodate myself to every circumstance and condition of life.

Quo mihi fortunas, si non conceditur uti? Lat. Hor. —"Of what use are fortune's gifts to me, if I am not permitted to enjoy them?"

Quo minus. Law Lat.—The appellation given to a writ issuing by fiction from the Court of Exchequer, on behalf of a person supposed to be the king's farmer or debtor, against another, where there is any cause of personal action.

Quo more pyris vesci jubet Calaber hospes. Lat Horace.—"In the same manner as a Calabrian would insist on your eating pears."—This fruit is so plenty in Calabria that it is chiefly used to feed hogs. The application is therefore to those, who officiously force on you that which is of little value, and for which you have no liking.

Quondam etiam victis redit in præcordia Virtus. Lat. Lucan.—"Valour sometimes returns even into the bosom of the conquered."—Nations have risen upon their victors, and regained their liberty.

Quondam his vicimus armis. Lat.—"We were once victorious with these arms."

Quoniam diu vixisse denegatur, aliquid faciamus quo possimus ostendere nos vixisse. Lat. Cic.—"As length of life is denied to us, we should at least do something to show that we have lived."

Quoniam id fieri quod vis non potest,
Id velis quod possis. Lat. Terence.
"As you can not effect that which you wish, you should wish for that which you may effect."—You should endeavour to divert your inclination from that which you can not possibly attain.

Quo nihil majus, meliusve terris. Lat. Horace.—"Than whom (or which) was never any thing greater, or better on earth."—A convenient phrase of compliment.

Quo res cunque cadent, unum et commune periculum,
Una salus ambobus erit. Lat. VIRGIL.
'Whatever may be the result, we (or they) shall share one common danger, or rejoice in mutual safety."

Quorum. Lat.—"Of whom," one of the *quorum.*—This description of a justice of peace, is taken from the words of his *Dedimus.* "*Quorum unum.*"—"One of whom," I have appointed N. S. Esq. to be.—It is also used in another sense: "Such a number to be a *quorum,*" *i. e.* to be of sufficiency to proceed in the business.

Quorum pars fui. Lat.—"Of whom I was one."—In which I have participated.

Quos Deus vult perdere, prius dementat. Latin.—"Those whom God has a mind to destroy, he first deprives of their senses."—This is a phrase most frequently applied to ministers, whose real or imputed faults are taken as the prelude to their approaching fall.

Quos ego . . . . . Lat. VIRGIL.
"Whom I," . . . . . (if I willed it, could destroy.) This is a figure of speech, in which through anger or earnestness, the speaker leaves out a part of the sentence, to be understood.

Quo semel est imbuta recens, servabit odorem
Testa diu. Lat. HORACE.
"The cask will long retain the flavour of that with which it was first filled."—The prejudices imbibed from early education, will probably last through life.

Quos spiritus gessisset, vultu ferebat. Lat. TAC.—"His countenance betrayed the affections of his mind."

Quota. Lat.—"How much—How many."—It is usually applied to the proportion of taxes or soldiers to be paid, or furnished by each member of a confederacy.

Quot capitum vivunt, totidem studiorum
Millia Lat. HORACE.

"The number of different pursuits and passions is equal to the number of men who live."—Each man has his own prevailing passion, which differs in some respects from that of his neighbour.

Quo teneam vultus mutantem Protea nodo? Lat HORACE.—"In what knot shall I hold this *Proteus*, who so often changes his countenance?"—How shall I confine to a specific point, the man who so often shifts his ground of argument?

Quot homines tot sententiæ. Lat. TERENCE.—"So many men, so many different opinions."—An allusion to the continued diversity of taste and opinion.

Quo warranto. Law Lat.—"By what warrant."—A writ lying against the person who has usurped any franchise of liberty, requiring him to show "by what authority" he exercises it.

Q. V. an abbreviation of *quod vide*, "which see.'

R

Rans de vache. Fr.—The name given to a favourite air among the Swiss shepherds, which they play upon their bagpipes, while tending their flocks. When in any foreign country, they hear this air, they become very much dejected, and melancholy.

Rara avis in terris, nigroque simillima cygno. Lat. OVID.—"A rare bird on the earth, and very like a black swan."—Something singular or wonderful. A *unique*, a prodigy.

Rara est adeo concordia formæ
Atque pudicitiæ. Lat. JUVENAL.
"So rare is the union of beauty and of virtue."

Rara fides, probitasque viris qui castra sequuntur Lat. LUCAN.
"Good faith and probity are rarely found amongst those who are the followers of camps."—A military life but too often relaxes the principles of men, and renders their feelings more callous.

Rarâ temporum felicitate ubi sentire quæ velis, et quæ sentias dicere, licet. Lat. TACITUS.—"Such being the happiness of the times, that you might think as you wished, and speak as you thought." —This strong description, so seldom realized, is given by the historians of the reigns of *Nerva* and *Trajan*.

Rari nantes in gurgite vasto. Lat. VIRG.—"Swimming dispersedly in the vast deep."—This was originally used in speaking of seamen escaping from a wreck. It is now applied to a literary performance where a few happy thoughts are nearly lost in an ocean of *no meanings*.

Rari quippe boni: numero vix sunt totidem, quot
Thebarum portæ, vel divitis ostia Nili.
Lat. JUVENAL.
"Good men are scarce indeed. They are scarcely more in number than the (seven) gates of *Thebes*, or mouths of the rich *Nile!*"

Rarò antecedentem scelestum
Deseruit pede pœna claudo. Lat. HORACE.
"Justice, though moving with a tardy pace, has seldom failed of overtaking the wicked in their flight."—It is one of the strongest arguments for the belief of a superintending Providence, that few men, guilty of enormous crimes, whether the scourge fall sooner or later, have finally escaped their deserved punishment.

Rarò magni errores nisi ex magnis ingeniis prodière. Lat. PETRARCH.—"Great errors seldom originate but with men of great minds."

Rarus concubitus corpus excitat, frequens solvit. Lat. CELSUS.—"The bodily powers are excited by occasional intercourse; by too frequent repetition they are relaxed."

Rarus enim ferme sensus communis in illâ
Fortunâ. Lat. JUVENAL.
"We do not commonly find men of common sense amongst those of the highest fortune"

Rarus sermo illis, et magna libido tacendi.
Lat. JUVENAL.
They seldom converse, and are much inclined to

be silent."—This is spoken of men who affect silence, as a characteristic of gravity and wisdom.

Ratio est anima legis. Lat. Law Maxim.—" Reason is the soul of the law."—There is, however, no reason in the " law's delay."

Ratio et consilium propriæ ducis artes. Lat. Tac.—" The essential qualities of a general are reason and deliberation."

Ratio, quasi quædam lux, lumenque vitæ. Lat. Cic. —" Reason is, as it were, the light and the ornament of life."

Ratio justifica. Lat.—" The reason which justifies."

Ratio suasoria. Latin.—" The reason which persuades."—These two phrases are used to distinguish, when a speaker is impelled by a different motive from that, by which he means to influence his auditory; when he secretly *justifies* his measures on one ground, and wishes to *persuade* his hearers on another.

Rebus angustis, animosus atque
Fortis appare. Lat.
" In adversity and difficulties, arm yourself with firmness and fortitude."

Rebus in angustis facile est contemnere vitam;
Fortiter ille facit, qui miser esse potest.
Lat. Martial.
" It is easy in adversity to despise death; he has real fortitude, who can dare to live and be wretched."

Rebus secundis etiam egregios duces insolescere. Lat. Tacitus.—" In the hour of prosperity, even the best generals become haughty and insolent."

Rectè et suaviter. Lat.—" Justly and mildly."

Rectus in curia. Lat.—" Upright in the court."—A man coming into a court of justice, as the phrase is, " with clean hands."

Reculer pour mieux sauter. Lat. Prov.—" To go backward in order to leap the better."—The metaphor is borrowed from the practice in what is called a running leap. To retreat with prudence for the purpose of coming forward with greater energy

Reddere personæ scit convenientia cuique. Lat. Hor. "He knows how to assign what is proper and becoming to each person."—As a dramatic poet he gives to every personage its apposite and characteristic expression.

Redire cum perit, nescit pudor. Lat. Seneca. "When modesty is once extinguished, it knows not a return."—The ingenuous sense of shame, when once lost, can never be restored.

Redolet lucerna. Lat.—"It smells of the lamp."—It is a laboured production.

Reductio ad absurdum. Lat.—A phrase in logic, when your adversary is, or is supposed to be, *reduced* to submission, by showing him the *absurdity* of his conclusions.

Regalia. Lat.—The ensigns of royalty, as the crown, the sceptre, &c.

Regula ex jure, non jus ex regula, sumitur. Law Max.—"We draw the rule from the law, and not the law from the practice."

Re infectâ. Lat. Cæsar.—"The affair not having been done."—He returned *re infectâ*—without accomplishing his purpose.

Re ipsâ reperi,
Facilitate nihil esse homini melius atque cle mentiâ. Lat. Terence

"I have found by experience, that nothing is more useful to man than a spirit of mildness and accommodation."—In the various contracts of human life, the man of bland and gentle manners will, in general, win his way, before the person who aims to gain his object by a coarse and undistinguishing austerity.

Reipublicæ forma, laudare facilius quam evenire, et si evenit, haud diuturna esse potest. Lat. Tac.—"It is much more easy to praise than to establish a republican government; and when it is established, it can not be of long duration."

Rem, facias rem,
Rectè, si possis· si non, quocunque modo, rem. Lat. Horace.

'A fortune—make a fortune, by honest means if you can; if not, by any means make a fortune."—This language is put by the poet into the mouth of a corrupt man.

Renovato nomine. Lat.—"By a revived name."

Repentè dives, nemo factus est bonus. Lat. SYRUS. "No good man ever became rich of a sudden."—Immense and rapid fortunes, generally speaking, are acquired by fraud or violence.

Repondre en Normand. Fr.—To give an indirect, or evasive answer.

Requiescat in pace. Lat.—"May he rest in peace."—This inscription is often found on tombstones. It is sometimes used ironically, as to a minister, departed from office.

Rerum copia verborum copiam gignit. Lat. CICERO. —"A copious supply of matter will produce an abundant flow of language" to a writer or speaker. —See *Verba provisam*, &c.

Rerum primordia. Lat.—"The first principles or elements of things."

Rerum suorum quidlibet est moderator et arbiter. Lat. Law Maxim.—"Every man is the regulator and disposer of his own property."

Res angusta domi. Lat. HORACE.—"Narrowed circumstances at home."—He was impelled by the *res angusta domi*—by the severe pressure of poverty.

Res est sacra miser. Lat. OVID.—"The person of affliction is sacred."—There is a hallowed respect due to the wretched, which should protect them from further insult or depression.

Res est soliciti plena timoris amor. Lat. OVID.—"Love is the perpetual source of fears and anxieties."

Res judicata pro veritate accipitur. Lat. Law Max. "A case once decided is considered as just," and will afford a precedent.

Respice finem. Lat.—"Look to the end."—Before

you enter on an affair, let the consequences be well considered.

Respicere exemplar vitæ, morumque jubebo
Doctum imitatorem, et veras hinc ducere voces
Lat. HORACE.

"I would advise him who wishes to imitate well, to look closely into life and manners, and thereby to learn to describe them with truth."—Characters to be striking, should be drawn from nature, not from fancy. This should be particularly observed upon the stage.

Respondeat superior. Lat. Law Maxim.—"Let the principal answer."—In civil cases, the master is always to be considered as responsible for the acts of his servant.

Respublica. Lat.—"The common-weal."—The general interest.

Res unius ætatis. Lat.—"A thing of only one age." This is a phrase used by civilians to denote a legal provision, which by no possibility can pass beyond the first generation.

Resurgam. Lat.—"I shall rise again."—A sepulchral inscription.

Retorquere non est respondere. Lat.—"To retort is not to reply."

Retraxit. Law Lat.—"He has recalled or revoked." —A term in law when the plaintiff or demandant says that he will proceed no farther.

Revenons à nos moutons. Fr. Phrase.—"Let us return to our sheep."—A French lawyer pleading the cause of a client who had lost some sheep, talked of every thing but the matter in question, when his unfortunate client recalled him, by the above exclamation. It is used in conversation, to check any impertinent wandering from the argument.

Rex datur propter regnum, non regnum propter regem Potentia non est nisi ad bonum. Lat. Law Maxim.—"A king is given to serve the kingdom, not the kingdom to serve the king —

Power is only conferred for the purpose of general advantage."

Rex est qui metuit nihil;
Rex est qui cupit nihil. Lat.

"He is a king who fears nothing: he is a king who covets nothing."—Such a man has erected in his own mind an independent sovereignty

Ridentem dicere verum,
Quid vetat? Lat. HORACE.

"What forbids a man, when laughing, to speak the truth?"—Why may not wholesome truths be conveyed under the garb of pleasantry?

Ride si sapis. Lat.—"Laugh, if you are wise."—En joy the ridicule which you will find is directed solely against error, ignorance, or folly.

Ridetur chordâ qui semper aberrat eadem. Lat. HOR.—"That person makes himself ridiculous, who is ever harping on one string."—Nothing is more disgusting than sameness in conversation, or writing.

Ridiculum acri
Fortius ac melius plerumque secat res.
Lat. HORACE.

"Ridicule is frequently employed with more power and success, than severity."—Playful satire may sometimes reform, where serious indignation would be of no avail.

Rien de plus estimable que la civilité, mais rien de plus ridicule et de plus à charge, que la cérémonie. Fr.—"Nothing is of more value than complaisance; nothing more ridiculous or troublesome than mere ceremony."

Rien n'empeche tant d'être naturel, que l'envie de le paroître. Fr. ROCHEFOUCAULT.—"Nothing prevents a person from being natural and easy, so much as the desire of appearing so."

Rien ne peut arrêter sa vigilante audace:
L'Eté n'a point de feux, l'hiver n'a point de glace. Fr. BOILEAU

"Nothing can arrest his daring vigilance. For him

the summer has no heat, the winter has no ice."—This was the eulogy of the poet on Louis XIV.

Rien ne s'anéantit; non, rien; et la matière,
Comme un fleuve éternal, roule toujours entière.
Fr. ROUCHER.

"Nothing whatever is annihilated. Matter, like an eternal river, still rolls on without diminution."

Rien n'est beau que le vrai, le vrai seul est aimable. Fr. BOILEAU.—"Nothing is beautiful but truth, and truth alone is lovely."

Rien n'est si dangereux qu'un indiscret ami;
Mieux vaudroit un sage ennemi.
Fr. LAFONTAINE.

"Nothing is more dangerous than an imprudent friend; it is better to have to deal with a prudent enemy."

Rira bien, qui rira le dernier. Fr. Proverb.—"He laughs successfully, who laughs the last."—Nothing is more ridiculous than when the anticipation of triumph is mocked by a defeat.

Risu inepto res ineptior nulla est. Lat. MARTIAL.—"Than silly laughter nothing is more silly."

Risum teneatis amici? Lat. HORACE.—"Can even friends abstain from laughter?"—Is not the thing so ridiculous, that even partiality must smile?

Risus abundat in ore stultorum. Lat.—"Laughter abounds in the mouth of fools."

Rixator de lanâ caprinâ. Lat.—"One who will quarrel about goat's wool,"—or, for a very trifle.

Role d'Equipage. Fr.—"A list of the crew."—An official list of the persons on board, which neutral vessels are compelled to produce in time of war.

Rostrum. Lat.—The stage or pulpit, in the Roman *forum*, or court, from which speeches or harangues were made.

Rudis indigestaque moles. Lat. OVID.—"A rude and unarranged mass."—A chaos of undigested matter.

Ruit mole suâ. Lat. HOR.—"It is crushed by its own weight."

Ruse contre ruse. Fr. Phrase.—" Trick against trick.' —A counterplot.

Ruse de guerre. Fr. Phrase.—" A trick of war."—A stratagem.

Rus in urbe. Lat.—" The country in town."—Describing a situation which partakes of the advantages of both.

Rusticus expectat dum defluat amnis; at ille
Labitur et labetur in omne volubilis ævum.
Lat. HORACE.

"The peasant sits waiting on the bank, until the river shall have passed away, but still the stream flows on, and will continue to flow forever."—This is used to mark the disappointed ignorance of those who seem to be of opinion, that the same causes will not continue to produce the same effects.

S

Sa boule est demeurée. Fr. Phrase.—" His bowl has stopt short of the jack."—He has failed of his object.

Sæpe intereunt aliis meditantes necem. Lat. PHÆDRUS.—" Those who plot the destruction of others, very often fall themselves the victims."—The mischiefs which men devise against others, very often recoil, and crush themselves.

Sæpe stylum vertas, iterum quæ digna legi sint
Scripturus: neque te ut miretur turba, laborcs,
Contentus paucis lectoribus. Lat. HORACE.

"You must often turn your style, if you mean to write any thing worthy of being read a second time: nor should you labour to be admired by the multitude, but be content with few readers."—The first part of this quotation alludes to the *stylum*, or instrument of steel, with the sharp end of which the Romans wrote on a tablet of wax, and with the flat end erased what they deemed imperfect. The meaning therefore is, that the writer who wishes for permanent fame, must submit to the labour of repeated correction.

Sæpius ventis agitatur ingens
Pinus, et celsæ graviore casu
Decidunt turres, feriuntque summos
Fulgura montes. Lat. HORACE.

"The lofty pine is oftenest agitated by the winds —high towers rush to the earth with a heavier fall —and the lightning most frequently strikes the highest mountains."—The proud and the exalted are more liable to the strokes of adversity than the lowly and humble.

Sævi inter se conveniunt ursi. Lat. JUV.—"Even savage bears will agree with each other."

Sævior armis luxuria incubuit. Lat. LUCAN.— "Luxury, more injurious than war, has cast her baleful influence over us."

Sævit amor ferri, et scelerata insania belli. Lat. VIRGIL.—"The passions are in arms, and nothing is heard of but the mad wickedness of war."

Sævitque animis ignobile vulgus;
Jamque faces et saxa volant: furor arma ministrat. Lat. VIRGIL.

"The rude rabble are enraged, now the fire-brands and stones are seen to fly about: their fury supplies them with arms."—A striking description of a popular tumult.

Saltabat melius quam necesse est probæ. Lat. SAL. —"She danced much better than became a modest woman."—Amongst the Romans to excel in this art was expected only from the public women.

Saltat Milonius, ut semel icto
Accessit fervor capiti, numerusque lucernis. Lat. JUVENAL

"Milonius dances as soon as the wine gets into his heated head, and the lights are doubled to his view." Used to describe a drunken frolic, where the actor is in other respects of a distinguished character.

Salus per Christum Redemptorem. Lat.—"Salvation through Christ the Redeemer."

Salus populi suprema est lex. Lat.—"To consult the welfare of the people is the first great law."—The main end of every government should be the well being of the people, the establishment of order and security, and the diffusion of social happiness.

Salvo jure. Lat.—"Saving the right."—A clause of exception.—Such a thing shall be granted, '*salvo jure Regis*, "saving the King's right," if it does not trench upon his rights or prerogatives.

Salvo pudore. Lat.—"Without offence to modesty" —I shall describe the matter "*salvo pudore*," without offending the decent eye or ear.

Sanctio justa, jubens honesta, et prohibens contraria. Lat.—"A just ordinance, commanding what is honest, and forbidding the contrary."—This is the proper definition, given by BRACTON, of our municipal law.

Sanctissima divitiarum majestas. Lat.—"The most holy majesty of wealth."—Used ironically in relation to the influence and respect, which riches obtain among men.

Sanctum Sanctorum. Lat.—"The Holy of Holies," —or, most holy place of the Jews.—A place which it is prohibited (except to the high priest) to enter, or look into.

Sang froid. French.—"Cold blood."—Indifference, apathy.

Sanguine junctus, mente tamen propior fuit. Lat OVID.—"Related by consanguinity, but of a yet more kindred mind."

Sans changer. Fr.—"Without changing."

Sans culottes. Fr.—"Men without breeches."— Ragamuffins.—A name given to one of the parties in France in the time of the revolution.

Sans Dieu rien. Fr.—"Nothing without God."

Sans peur et sans reproche. Fr.—"Without fear, and without reproach."

Sapere aude. Lat. HOR.—"Dare to be wise."—Pursue the path of wisdom, without regarding the obstacles which may be thrown in your course.

Sapiens dominabitur astris. Lat.—"The wise man will govern the stars."—His prudence and foresight will enable him to counteract that which, with vulgar minds, is suffered to pass for fate or destiny.

Sapientem pascere barbam. Lat. HOR.—"To nurse a wise beard."—To assume the outward indications of wisdom.

Sapientes principes sapientum congressu. Lat. from PLATO.—"Princes become wise from their intercourse with wise men."—The good sense of a monarch may be judged of by that of those whom he takes for his advisers.

Sapientis est providere; ex quo sapientia est appellata prudentia. Lat. CICERO.—"It is the part of a wise man to be cautious and circumspect; and hence wisdom has derived the name of prudence."

Sapientia prima est stultitiâ caruisse. Lat. HOR.—"The first step to wisdom is, to be exempt from folly."—No man can be called wise who makes occasional lapses in point of prudence.

Satis dotata, si benè morata. Lat. Prov.—"She is well enough dowered, if possessed of good morals."

Satis eloquentiæ, sapientiæ parum. Lat. SALLUST.—"A sufficient share of eloquence, with little wisdom."—A fluent elocution is not always a proof of intrinsic good sense.

Satis, superque. Lat.—"Enough, and more than enough."

Satius est petere fontes, quam sectari rivulos. Lat.—"It is better to seek the fountain, than to follow the stream."

Saturnalia. Lat.—A Roman festival in honour of Saturn, celebrated on the 16th or 17th of December; which was attended by a general freedom from restraint, when slaves were allowed to take liberties with their masters, and scholars with their teachers.

Sauve qui peut. Fr.—"Save himself who can."—The phrase of flight, when a French army is routed.

Scan. Mag. (*Scandalum Magnatum.*) Law Lat.—"The scandal of the Peerage."—The name given to a statute of Richard II. by which, punishment is to be inflicted for any scandal or wrong offered to, or uttered against a noble personage.

Scavoir faire. Fr.—" Ability, skill, industry,"—and,

Scavoir vivre. Fr.—" Good breeding, polite behaviour."

Scelere velandum est scelus. Lat. SEN.—" One crime must be concealed by the commission of another."

Scelus intra se tacitum qui cogitat ullum,
Facti crimen habet. Lat. JUVENAL.
" He who meditates the commission of a crime, has all the guilt of the deed."—The intention, in certain cases, is as guilty as the act itself.

Scilicet ut fulvum spectatur in ignibus aurum,
Tempore sic duro est inspicienda fides. Lat. Ov.
" As the yellow gold is tried in the fire, so the faith of friendship can only be known in the season of adversity."

Scinditur incertum studia in contraria vulgus. Lat. VIRGIL.—" The wavering multitude is divided by opposite opinions."—The populace incapable of judging for themselves, and generally taking their opinions from others, are seldom to be found in a state of unanimity.

Scio, coactus tuâ voluntate es. Lat. TERENCE.—" I know, thou art compelled by thy own will."—You plead necessity, when in fact you are biassed only by your own inclination.

Scire facias. Law Lat.—" Cause it to be known."—The name given to a judicial writ, ordering the defendant to show cause, why the execution should not be made out on a judgment which has passed.

Scire tuum nihil est, nisi te scire hoc sciat alter. Lat. PERSIUS.—" Your own knowledge is as nothing, unless others know you to possess that knowledge."

Scire volunt omnes, mercedem solvere nemo. Lat. JUV.—" Every man wishes to be informed, but few are willing to pay the price;"—to undergo the study and expense.

Scribendi rectè, sapere est principium et fons. Lat. HORACE.
"The first principle and source of all good writing is, to think justly."

Scribimus indocti, doctique, poemata passim. Lat. HORACE.
"We, both learned, and unlearned, are in the habit of writing poetry."—Other pursuits are supposed to require some previous study, but most men suppose themselves as it were instinctively qualified to become poets, as well as politicians.

Secretè amicos admone, lauda palam. Lat. SYRUS.
"Admonish your friends secretly, but praise them openly."

Secundum artem. Lat.—"According to art."—To die *secundum artem*—to expire under the doctor's hands..

Secundum formam statuti. Law Lat.—"According to the form of the statute."

Secundum naturam. Lat.—"According to the course of nature."

Se defendendo. Law Lat.—"In defending himself."—A plea for him who is charged with the death of another, that it was necessary in his own defence.

Secundis dubiisque rectus. Lat.—"Preserving my integrity, both in prosperity and in adversity."

Sed fugit interea, fugit irreparabile tempus. Lat. VIRGIL.
"But in the mean while time flies;—time, whose loss is never to be retrieved."—Used as an admonition against procrastination or delay.

Sed nunc amoto quæramus seria ludo. Lat. HOR.—"But, now laying sportiveness aside, let us attend to more serious matters."—Putting wit and raillery out of question, let us come to facts and arguments.

Sed notat hunc omnis domus et vicinia tota,
Introrsum turpem, et speciosum pelle decora. Lat. HORACE.
"Yet all the house and the whole neighbourhood

see the inward baseness and the outward speciousness of this man."—Applied to a plausible but detected hypocrite.

Sed nunc non erat his locus. Lat. Hor.—"But there was at this time no place for these matters."—The observations were sufficiently well in themselves, but they were extraneous and inapplicable to the subject.

Sed post est occasio calva. Lat.—"But opportunity is bald behind."—This alludes to the figure of Time, as represented by painters, with a *forelock* only, to intimate that when once past, he can not by any means be caught or recalled.—An opportunity once missed, is most frequently lost forever.

Sed te
Nos facimus, Fortuna, Deam, cæloque locamus. Lat.
"We, Fortune, make thee a goddess, and place thee in the heavens."—Or, as Dryden has it;
"Fortune a goddess is to fools alone,
The wise are always master of their own."

Sed ubi plura nitent in carmine, non ego paucis
Offendar maculis. Lat. Horace.
"But if there are many brilliancies in the poem, I shall not be offended with a few faults."—Where there are many beauties, we should pardon a few defects.

Segnem ac desidem, et Circo et Theatris corruptum Militem. Lat. Tacitus.—"A slothful and listless soldiery, debauched by the circus and the theatres"—by the dissipation of a long peace.

Segniùs irritant animos demissa per aurem,
Quam quæ sunt oculis subjecta fidelibus.
Lat. Horace.
"The facts, which are merely told, produce a slight impression, compared with that of those which are presented to the eye."—We are indifferent hearers of acts, which, had we been eye-witnesses, would have excited our lively indignation.

Selon les règles. Fr.—"According to rule."

Semel insanivimus omnes. Lat.—"We have all at

some time been mad."—Every man must recollect some period in his life, when his conduct was not influenced by his reason.

Semel malus, semper præsumitur esse malus. Lat. Law Maxim.—"Those who are once evil, are always presumed to be so."—This is to be understood *in eodem genere mali,* "in the same kind of evil:" as, persons convicted of perjury are not to be admitted as witnesses in any cause, after having once so offended.

Semita certè
Tranquillæ per virtutem patet unica vitæ.
Lat. JUVENAL.
"Virtue offers the only path, which, in this life, leads to tranquillity."

Semper avarus eget. Lat. HORACE.—"The miser is ever in want."

Semper ego auditor tantum, nunquamne reponam? Lat.—"Must I still be compelled to hear, and be refused the privilege of replying?"—Shall I not be allowed to repel such calumnies?

Semper habet lites, alternaque jurgia lectus,
In quo nupta jacet: minimum dormitur in illo.
Lat. JUVENAL.
"That bed in which a married woman lies, is full of scolding and disputes: it will therefore admit of little sleep."

Semper honos, nomenque tuum, laudesque manebunt. Lat. VIRGIL.—"Your honour, your name and your praises shall ever remain."—Your fame shall be eternized.

Semper idem—Semper eadem. Lat.—"Always the same."—The former phrase is of the masculine and neuter, the latter of the feminine gender.

Semper inops quicunque cupit. Lat. CLAUDIAN.
"The man who desires more, is ever poor."—The avaricious, who are continually extending their wishes, are poor even in the midst of affluence.

Semper nocet differre paratis. Lat. LUCAN.—"Delay is always injurious to those who are prepared."—

When you are ready, you should leave to your adversary no further time for preparation.

Semper fidelis. Lat.—" Always faithful "

Semper paratus. Lat.—" Always ready."

Semper timidum scelus. Lat.—" Guilt is ever cowardly."

Semper vivit in armis. Lat.—" He ever lives in arms;"—or, in continual hostility.

Semper il mal non vien per nuocere. Ital. Prov.—" Misfortune does not always come to injure."—That which we take for an infliction, sometimes comes as a blessing.

Senatus consulta. Lat.—" The public acts or laws passed by the Roman Senate."

Senectus est naturâ loquacior. Lat. Cic.—" Old age is naturally more talkative."

Si non è vero; è ben trovato. Ital. Prov.—" If it be not true, it is at least well invented."—It has the appearance of truth, if it be not true in reality.

Sequari vestigia rerum. Lat.—" To follow the footsteps of things."—To trace up effects to their causes.

Sequi debet potentia justitiam non præcedere. Lat. Law Maxim.—" Power should follow, not precede, justice."

Sequiturque patrem non passibus æquis. Lat. Virg. " He follows his father, but not with equal paces." —He follows his predecessor, but with an inferior share of vigour or ability.

Seria cum possim, quod delectantia malim
Scribere, tu causa es lector. Lat. Martial.
" That I dwell on lighter topics, when I could handle those more serious, thou, reader, art the cause."—An author must strive to gratify the taste of his readers.

Seriatim. Lat.—" In order."—According to place or seniority.

Series implexa causarum. Lat. Seneca.—" The complicated series of causes."—By this is signified what the ancients expressed by the general term—*Fate.*

Sermo datur cunctis, animi sapientia paucis. Lat. CATO.—"All have the gift of speech, but few are possessed of wisdom."

Sero respicitur tellus, ubi fune soluto,
Currit in immensum panda carina salum.
Lat. OVID.
"It is too late to look back upon the land, when the cable being loosed, the vessel is making her way into the immense deep."—We should use all previous circumspection, when about to commit an act which in its consequences, may be irretrievable

Serò sed serio. Lat.—"Late, but seriously."

Serò venientibus ossa. Lat.—"The last comer shall have the bones."—A word of reproach to those who do not steadily maintain their dinner appointments.

Serpentes avibus geminentur, tigribus agni. Lat. VIRGIL.—"Let serpents couple with birds, and lambs with tigers."—Let things the most dissonant agree, ere this harsh union be completed.

Serum est cavendi tempus in mediis malis. Lat. SENECA.—"The season of caution is past, when we are in the midst of evils."

Serus in cœlum redeas, diuque læto
Intersis populo. Lat. HORACE.
"Late may you return to heaven, and long may you continue to gladden your people with your presence."—This was the flattering invocation ot the poet, to the emperor *Augustus.*

Serva jugum. Lat.—"Preserve the yoke."

Servabo fidem. Lat.—"I will keep faith."

Servare cives, major est virtus patriæ patri. Lat. SEN.—"To preserve the lives of citizens, is the greatest virtue in the father of his country."

Servare modum. Lat.—"To keep within bounds."-To preserve a propriety of conduct"

Servata fides cineri. Lat.—"Faithful to the memory of my ancestors."

Servetur ad imum,
Qualis ab incæpto processerit, et sibi constet.
Lat. HORACE.
"Let the character be preserved to the last, as it set out from the beginning, and be consistent with itself."—Let not your conduct, or that of the character which you pourtray, be disgraced by inconsistency.

Serviet æturnum, qui parvo nescit uti. Lat. HOR.—"He must be a perpetual slave, who knows not how to live upon a little."—Prodigality in the first instance, is the natural parent of baseness, and servility in the second.

Sesquipedalia verba. Lat.—"Words a foot and a half long."—Big, vaunting words—swollen and bombastic expressions.

Sexu fœmina, ingenio vir. Lat. (Epitaph of Maria Theresa of Austria.)—"A woman by sex, but a man in mind."

Si ad naturam vivas, nunquam eris pauper; si ad opinionem, nunquam dives. Lat. SEN.—"If you live according to the dictates of nature, you will never be poor; if according to the world's caprice, you never will be rich."

Si antiquitatem spectes est vetustissima, si dignitatem est honoratissima, si jurisdictionem est capacissima. Lat. COKE.—"If you look to its antiquity, it is most ancient—if to its dignity, it is most honourable—if to its jurisdiction, it is most extensive."—This is the description given, by one of the ablest law-writers, of the English House of Commons.

Si cadere necesse est, occurrendum discrimini. Lat. TACITUS.—"If a man must fall, he should manfully meet the event."—When the danger is extreme, it should be met with a proportioned energy

Si caput dolet, omnia membra languent. Lat.—"If the head aches, all the members of the body sympathize with it."

Si ceux, qui sont ennemis des divertissimens honnêtes, avoient la direction du monde, ils vou-

droient ôter le printemps et la jeunesse,—l'un de l'année, et l'autre de la vie. Fr. BALZAC.—"If those, who are the enemies of innocent amusements, had the direction of the world, they would take away the spring and youth—the former from the year, and the latter from human life."

Sic itur ad astra. Lat. VIRGIL.—"Thus men ascend to the skies."—Such is the way to immortality.

Sic omnia fatis
In pejus ruere, et retro sublapsa referri.
Lat. VIRGIL.

"Thus all things are changed for the worse, and at length borne down by fate."—By the greater number of the ancient poets in particular, every signal misfortune was supposed to spring from a fixed and irrevocable destiny.

Sic passim. Lat.—"So every where."—This is used to denote, that the same sentiment occurs in several passages of the same work.

Sic præsentibus utaris voluptatibus, ut futuris non noceas. Lat. SENECA.—"Enjoy your present pleasures, so as not to injure those which are to follow."—Take care in every indulgence, not to destroy your powers by excess.

Sic quisque pavendo,
Dat vires famæ, nulloque auctore malorum,
Quæ finxēre timent. Lat. LUCAN.

"Thus each person by his fears, gives wings to rumour, and without any real source of apprehension, men fear what they themselves have feigned."—The popular apprehension too often makes the mischief which it fears.

Sic semper tyrannis. Lat.—"May this ever be the fate of tyrants."—May a similar punishment always await them.—Motto of the state of VIRGINIA.

Sic transit gloria mundi. Lat.—"Thus fades the glory of this world."—Such are the transitions and fluctuations of worldly splendour, and of human happiness.

Sicut ante. Lat.—"As before."

Sic utere tuo ut alienum non lædas. Lat. Law Max. —"Make use of your own property in such a manner as not to injure that of another."—This is often applied in case of nuisances, &c.

Sic volo, sic jubeo, stat pro ratione voluntas. Lat.— "Thus I wish and order; my will stands in the place of reason."—This characteristic language is generally put into the mouth of a despot.

Sic vos non vobis. Lat. VIRGIL.—"So you do not labour for yourselves."—This is merely the commencement of some stanzas, in which the poet complains, that as bees do not make honey, or sheep bear fleeces, for their own use, so the profit and honour of his labours had been usurped by others —The application is to those who have suffered by a similar usurpation.

Si Deus nobiscum, quis contra nos? Lat.—"If God be with us, who shall be against us?"

Si dixeris æstuo, sudat. Lat.—"If you say that you are warm, he sweats."—Spoken of such sycophants, or "water-flies" as *Osrick* in *Hamlet*, who amongst other modes of adulation, are ever of the same opinion with those to whom they address themselves.

Si duo in testamento pugnanti reperiuntur, ultimum est ratum. Lat. Law Max.—"If in a will, any two clauses are found at variance with each other, the last is to be sustained."

Si fas est magnis componere parva. Lat. VIRGIL.— "If it be allowable to compare small things with great."

Si foret in terris, rideret Heraclitus. Lat.—"If Heraclitus were on earth, he would laugh."—The philosopher of antiquity, who was only remarkable for weeping, must laugh *per force*, at the absurdity of these arguments or proceedings.

Si fortuna juvat, caveto tolli,
Si fortuna tonat, caveto mergi. Lat. AUSON.
"If fortune favours you, do not be elated;—if she should frown, do not despond."—Preserve an equal mind in all situations.

Si genus humanum et mortalia temnitis arma,
At sperate Deos memores fandi atque nefandi.
Lat. VIRGIL.
"If you despise the human race, and mortal arms, yet be aware that there is a God who is mindful of right and wrong."—Recollect that there is a future state of reward and punishment.

Si je puis. Fr.—"If I can."

Si judicas, cognosce; si regnas, jube. Lat. SENECA.—"If you judge, inquire; if you reign, command."—If your office be judicial, inform yourself; if ministerial, you may decide without inquiry.

Silent leges inter arma. Lat. CIC.—"The laws are silent in the midst of arms."—The violence of war ofttimes prevents the equitable administration of the laws.

Si mens non læva fuisset. Lat. VIRGIL.—"If my (or the) mind had not been perverted," literally, had not been on the *left* side.—If I had not been infatuated.

Simia quam similis, turpissima bestia, nobis! Lat.—"How like to a man, in shape and action, is that vile beast the monkey!"

Si mihi pergit quæ vult dicere, ea quæ non vult
Audiet. Lat. TERENCE.
"If he proceeds to state what he pleases against me, he shall have something in return, which it will not please him to hear."

Similis simili gaudet. Lat.—"Like is pleased with like."—Those of similar tastes, or dispositions, will associate.—"Birds of a feather will flock together."

Simplex munditiis. Lat. HORACE.—"Simple in neatness."—Recommended by propriety of dress, but unincumbered with superfluous ornament.

Simplicissimâ mente, et verâ fide. Lat. PETRON.—"Of the most pure intentions, and strict integrity."

Simplicissimi omnium habentur iracundi. Lat. SENECA.—"Of all persons, they, who are prone to anger and petulancy, are the most silly."

Simul et jucunda et idonea dicere vitæ. Lat. Hor.—"To tell at once what is pleasant and proper in life."—This is the task of the didactic poet, whose business it is to blend amusement with instruction.

Si natura negat, facit indignatio versus. Lat. Juv. —"If nature does not, anger makes us write."

Sincerum est nisi vas, quodcunque infundis acescit. Lat. Horace. "Unless the vessel be pure, whatever you put in will turn sour."—If the young mind be not duly prepared, all after instructions are thrown away.

Sine Cerere et Baccho, friget Venus. Lat.—"Without the aid of *Ceres* and *Bacchus*, *Venus* freezes." —Love will speedily cool, says the poet from the school of *Epicurus*, without the aid of wine and good living.

Sine cura. Lat.—"Without charge."—A sinecure.—This is a denomination given to an office which does not require any *duty* to be performed by the incumbent.

Sine die. Lat.—"Without a day."—The business was deferred *sine die:*—no day was named for its reconsideration, or for a further meeting.

Sine dubio. Lat.—"Without doubt;"—assuredly.

Sine invidiâ. Lat.—"Without envy."—Not speaking invidiously.

Sine odio. Lat.—"Without hatred."—I speak *sine odio*—I feel divested of all animosity.

Sine quâ non. Lat.—"A thing without which another can not be."—An indispensable condition.—An ingredient absolutely necessary.

Sine virtute esse amicitia nullo pacto potest; quæ autem inter bonos amicitia dicitur, hæc inter malos factio est. Lat. Sallust.—"There can be no friendship without virtue; for that intimacy, which amongst good men is called friendship, becomes faction, when it subsists among the unprincipled."

Singula de nobis anni prædantur euntes. Lat. Hor.

"Each passing year robs us of a share of what we possessed."—Talents, beauty, and health, the most valuable possessions of human nature, all fall a prey to the ravages of time.

Singula quæque locum teneant sortita decenter. Lat. HOR.—"Let each thing keep the place it occupies with propriety."—The poet is instructing the dramatist not to go into any deviation from propriety of character. The phrase is also used in a political sense, to recommend that all things may preserve their due place and order.

Si non errâsset, fecerat ille minus. Lat. MARTIAL. "Had he not erred, he would have done less."—Applied to one who has atoned for a temporary lapse, by great efforts of industry or virtue.

Si nous n'avions point de défauts, nous ne prendrions pas tant de plaisir à en remarquer dans les autres. Fr. ROCHEFOUCAULT.—"If we had no defects in ourselves, we should not take so much pleasure in remarking those of others."

Si nous ne nous flattions pas nous-mêmes, la flatterie des autres ne nous pourroit nuire. Fr. BOUHOURS.—"If we did not flatter ourselves, the flattery of others could do us no harm."—Their incense would be thrown away, if it was not grateful to our self-love.

Si parva licet componere magnis. Lat. VIRGIL.—"If small things may be compared with great."—If I may be permitted to use the comparison.

Si qua vis aptè nubere, nube pari. Lat. OVID. "If you wish fitly to marry, then marry your equal."—The Poet alludes to an equality of years; but it may also refer to an equality of conditions.

Si quæris monumentum, circumspice. Lat.—"If you seek my monument, look around."—This is the epitaph of the architect, (Sir C. Wren) in the church of St. PAUL, which he designed and erected. If you question my merit, behold my works.

Si quid ego adjuvero, curamve levasso,
Quæ nunc te coquit, et versat sub pectore fixa,
Ecquid erit prætii? Lat. ENNIUS.

"If I can by any means assist you, or lighten the cares which now oppress you, and incessantly harass your anxious breast, what shall be my reward?"

Si quid novisti rectius istis,
Candidus imperti; si non his utere mecum.
Lat. HORACE.

"If you know of any thing more proper than these (precepts), be so candid as to communicate your knowledge—if not, make use of what I have furnished."—Thus translated:

"——— If a better system's thine,
Impart it freely, or make use of mine."

Si sine amore, jocisque
Nil est jucundum, vivas in amore, jocisque.
Lat. HORACE.

"If nothing appears to you delightful without love and sports, then live in sports and love."—A maxim from the *Epicurean* school.

Si sit prudentia. Lat.—"If there be but prudence."

Si tibi deficiant medici, medici tibi fiant
Hæc tria: mens hilaris, requies, moderata diæta. Lat.

"If you need a physician, employ these three—a cheerful mind, rest, and a temperate diet."

Sit mihi quod nunc est, etiam minus, ut mihi vivam
Quod superest ævi—si quid superesse volunt dii.
Lat. HORACE.

"Let me, I pray, possess what I now have, or even less, that I may enjoy myself for my remaining days, if Heaven grants any to remain."

Sit mihi fas audita loqui. Lat.—"Let me have permission to state what I have heard."

Sit piger ad pœnas princeps, ad præmia velox. Lat. OVID.—"A ruler should be slow to punish, and swift to reward."

Sit tibi terra levis. Lat.—"Light lie the earth upon thy grave."—This was the wish of the Romans to a departed friend, from an idea that the clay which covered the guilty dead, was heavy, painful, and oppressive.

Si veris magna paratur
Fama bonis, et si successu nuda remoto
Inspicitur virtus, quicquid laudamus in ullo
Majorum, fortuna fuit. Lat. LUCAN.
"If honest fame awaits upon the truly good—if setting aside the ultimate success, virtue and valour are alone to be considered, then was his fortune as proud as any to be found in the records of our ancestry."—This is the poetic incense offered at the shrine of Pompey.

Si vis incolumem, si vis te reddere sanum,
Curas tolle graves, irasci crede profanum. Lat.
"If you wish to preserve yourself in health and safety, avoid all serious cares, and never give way to vehement passion."

Si vis me flere, dolendum est
Primum ipsi tibi. Lat. HORACE.
"If you wish me to weep, you must first appear to be yourself affected."—This was the precept of the didactic to the tragic poet. It is equally applicable to the actor in tragedy, and to every public speaker.

Si volet usus,
Quem penes arbitrium est, et jus et norma loquendi. Lat. HORACE.
"If usage so wills it, within whose power is the rule and law of speech."—The use and pronunciation of particular words and expressions are arbitrary, and must be governed by the fashion of the day.

Sobriquet. Fr.—"A nick-name."

Soi-disant. French.—"Self-called."—The *soi-disant* Marquis—the self-styled Marquis.

Soirée. Fr.—"An evening."—an evening appropriated to literary conversation.

Sola juvat virtus. Lat.—"Virtue alone assists me."

Solamen miseris, socios habuisse doloris. Lat. VIRG.
"It is a comfort to the wretched to have companions in misery."

Sola nobilitas virtus Lat.—"Virtue alone is true nobility."

Sola salus servire Deo. Lat.—" Our only safety is in serving God."

Sola virtus invicta. Lat.—" Virtue alone is invincible."

Solitudinem faciunt, pacem appellant. Lat. TAC.—" They make a desert, and call that tranquillity." —They exterminate a people, and then say that peace is restored.

Sol occubuit; nox nulla secuta est. Lat.—" The sun set, but no night followed."—An ingenious stroke of flattery, addressed to the successor to a throne. The meaning is, " The sun of your father's glory is set, but we feel not the loss, whilst enlightened by your radiance."

Solvit ad diem. Lat. Law Term.—" He paid it to the day."—This is a plea to an action of debt on a bond or penal bill, by which it is alleged that the money was paid on the day assigned.

Solvuntur tabulæ. Lat.—" The bills are dismissed." —The defendant is acquitted.

Sonat vitium. Lat. PERS.—" It sounds as if cracked."—There is a hidden defect or mischief in it.

Soyez ferme. Fr.—" Be firm."—Persevere.

Spargere voces in vulgum ambiguas. Lat. VIRGIL. " To scatter ambiguous sounds among the crowd." To circulate deceptive rumours amongst the populace.

Spectantes plaudebant in re fictâ; quid arbitramur in verâ fuisse facturos? Lat.—" The spectators applauded the *representation*—how would they have been affected, if they had witnessed the *fact?*"

Spectas, et tu spectabere. Lat.—" You see, and you shall be seen."—You witness here the exhibition of character, but if your faults deserve it, you shall be exhibited in your turn.

Spectatum admissi, risum teneatis amici? Latin. HORACE.—" Can even the friends who are admitted to see (the picture), refrain from laughter?"

—Must not the risible mucles, even of partiality, give way at an exhibition so ridiculous.

Spectemur agendo. Lat.—"Let us be tried by our actions.—"Let us be examined by our conduct.

Spem bonam certamque domum reporto. Lat.—"I bring home with me a good and certain hope." —The prospect which I am to open is highly soothing and encouraging.

Spem pretio non emo. Lat. TERENCE.—"I do not give prompt payment for hope."—I do not annex any value to idle expectations.

Sperate, et vosmet rebus servate secundis. Lat. VIRG. —"L. ve in hope, and reserve yourselves for more prosp. rous circumstances."—An appeal from the only source of consolation left, to companions in severe adversity.

Sperate, miseri, cavete felices. Lat.—"Let the wretched live in hope, and the happy be upon their guard."—The mutability of fortune is such, that the lowest have nothing to expect, and the highest something to fear.

Sperat infestis, metuit secundis
Alteram sortem, bene preparatum
Pectus. Lat. HORACE.

"The breast which is well prepared, hopes every thing in adversity, and fears every thing in prosperity."—The philosophic mind can buoy up in distress by hope, and curb the insolence of success, by reflecting on its instability.

Speravimus ista,
Dum fortuna fuit. Lat. VIRGIL.

"We too have hoped for such things, when favoured by fortune."—We presumed as far in our better days.

Sperne voluptates—-nocet empta dolore voluptas. Lat. HORACE.—"Despise all vain enjoyment,—it is injurious when purchased at the price of pain."—The pursuit of pleasure to excess, not only takes away the faculty of enjoyment, but leaves a permanent sting behind.

Spero meliora. Lat.—"I hope for better times, or things."

Spes durat avorum. Lat.—"The hope of my ancestors continues."

Spes mea Christus. Lat.—"Christ is my hope."

Spes mea in Deo. Lat.—"My hope is in God."

Spes tutissima cœlis. Lat.—"The safest hope is in Heaven."

Spolia opima. Lat.—When a Roman general slew a general of the enemy in single combat, the spoils which he took from him were called *spolia opima*, and were hung up in the temple of Jupiter Feretrius.—"The rich booty."

Sponte sua, sine lege, fidem rectumque colebant. Lat.—"Freely, and without the injunctions of law, they maintained good faith, and justice."

S. P. Q. R. an abbreviation of *Senatus Populus Que Romanus.*—"The Senate and Roman people."

Spretæ injuria formæ. Lat. VIRGIL.—"The insult offered to her despised beauty."—This is spoken of the resentment of *Juno*, in consequence of the well-known judgment of *Paris*. The intrigues of courts, where women bear sway, has made it a phrase of modern application.

Stans pede in uno. Lat. HOR.—"Standing upon one leg."—A work composed *stans pede in uno*—with no more than an ordinary degree of exertion.

Stant cætera tigno. Lat.—"The rest stand on a beam."

Stare decisis, et non quieta movere. Lat. Law Max.—"To stand by things as decided, and not to disturb those which are tranquil."—It is advisable to act upon the ground of precedent, and to resist all innovation.

Stare super vias antiquas. Lat.—"To stand firm on the old paths,"—and not give way to any bold novelties.

Statim daret, ne differendo videretur negare. Lat. CORN. NEP.—"He would give at once, lest by delaying he should seem to deny the favour.'

Stat magni nominis umbra. Lat. LUCAN.—"He stands the shadow of a mighty name."—He exhibits only a faint image of his former greatness—and,

Stat nominis umbra. Lat.—The same as the preceding, omitting "mighty."

Stat promissa fides. Lat.—"The promised faith remains."

Stat pro ratione voluntas. Lat.—"My will stands in the place of reason."—Applied to a despot, who ordains that his caprices should be obeyed as law See "*Sic volo,*" &c.

Stat sua cuique dies; breve et irreparabile tempus
Omnibus est vitæ; sed famam extendere factis,
Hoc virtutis opus. Lat. VIRGIL.
"Every man has his brief portion of life, and of time, which can not be recalled; but it belongs to virtue (or valour) alone, to extend our fame by our deeds."—Superior genius or virtue can overleap the brief span of human life, and consecrate the name of its possessor to immortality.

Status quo. Lat.—"The state in which," or *status quo ante bellum.*—"The state in which both parties were before the war."—This is used in speaking of belligerent powers when they agree, as a preliminary to peace, to restore their conquests, and to return to that condition in which the parties respectively stood, before the commencement of hostilities.

Stavo bene, ma, per star meglior, sto qui. Ital.—"I was well, but by endeavouring to be better, I am here."—The epitaph on an hypochondriac, who, though well in health, was not easy until he had quacked himself into his grave.—Used to mark the discontent of those who are dissatisfied when in an eligible situation.

Stemmata quid faciunt? quid prodest, Pontice, longo
Sanguine censeri. Lat. JUVENAL
"Of what avail are pedigrees, or to derive one's blood from a long train of lofty ancestors?"—With

out virtue or genius, what are the boasted advantages of high birth?

Sternitur, infelix, alieno vulnere. Lat. VIRGIL.—"Ill-fated man! he is slain by a blow aimed at another."

Stet. Lat.—"Let it stand."—A marginal direction on a *proof-sheet*, to let a word or letter, which had been obliterated, remain.

Stimulos dedit æmula virtus. Lat. LUCAN.—"He was spurred on by rival valour."—An honourable emulation is the best incentive to acts of greatness.

Stratum super stratum. Lat.—"One layer upon another."—Beds of matter ranged alternately one upon the other.

Strenua nos exercet inertia; navibus atque
Quadrigis petimus bene vivere. Quod petis hic
est. Lat. HORACE.

"We are here but idly busy; our ships and carriages are employed to take us to happiness. That which we seek is on the spot."—It is not for change of place to afford that happiness, which is only to be found in the bosom of honest consciousness.

Studiis et rebus honestis. Lat.—"By honest pursuits and studies."

Studio fallente laborem. Lat. HOR.—"With zeal so ardent as to beguile the labour or fatigue."

Studium immane loquendi. Lat.—"The insatiable rage for talking."

Stulti malorum memoria torquentur. Lat. CICERO.—"Fools suffer themselves to be tormented by the remembrance of past evils."

Stultitia plerumque exitio est. Lat.—"Foolery is often fatal."

Stultitiam patiunter opes. Lat.—"Riches will bear out folly."—The rich fool is suffered to play such pranks with impunity, as if played off by one in an inferior station, would meet not only with derision, but punishment.

Stultitiam simulare loco, sapientia summa est: Lat. Prov.—"To assume the garb of folly is, in certain situations, the most consummate wisdom."—Such was the conduct of the first *Brutus*, who, by affecting to be mad, eluded the vengeance of *Tarquin*, and ultimately succeeded in expelling that tyrant.

Stultorum incurata malus pudor ulcera celat. Lat. HORACE.—"The false shame of fools makes them conceal their uncured sores."—It is the height of folly, to conceal our faults from those, from whom we may derive amendment.—This maxim applies itself both morally and physically.

Stultum est timere, quod vitare non potes. Lat. SYRUS.—"It is idle to dread that which you can not avoid."—In such a case, instead of giving way to fear, we should summon all our fortitude.

Stultus labor est ineptiarum. Lat. MART.—"The labour is silly which is bestowed on trifles."—Industry is respectable only when it is applied to useful objects.

Stultus, nisi quod ipse facit, nil rectum putat. Lat. Prov.—"The fool thinks nothing well done, but what is done by himself."

Sua cuique voluptas. Lat. Prov.—"Each man has his own pleasure."—Every person has a taste for some particular enjoyment.

Suam quisque homo rem meminit. Lat. PLAUTUS.—"Every one can remember that which has interested himself."

Sua quisque exempla debet æquo animo pati. Lat. PHÆDRUS.—"Every man is bound to tolerate the act of which he has himself given the example."—No man can fairly complain of that, as an injustice, of which he has himself furnished a previous specimen.

Suave est ex magno tollere acervo. Lat. HORACE.—"It is pleasant to take from a large heap."—The poet speaks sarcastically of a miser, whose perverse delight it is to take from a large hoard, the little which he dares to use.

Suave, mari magno, turbantibus æquora ventis,
E terrâ magnum alterius spectare laborem
Lat. LUCRETIUS

"It is pleasant, when the sea runs high, to view from land the great distresses of another."—It is not uncommon for men to enjoy the distresses of others, when they can indulge the sense of their own security.

Suaviter in modo, fortiter in re. Lat.—"Gentle in the manner, but vigorous in the deed."—In affairs of importance, outward complacency should be joined with inward firmness.

Sub hoc signo vinces. Lat.—"Under this sign thou shalt conquer."—Alluding to the cross which appeared in the air, as the signal of victory, to CONSTANTINE.

Sublatâ causâ, tollitur effectus. Lat.—"When the cause is removed, the effect must cease."

Sublimi feriam sidera vertice. Lat. HORACE.—"My lofty head shall strike the stars."—This flight of the poet is now employed as a common place pleasantry.

Sub pœnâ. Law Lat.—"Under a penalty."—The name given to a writ for the summoning of witnesses; and,

Subpœnâ duces tecum. A writ commanding a man to appear, and "bring with him" some piece of evidence that the court wishes to see.

Sub silentio. Lat.—"In silence."—The matter passed *sub silentio*—without any notice being taken.

Sub rosâ. Lat.—"Under the rose."—Secretly.

Substantia prior et dignior est accidente. Lat. Law Maxim.—"The substance should be considered as prior to, and of more weight than the accident."—No judgment, it is held, shall be arrested in any court of record for any defect in point of *form*, or unless it be a matter of *substance* on which the judges of those courts are to decide.

Succedaneum. Lat.—"A substitute."—A matter substituted.—Impudence is frequently used as a *succedaneum* for argument.

Sufficit ad id, Natura quod poscit. Lat. SENECA.—"We have a sufficiency, when we have what Nature requires."—Her wants are but few, and the consciousness of this should each us limitation and content.

Suggestio falsi. Lat.—"The suggestion of a falsehood."—This, and the *suppressio veri*, or "suppression of the truth," are the strongest charges which can be made against a public orator or writer.

Sui cuique mores fingunt fortunam. Lat. CORN. NEPOS.—"His own morals (or manners) shape the fortune of every man."—Thus, the English proverb, "manners make the man."

Sui generis. Lat.—"Of its own kind."—Not to be classed under any ordinary description.

Sumite materiam vestris, qui scribitis, æquam
Viribus. Lat. HORACE.
"Let those who write, fix on a subject to which their force is equal."—Every author should look to his mental powers, and consider whether they are equal to the task which he is about to undertake.

Summum nec metuas diem, nec optes. Lat. MART.—"You should neither fear, nor wish for, your last day."—The philosophic mind neither timidly shrinks from death, nor desperately wishes to accelerate its approach.

Summum bonum. Lat.—"The chief good."—The object of attainment most desirable, which some of the ancient philosophers stated to be pleasure, and others virtue.

Summum crede nefas, animam præferre pudori,
Et propter vitam, vivendi perdere causas.
Lat. JUVENAL.
"Believe it to be the last of all infamies, to prefer your existence to your honour, or, for the sake of life, to lose every inducement to live."

Summum jus, summa injuria. Lat.—"Strictness of law is sometimes the greatest injustice."—A too rigorous interpretation of the law is not unfrequently productive of results which do not accord with equity.

Sum quod eris, fui quod sis. Lat.—" I am what thou shalt be, as I have been what thou now art."—An admonition frequently met with as a sepulchral inscription.

Sunt lachrymæ rerum, et mentem mortalia tangunt. Lat. VIRGIL.—" Tears are due to human misery, and the woes of mortality affect the mind."—Every virtuous mind on hearing of such calamities, must be touched by sympathy.

Sunt superis sua jura. Lat. OVID.—" The gods or supreme powers have their own laws."—This is sometimes quoted in political discussions, to intimate that the higher powers often overlook those duties and promises, which are supposed to be binding on the lower orders of the community.

Suo Marte. Lat.—" By his own exertion."—He performed it *suo Marte*—by his own unaided skill and ability.

Suo sibi gladio hunc jugulo. Lat. TER.—" With his own sword do I stab this man."—I defeat him, in argument, with the weapons and the admissions which he has himself furnished.

Superanda omnis fortuna ferendo est. Lat. VIRGIL. " Every misfortune is to be subdued by patience."

Supersedeas. Law Lat.—" You may remove or set aside."—A writ to stay proceedings.

Super subjectam materiam. Lat.—" On the subject submitted."—A lawyer is not responsible for his opinion, when it is given *super subjectam materiam*—on the circumstances, as they are laid before him by his client.

Super visum corporis. Law Lat.—" Upon a view of the body."—A coroner holds his inquest, *super visum corporis.*

Supremum
Carpere iter comites parati. Lat. HORACE. " Friends, prepared to take the last journey together"—to die with each other.

Suppressio veri. Lat.—See *suggestio falsi.*

Surgit amari aliquid, quod in ipsis floribus angat. Lat. LUCRETIUS.—"Something bitter ever arises, and alloys our highest pleasures."

Surgo ut prossim. Lat.—"I rise to do good."—I exert myself for the public benefit.

Suspectum semper invisumque dominantibus, qui proximus destinaretur Lat. TACITUS.—"The next in succession is ever hated and suspected by those, who are actually in possession of the supreme power."

Suum cuique. Lat.—"Let each man have his own." —Let the laws of property be strictly observed.

Suum cuique incommodum ferendum est, potius quam de alterius commodis detrahendum. Lat. CIC.—"Every man should bear his own grievance and inconveniences, rather than detract from, or abridge the comforts of, another."

Suus cuique mos. Lat. TERENCE.—"Each man has his particular habit."—In opinions and habitudes, there is a permanent diversity, and every person should in fairness, be left to the free exercise of his own.

T

Tabula rasa. Lat.—"A shaved or smoothed tablet." —His mind is a *tabula rasa*—it is a mere blank. The idea is taken from the waxed tablets of the ancients, on which they made their *memoranda* with a sharp instrument called a *stylus*, with the other flatted end of which they afterwards erased what they had written.

Table d'hote. Fr.—"A public eating house—An ordinary."

Tacent, satis laudant. Lat. TER.—"Their silence is sufficient praise."—It is ample proof of worth, when the censorious have nothing to allege.

Tâche sans tâche. Fr.—"A work without a stain."

Tacitum vivit sub pectore vulnus. Lat. VIRGIL —"The secret wound still lives within the breast." —The injury is not forgotten, but is treasured up for an opportunity of revenge.

Tædium vitæ. Lat.—"A weariness of life."—A disgust of existence.—This, in France, is called *Ennui*, but this does not amount to the full force of the Latin term.

Tale tuum carmen nobis, divina Poeta,
Quale sopor fessis. Lat. VIRGIL.
"As pleasing are thy verses to us, divine Poet, as sleep is to the wearied," &c."—This compliment, for such it is meant in the original, is sometimes ironically turned against a different description of Poets, who are

"*Sleepless* themselves, to give their readers *sleep!*"

Talibus ex adyto dictis, Cumæa Sibylla
Horrendas canit ambages, antroque remugit,
Obscuris vera involvens. Lat. VIRGIL.
"In words like these, the Sybil utters her fearful oracles of dubious import, and sounds them forth from her cavern, blending truth with obscurity."—This quotation is frequently used to reprobate a style which is at once pompous and ambiguous.

Tam deest avaro quod habet, quam quod non habet. Lat. SYRUS.—"The miser is as much in want of that which he has, as of that which he has not!"—for he fears to make use of what he has.

Tam Marte quam Minervâ. Lat.—"As much by Mars as by Minerva."—He has succeeded "*tam Marte quam Minervâ*,"—equally by his courage and his genius.

Tam Marti quam Mercurio. Lat.—"As much for Mars as for Mercury."—As well qualified for war as for merchandise.

Tandem fit surculus arbor. Lat.—"A shoot at length becomes a tree."

Tantæne animis cœlestibus iræ? Lat. VIRGIL.—"Can heavenly minds such anger entertain?"—Is it possible for exalted minds to descend to such low resentments?

Tanti eris, quanti tu te facias. Lat.—"You shall be esteemed in proportion to your merit."

Tantis parta malis, cura majore metuque
Servantur. Lat. JUVENAL
"That wealth, which is acquired by so much labour and so many privations, can be preserved only by greater anxiety and solicitude."

Tant mieux. Fr.—"So much the better."

Tanto buon, che val niente. Ital. Prov.—"So good, that he is good for nothing."—Applied to that weak good nature, which is injurious to the possessor, without being of advantage to any other person.

Tanto homini fidus, tantæ virtutis amator. Lat.—"A faithful friend to so great a man, and a steady admirer of such distinguished excellence."

Tant pis. Fr.—"So much the worse."

Tantum de medio sumptis accedit honoris. Lat. HORACE.—"So much of honour is due to subjects taken from middle or common life."—This is a phrase very justly granted to the authors of such plays as "*George Barnwell,*" or, the "*Gamester,*" where the sentiments come home to every man's business and bosom, as contra-distinguished to those, where emperors, queens, and heroes fill the scene; and whose sorrows astound for the moment, but in a moment are forgotten.

Tantum se fortunæ permittunt, etiam ut naturam dediscant. Lat. QUINT. CURT.—"They give themselves up so much to fortune, as even to forget their nature."

Tantum series juncturaque pollet. Lat. HORACE.—"Of so much force is system and connexion."

Tarda sit illa dies, et nostro serior ævo. Lat. OVID.—"Long may it be before that day arrives, and after our period of existence."

Tardè, quæ credita lædunt, credimus. Lat. OVID—"We are slow to believe that, which, if believed, would hurt our feelings."

Te Deum (laudamus). Lat.—"Thee, Lord, (we

praise)."—These are the initial words of a musical service, usually celebrated in the churches, in Catholic countries, on the occasion of a victory, or any other great national event.

Tel brille au second rang, qui s'éclipse au premier. Fr.—"A man my shine in the second rank, who would be eclipsed in the first."—Many who conceive themselves fitted for first-rate characters in life, would in fact appear to more advantage in subordinate situations.

Tel en vous lisant, admire chaque trait,
Qui, dans le fond de l'ame, et vous craint et vous haït. Fr. Boileau.
"Such a one on reading your work, admires every stroke, but from the bottom of his soul, he fears and hates you."—The living satirist excites more of fear than of regard.

Tel maître, tel valet. Fr. Prov.—"Like master, like man."

Τελος οραν μαχρου Βιου. Gr. *Telos oran macrou Biou.*—"To see the end of a long life."—This was the wish of Chilias, one of the celebrated seven wise men of Greece.

Telum imbelle sine ictu. Lat. Virgil.—"A feeble weapon thrown without effect."—Applied metaphorically, to a weak or imbecile argument.

Tel vous semble applaudir, qui vous raille et vous joue;
Aimez qu'on vous conseille, et non pas qu'on vous loue. Fr. Boileau
"That man appears to applaud you, who in fact makes you his jest and sport. Let your inclination be to those who advise, rather than to those who praise your conduct."

Temeritas à sapientiâ dissidet plurimum. Lat. Cic —"Rashness differs widely from wisdom."

Temeritas est florentis ætatis, prudentia senectutis. Lat. Cic.—"Rashness is the characteristic of ardent youth, and prudence that of mellowed age."

Templa quam dilecta! Lat.—"Temples how beloved!"

Tempora mutantur, et nos mutamur in illis. Lat —"The times are changed, and we are changed with them."—There is nothing fixed or stable, either in situations or opinions.

"Men change with fortune, manners change with climes,
Tenets with books, and principles with times."

Tempora si fuerint nubila, solus eris. Lat. OVID. "If the stormy season should arrive, you will be alone."—Adversity finds but few companions or comforters.

Tempore ducetur longo fortasse cicatrix:
Horrent admotas vulnera cruda manus.
Lat. OVID.

"The wound will perhaps be healed by the process of time, but it shrinks from the touch, whilst it is yet recent."—This is figuratively applied to sorrow, which, in the first burst, will reject the most friendly attempt at consolation.

Tempore felici, multi numerantur amici;
Si fortuna perit, nullus amicus erit. Lat. Ov.
"In prosperity we can discover many friends; but if fortune fails, not one is to be found."

Tempus edax rerum. Lat. HORACE.—"Time that devours all things."

Tempus omnia revelat. Lat.—"Time reveals all things."—Few things, these two proverbs say, escape the disclosure of time, and nothing, its ravages.

Tenacem propositi. Lat.—"Firm to his purpose."

Tenet insanabile multos
Scribendi cacoëthes, ægroque in corde senescit.
"Many have an incurable itch for writing, which takes full possession of their disordered faculties." —The race has been numerous, in every age, of those

"——— who in despite
Of nature, and their stars, will write."

Tentanda via est, quâ me quoque possim
Tollere humo. Lat. VIRGIL.
"I also must endeavour, by some means, to raise

myself from obscurity."—This is a motto very frequently prefixed to the maiden productions of young authors.

Terræ filius. Lat.—" A son of the earth."—An Oxford phrase, signifying a man of no birth.

Terra firma. Lat.—" Solid earth,"—safe footing.

Terra incognita. Lat.—" An unknown land or coun try."—Such as the central parts of Africa.

Terra malos homines nunc educat, atque pusillos. Lat. JUVENAL.
" This earth now maintains, as before, both bad and weak men."—The condition of the human species in all ages, is nearly the same.

Tertium quid. Lat.—" A third something."—Struck out by the collision of two opposite forces or principles.

Tertius è cœlo cecidit Cato. Lat. JUV.—" A third Cato has dropped down from heaven."—Another rigid moralist has made his appearance.

Testamentum, nisi post mortem testatoris, vim non habet. Lat. Law Max.—" No will can have any force, until after the death of the testator."

Της φυσεος γραμματευς ην, τον καλαμον αποβρεξον εις νουν. Gr. SUIDAS. *Tes Phuseos grammateus en, ton calamon apobrexon eis noun.*—" He was the writer, or interpreter of nature, dipping his pen into *Mind.*"

Tête à tête. Fr.—" Head to head."—In close conversation.

Tibi nullum periculum esse perspicio, quod quidem sejunctum sit ab omnium interitu. Lat. CIC.—" I can see no danger to which you are personally exposed, separately and apart from the destruction of us all "

Tiens ta foy. Fr.—" Keep thy faith."

Timeo Danaos et dona ferentes. Lat. VIRGIL.—" I fear the Greeks, even when they offer presents. '—I am on my guard against an enemy, and particularly, when he proffers kindness.

Timet pudorem. Lat.—" He fears shame."

Timidus se vocat cautum, parcum sordidus. Lat. Prov.—"The cowardly man says that he is cautious, the miser that he is frugal."—We have each an excuse, or palliation for our respective faults.

Tirer le diable par le queue. Fr. Prov.—"To pull the devil by the tail."—To be put to one's shifts for a livelihood.

Toga virilis. Lat.—"The manly robe."—This was the dress, which the Roman youth assumed on reaching a certain period of life.—He has assumed the *toga virilis*—he has entered into a state of manhood

Το ὅλον. Gr. *To holon.*—"The whole."—Unity.

Το χαλον. Gr. *To Kalon.*—"The *summum bonum,*"—The supreme good.

Tolle jocos—non est jocus esse malignum. Lat.—"Away with such jests—there is no jest in being malignant."—This is properly applied to that sarcastic merriment, which wounds the peace or feelings of the individual, for the purpose of giving entertainment to the many.

Tolle moras—semper nocuit differre paratis. Lat. Lucan.—"Away with all delays—it is ever injurious to postpone, when you are in readiness."—The application is in particular to war. When you are ready, you should allow the enemy no time for preparation.

Tolluntur in altum,
Ut lapsu graviore ruant. Lat. Claudian.
"They are raised to such a height, that they may tumble with a heavier fall."—Some men seem to have been raised to the summit of their ambition, only to aggravate their subsequent reverses.

Το πρεπον. Gr. *To prepon.*—"That which is decorous."—Decency, decorum.

Totam Philosophiam revocavit ad mores. Lat. Sen. "He (Socrates) made all his philosophy subservient to morality."

Tot homines quot sententiæ. Lat.—"So many men, so many opinions."—There will be as many different suffrages as heads.

Totidem verbis. Lat.—"In just so many words."

Toties quoties. Lat.—"As many times as, then so often."—A term frequently used in law proceedings, as thus;—If A. B. commit a certain offence, he shall be fined $10., and so on, *toties quoties*, viz. on every repetition of the offence, he shall incur a similar penalty.

Totis viribus. Lat.—"With all his might or force."

Totius injustitiæ nulla capitalior est, quam eorum, qui cum maximè fallunt, id agunt, ut viri boni esse videantur. Lat. Cic.—"There is no species of injustice so vile as that of those, who, while they practise the grossest frauds, assume the appearance of good men."

Toto cœlo. Lat.—"By the whole heavens."—The men differ *toto cœlo*—their dispositions, (or opinions,) are as opposite as the two poles.

Totus hic locus est contemnendus in nobis, non negligendus in nostris. Lat. Cic.—"This place (the place of our sepulture) is wholly to be disregarded by us, but not to be neglected by our surviving friends."

Totus in toto, et totus in qualibet parte. Lat.—"Whole in itself, and whole in every part."—This was the definition given by the ancient scholiasts, of the human mind.

Totus mundus agit histrionem. Latin.—"All the world acts the player."—All the world's a stage.

Totus teres atque rotundus. Lat.—"Every way round and smooth."—A man so polished as to roll through the world unbiased by any asperity.

Toujours prêt. Fr.—"Always ready."

Toujours propice. Fr.—"Ever propitious."

Tour d'expression. Fr.—"A peculiar turn or mode of expression."—An idiom.

Tourner casaque. Fr.—"To turn a man's coat."—This in former times was regarded as a disgrace.

Tous frais faits. Fr.—"All expenses paid."

Tous les hommes sont fous, et malgré leurs soins,
Ne diffèrent entr'eux, que du plus ou du moins.
Fr. Boileau.

"All men are fools, and with every effort, they can only differ in the degree."—There will only be the more foolish, and the less foolish.

Tout bien ou rien. Fr.—"The whole or nothing."

Tout éloge imposteur blesse une ame sincère. Fr. Boileau.—"Nothing wounds a feeling mind more than praise unjustly bestowed."

Tout ensemble. Fr.—"The whole taken together."

Tout est pris. Fr.—"All is taken."—Every avenue to fame and to fortune is pre-occupied.

Tout le monde se plaint de sa mémoire, et personne ne se plaint de son jugement. Fr. Rochefoucault.—"Every man complains of his memory, but no man complains of his judgment."—Our pride will not suffer us to impeach the latter.

Tout lui rit. Fr.—"All goes well with him."

Trahimur omnes laudis studio. Lat. Cic.—"We are all incited by the love of praise."

Trahit ipsa furoris
Impetus, et visum est lenti quæsisse nocentem.
Lat. Lucan.

"They are borne away by the violence of their rage, and they think it a waste of time to inquire who are the guilty."—This is a forcible description of popular and indiscriminate vengeance.

Trahit sua quemque voluptas. Lat. Virg.—"Each man is led by his own peculiar taste or pleasure."—A remark on the ever-prevailing diversity of tastes and passions.

Trahit quodcunque potest, atque addit acervo. Lat. Hor.—"Brings what he can, and adds it to the heap."

Transeat in exemplum. Lat.—"May it pass into an example."—May an act so meritorious stand recorded as a precedent for others to follow.

Tria juncta in uno. Lat.—"Three joined in one."—This is sometimes used in speaking of the Trini ty;—oftener in speaking of a political coalition, consisting of three members.

Tribus Anticyris caput insanabile. Lat. HORACE.—"A head incurable by three Anticyræ."—The island of Anticyra, in the Archipelago, was famous for the growth of hellebore, which is administered to purge the head.—The phrase therefore means an incurable madman.

Triumpho morte tam vita. Lat.—"I triumph in death, as in life."

Tros, Tyriusve, mihi nullo discrimine agetur. Lat. VIRGIL. "The Trojan and the Tyrian shall be treated by me without distinction."—I profess no attachment to either of the contending parties, and shall of course speak of them with due impartiality.

Truditur dies die. Lat. HORACE.—"One day is pressed onward by another."—The progress of time, however neglected by man, is silent and irresistible.

Trunco, non frondibus, efficit umbram. Lat.—"It casts a shade, not with its foliage, but with its trunk."

Tua res agitur, paries cum proximus ardet. Lat. HORACE.—"Your affairs are at stake, when the next house is on fire."—We should remember, that the calamity, which afflicts our neighbour, most seriously threatens ourselves.

Tuebor. Lat.—"I will defend."

Tu ne cede malis, sed contra audentior ito. Lat. VIRGIL.—"Do not yield to misfortunes, but meet them on the contrary with fortitude."—You can only subdue adversity by bearing up against it.

Tuo tibi judicio est utendum. Virtutis et vitiorum grave ipsius conscientiæ pondus est; quâ sublatâ, jacent omnia. Lat. CIC.—"You must use your own judgment on yourself. Great is the weight of conscience in deciding on your own virtues and vices: if that be taken away, all is lost."

Tu pulmentaria quære sudando. Lat. HOR.—"Do

you seek an appetite for plain food, by sweat-inducing labour."

Tu quoque, Brute! Lat.—"And thou too, *Brutus!*" —This was the exclamation of Julius Cæsar, when he discovered Brutus among the conspirators in the senate-house.

Tu recte vives, si curas esse quod audis. Lat. Hor. "You will be truly a good man, if you are careful to be what you are supposed to be," or, to act up to your professions.

Turpe est aliud loqui, aliud sentire; quanto turpius aliud scribere, aliud sentire? Lat. Seneca.—"It is dishonourable to speak one thing, and to think another; but how much more base is it, to write that which is contrary to a man's real sentiments?" —The act of *writing* is of greater deliberation, and of broader tendency. An attempt to deceive in this way, is therefore more highly criminal.

Turpe est in patriâ peregrinari, et in iis rebus quæ ad patriam pertinent, hospitem esse. Lat. Manutius.—"It is shameful for a man to live as a stranger in his own country, and to be uninformed of her affairs and interests."

Turpe est laudari ab illaudatis. Lat.—"It is degrading to be commended by those, who are not themselves worthy of praise."

Turpe est relinqui. Lat.—"It is shameful to be left behind."—To be excelled by all others.

Turpe est viro, id, in quo quotidie versatur, ignorare. Lat.—"It is shameful that a man should be ignorant of that, in which he is every day employed."

Turpis et ridicula res est elementarius senex: juveni parandum, seni utendum est. Lat. Sen.—"Nothing can be so ridiculous or absurd, as to see an old man in his rudiments. It is for youth to acquire, and for age to employ those acquirements."

Turpiter obticuit, sublato jure nocendi. Lat.—"He was shamefully silent when he had lost the power to injure."

Tu si hic sis, aliter sentias. Lat.—"If you were in my place, you would think otherwise."

Tussis pro crepitu. Lat.—A poor pretext to cover a foul act, or design.

Tuta timens. Lat.—"Fearing even that which is safe."—Men, who are at the pinnacle of fortune, should know that they are not out of the reach of its vicissitudes.

Tutor et ultor. Latin.—"The protector and the avenger."—A compliment of little meaning, but which is generally found on the medals inscribed to a successful prince or potentate.

Tuum est. Lat.—"It is your own."

U

Uberibus semper lachrymis, semperque paratis
In statione suâ, atque expectantibus illam
Quo jubeat manare. Lat.
"She has an inexhaustible fund of tears ready at a call, and the flow of which she has only to direct."

Uberrima fides. Lat. Phr.—"A full growth of confidence."—An implicit faith or reliance.

Ubicunque ars ostentatur, veritas abesse videtur. Lat.—"Wherever art is displayed, truth seems to be wanting."—We seldom witness a laborious exertion to excite interest or to give pleasure, that we do not begin to doubt the reality of the interest or pleasure, which is thus forced upon us.

Ubi jus incertum ibi jus nullum. Lat. Law Max.—"Where the law is uncertain, there is no law."—No legal decision can properly be made on vague and undefined enactment.

Ubi lapsus?—Quid feci? Lat.—"Where am I fallen? What have I done?"

Ubi libertas, ibi patria. Lat.—"Where liberty dwells, there is my country."

Ubi major pars est, ibi est totum. Lat. Law Max.—"Where the greater part is, there, by law, is the whole."—The only way of determining the acts of many, is by the major part, or the majority; as the majority in parliament enact laws, &c.

Ubi mel, ibi apes. Lat. PLAUTUS.—"Where there is honey, there will be bees."—Where there is a pleasing attraction, there will be no want of followers.

Ubi non est lex, ibi non est transgressio. Lat. Law Maxim.—"Where there is no law, there can be no trespass."

Ubi plura nitent in carmine, non ego paucis
Offendar maculis, quas aut incuria fudit,
Aut humana parum cavit natura. Lat. HOR.
"Where there are many beauties in a work, I shall not cavil at a few faults, proceeding either from negligence, or from the imperfection of our nature."

Ubi plus mali, quam boni, reperio, id totum abjudico atque rejicio. Lat. CIC.—"Whenever I discover in any thing, more of evil than of good, I wholly refuse and reject it."

Ubique patriam reminisci. Lat.—"Every where to remember our country."

Ubi reddunt ova columbæ. Lat. JUVENAL.—"Where the pigeons lay their eggs."—This at Rome, was in the interstices under the roofs of houses, in the garrets of which then, as now, poets had that honourable residence, which by some is called "the first floor down the chimney," and by others, "the roost of eminence," and still more generally, "the *Attic* story."

Ubi supra. Lat.—"Where above-mentioned."—A reference to a preceding quotation.

Ubi velis nolunt, ubi nolis volunt ultro;
Concessâ pudet ire viâ. Lat. TERENCE.
"When you are willing, they are disinclined—when you are averse, they are willing. They are loth to tread in that path where it is permitted."—This is rather a severe description of the caprices of woman.

Ultima ratio regum. Lat.—"The last reasoning of kings."—An appeal to violence and hostility. This inscription, if we rightly recollect, was ordered to be graven by Louis XIV. on his cannon.

Ultima semper
Expectanda dies homini est, dicique beatus
Ante obitum nemo supremaque funera debet.
Lat. Ovid.

"Man should ever look to his last day, and no man should be accounted happy before his decease, or until his funeral rites are performed."—Such is the instability of human affairs, that no man should be deemed fortunate, until death has precluded any further possibility of change.

Ultima Thule. Lat.—Thule was the name of the most northern island known to the Romans, supposed to be one of the Shetland isles.—*Ultima Thule* is therefore used to express the limits of our geographical discoveries; and figuratively, the boundary of our knowledge on any subject.

Ult—ultimus. Lat.—"The last."

Ultimus hæres. Law Lat.—"The last heir;" which, in monarchies, is the king, and in other governments, the State, to whom the property of a deceased intestate *escheats,* in failure of relations.

Ultimatum. Lat.—"The last,"—or the only condition.

Ultimum et unicum remedium. Lat.—"The last and only remedy."

Ultimus suorum moriatur! Lat.—"May he die the last of his kindred!"—May he be so miserable as to survive all his friends!—This was an imprecation used by the Romans upon a man who had been guilty of some enormity.

Una salus victis, nullam sperare salutem. Lat. Virgil.—"The only hope for the conquered is to expect no safety."—The resolute despair of the vanquished sometimes brings about a relief, not to be effected by any other means.

Unde habeas quærit nemo; sed oportet habere. Lat. Juvenal.—"No man inquires how you have got your wealth, (or learning) but it is necessary to possess it."—All men pay respect to riches, without inquiring very scrupulously into the means by which they have been obtained.

*Unde tibi frontem libertatemque parentis,
Cum facias pejora senex.* Lat. JUVENAL. "Whence do you derive the power and privilege of a parent, when you, though an old man, fall into greater errors."—How can you presume to chide your juniors, when you, though advanced in years, set the vicious example.

Un enfant en ouvrant ses yeux, doit voir sa patrie, et jusqu'à la mort, ne voir qu'elle. Fr. ROUSSEAU. —"The infant on first opening his eyes, ought to see his country, and to the hour of his death never to lose sight of it."—The love of our country should be implanted early, and nourished through life.

Unguibus et rostro. Lat.—"With talons and beak." He fought it *unguibus et rostro*—tooth and nail.

Unguis in ulcere. Lat. CIC.—"A nail in the wound." —This strong phrase was applied by the orator to the conspirator *Catiline.* "Your country," he would have said in a periphrase, "has received a dangerous wound, into which, you, vulture-like, infix your talons, for the purpose of irritating and keeping it open."

Un homme d'esprit seroit souvènt bien embarrassé sans la compagnie des sots. Fr. ROCHEFOUCAULT. —"A man of wit would be often embarrassed without the company of fools."—He would lack a butt for his sarcasm.

Un homme, toujours satisfait de lui-meme, peu souvent l'est des autres: rarement on l'est de lui. Fr. ROCHEFOUCAULT.—"A man who is always well satisfied with himself, is seldom so with others, and others are as little pleased with him." —A man, who has an overweening conceit of himself, is too proud to be pleased with the efforts of others, and by that pride, is sure to excite a general disgust against himself."

Uni æquus virtuti, atque ejus amicis. Lat. HOR. "Friendly to virtue alone, and to the friends of virtue."

Unica virtus necessaria. Lat.—"Virtue is the only thing necessary."

Uni quippe vacat, studiis odiisque carenti,
Humanum lugere genus. Lat. LUCAN
"There is only one man, who being equally free from attachments and resentments, is at leisure to weep for the miseries of the human race."—This praise, which the poet has given to *Cato*, applies to the disinterested patriot, who sighs only for the sufferings of his country.

Unique. Fr.—"Sole, singular, extraordinary."—It is an *unique*—it is the *only* thing of its kind.

Uno absurdo dato, infinita sequuntur. Lat.—"One absurdity being admitted, you must submit to all that follow."

Uno avulso, non deficit alter. Lat. VIRG.—"When one is plucked away, another shall not be wanting."—Used in a political sense—remove that man, and you shall have his like for a successor.

Uno tiené la fama, y otro carda la lana. Sp. Prov. —"One man gets the credit, while another cards the wool."—One does the labour, and another bears away the reward.

Unoculus inter cæcos. Lat.—"A one-eyed man among the blind."—A man whose very slender abilities are perceptible only among the grossly ignorant.

Un sot à triple étage. Fr.—"A fool of the third story."—An egregious blockhead.

Un sot trouve toujours un plus sot qui l'admire.
Fr. BOILEAU.
"A fool always finds a greater fool to admire him."—Used in reproaching a silly, or adulatory commendation of an indifferent work."

Un "tiens" vaut mieux que deux "tu l'auras." Fr. Prov.—"One 'hold fast' is better than two 'I'll give thee."—A bird in the hand, &c.

Unus homo nobis cunctando restituit rem,
Non ponebat enim rumores ante salutem.
Fragment of ENNIUS.
"One man by delay retrieved our affairs, for he preferred the public safety to idle report."—This was applied to Fabius, who, by prudently avoiding a battle, at length wasted away the army of Han-

nibal, the inveterate and sworn enemy of the Romans. It is now sometimes quoted, when caution or delay is to be justified on the part of a general or a statesman.

*Unus utrique
Error; sed variis illudit partibus.* Lat. HOR. "The same error belongs to each, but it mocks them in different ways."—Several men may engage in a pursuit of the same folly, yet each travel by a different road.

Urbem lateritiam invenit, marmoream reliquit. Lat. SUETONIUS.—"He found a city built of bricks, and he left it constructed of marble."—This was the boast of *Augustus*, with respect to the city of Rome.

*Urit enim fulgore suo, qui prægravat artes
Infra se positas: extinctus amibitur idem.*
Lat. HORACE.
"He is consumed by his own brightness, who depresses the arts beneath him—yet he, after his decease, shall be admired."—The man of exalted genius, throws, by the splendour of his talents, all inferior merits into shade. He is exposed therefore, to all the shafts of contemporary jealousy His death alone can deprive envy of her sting; then, those who were most forward to detract, will be the first to do justice to his merits.

*Usque adeone
Scire tuum nihil est, nisi te scire hoc sciat alter?*
Lat. PERSIUS.
"Is therefore your own knowledge to pass for no thing, unless others are aware of that knowledge?" —Is it not the sole object of your studies, to im press others with a sense of your acquirements?

Usque adeone mori miserum est? Lat. VIRG.—"Is it then so terrible a thing to die?"—Are the thoughts of mortality then so very dreadful?

Ut ameris, amabilis esto. Lat Ov.—"That you may be beloved, be deserving of love."—To merit re gard, is the surest mode of obtaining it.

Ut apes geometriam. Lat.—"As bees practise geometry."

Utatur motu animi, qui uti ratione non potest. Lat. —"Let him be guided by his passions, who can make no use of his reason."—Fools must be impelled by their passions, but the man of reason is left without an excuse.

Ut coëat par, jungaturque pari. Lat. HORACE. "That men, of similar tastes and pursuits, may be assembled and classed together."

Utcunque placuerit Deo. Lat.—"As it shall please God."

Utendum est ætate, cito pede præterit ætas;
Quàm cuperes votis hunc revocare diem?
Lat. OVID.
"You should employ your youth, which passes swiftly away. With how many wishes will you not then endeavour to recall the present day?"

Uterque bonus belli pacisque minister. Lat. VIRG. —"Both fit for governing in peace and war."—This is a high but rather a scarce character.

Ut homo est, ita morem geras. Lat. TERENCE.—"As the man is, so you should conduct yourself."—This is a practical maxim of the most useful kind. The dexterous man who has a purpose to carry, will be full of deference before the lofty, easy with the free, and complacent with the humble.

Utile dulci. Lat.—"The useful with the pleasant."—To say that he has combined the *utile dulci*—is to give the very first praise to a writer.—See the line at length—"*Omne tulit punctum*," &c.

Utilium sagax rerum. Lat. HORACE.—"Sagacious in making useful discoveries."

Utinam tam facile vera invenire possem, quam falsa convincere. Lat. CICERO.—"I wish that I could as easily discover the truth, as I can detect the falsehood."—I have no clue to the former, but the latter betrays itself by its inconsistency.

Uti possidetis. Lat.—"As you possess."—A diplomatic phrase, used when two sovereigns, after sacrificing a number of human lives, &c. choose to make peace, " both retaining the possessions which they have acquired."—Its opposite is the *status quo*, when both parties re-enter into the condition in which they stood, before the war.

Ut nec pes, nec caput uni
Reddatur formæ. Lat. HORACE.
" So that neither the foot nor the head shall belong to the same form."—Applied to a dramatic piece, or to a picture, where all is incongruity.

Ut pictura, poesis erit. Lat. HOR.—" It will ever be in poetry, as in painting."—There must always be an affinity between those sister arts.

Ut prosim. Lat.—" That I may do good."

Ut pudicè verba fecit! cogitatè et commodè!
Ut modestè orationem prebuit. Lat. PLAUTUS.
" With how much chasteness, good sense, propriety and modesty, did he speak!"

Utque alios industria, ita hunc ignavia ad famam protulerat. Lat. TAC.—" Other men have been advanced to fame by industrious exertion, but this man has succeeded by mere sluggishness and indolence."—The person in question, owes not his elevation to his deserts.

Ut quimus, quando ut volumus non licet. Lat. TER. —" When we can not act as we wish, we must act as we can."

Ut quisque suum vult esse, ita est. Lat. TERENCE. " As every man wishes his (offspring) to be, so it is."—The minds of children are of so plastic a nature, that if they do not answer the hopes of the parent, it is in the greater number of instances, to be attributed to the neglect of their education.

Ut quocunque paratus. Lat.—" Prepared on every side."

Ut redeat miseris, abeat fortuna superbis. Lat. HOR.—" That fortune may quit the proud, and return to the wretched."—That something like the natural equality of condition may be restored.

Ut adversas res, sic secundas immoderatè ferre, levitatis est. Lat. CIC.—" It is indicative of a weak mind, to be much depressed by adversity, or elated by prosperity."

Ut omnes facilius laudare possint, quam æmulari! Lat. Cic.—"How much easier do we find it, to commend, than to imitate" good actions!

Utrum horum mavis, accipe. Lat.—"Take whichever of those you prefer."—A conclusion generally made in argument, after having offered a choice of difficulties.

Ut sæpe summa ingenia in occulto latent. Lat. Plautus.—"How often men of the greatest genius are lost in obscurity."—The exercise and use of surpassing talents are frequently lost to the world, through the want of protection and cultivation.

Ut sementem feceris, ita et metes. Lat. Cic.—"As you have sown, so shall you reap."—As your conduct has been, so shall be its fruits.

Ut vellem his potius nugis, tota illa dedisset
Tempora sævitiæ. Lat. Juvenal.
"Would to heaven, he had given up to trifles like these, *all* the time which he devoted to savage and cruel purposes."—Spoken of a tyrant, whose days were divided between frivolous pursuits, and barbarous inflictions.

V

Vacuus cantat coram latrone viator. Lat. Juvenal. "The man with an empty purse, may sing before the robber."—He of course can lose nothing.

Vade mecum. Lat.—"Go with me."—A young man's *vade mecum*,—that which should be his constant companion.

Væ victis! Lat.—"Wo to the conquered!"—If it should come to that point, *væ victis*—it will be a war of extermination.

Valeat quantum valere potest. Lat.—"Let it prevail as far as it may."—Let the argument pass for as much as it is worth.

Valeat res ludicra. Lat. HOR.—"Farewell to the ridiculous."—Let us leave off all foolery.

Valeant, qui inter nos dissidium volunt. Lat. TER. "Shame upon those, who would create dissension between us."

Valet de chambre. Fr.—"A servant, a waiting-man."

Valete ac plaudite. Lat. TER.—"Farewell and applaud."—This was the conclusion of the Latin comedy. It is now sometimes used in the way of triumphant irony, at the conclusion of a political discourse.

Valet ima summis
Mutare, et insignem attenuat Deus,
Obscura promens. Lat. HORACE.
"The Deity can change the lowest into the highest—can extinguish the proud, and bring forward the humble."—Every sublunary change is marked out by the finger of Providence.

Vana quoque ad veros accessit fama timores. Lat. LUCAN.
"Idle rumours were also added to well-founded apprehensions."—This is a phrase often quoted, as the circumstance constantly recurs, in every great crisis of national difficulty or danger.

Varium et mutabile semper
Fœmina. Lat. VIRGIL.
"A woman is always changeable and capricious."—The opinions of that sex are ever fluctuating.

Vasa vacua plurimum sonant. Lat. Prov.—"Empty vessels give out the loudest sound."—Ignorance is always most loquacious and noisy.

Vedettes. Fr. Mil. Term.—"Sentinels on horseback," to watch and give notice of the approach of an enemy.

Vehimur in altum. Lat.—"We are borne on high."—We have a propensity for the sublime.

Velim mehercule cum istis errare, quam cum aliis rectè sentire. Lat.—"I would rather, in fact, err with those men, than think rightly with others."—I so much approve of their general consistency, that though they may be erroneous in the single point, they still shall have my concurrence.

Velis et remis. Lat.—" With sails and oars."—He pushed forward *velis et remis*—by every possible means.

Velle suum cuique, nec voto vivitur uno. Lat. PERSIUS.—" Each man has his own wish—the inclinations of all can not be the same."—Taste and opinion must differ in men and in nations.

Velocius ac citius nos [*nis*
Corrumpunt vitiorum exempla domestica, mag-
Cum subeant animos auctoribus. Lat. HORACE. " We are more speedily and fatally corrupted by domestic examples of vice, and particularly, when they are impressed on our minds as from authority."—Such is the effect, for instance, of bad example, held forth by a father or mother, to children of either sex.

Velox consilium sequitur pœnitentia. Lat. LABER. " Hasty counsels are generally followed by repentance."

Vel pace, vel bello, clarum fieri licet. Lat. SALLUST. " A man may acquire celebrity, either in war, or in peace;"—in cultivating the peaceful arts, or directing " the storm of war."

Vel prece, vel pretio. Lat.—" Either for love, or for money."

Veluti in speculum. Lat.—" As if in a mirror, or looking-glass."—You shall see here your follies reflected.

Venalis populus, venalis curia patrum. Lat.—" The people are venal, and the senate is equally venal." —A description once given of *Rome.*

Vendentem thus et odores. Lat. HORACE.—" Selling frankincense and perfumes."—Applied to such pamphlets, as are destined to wrap up groceries, line trunks, &c.

Vendidit hic auro patriam. Lat. VIRGIL —" This man sold his country for gold."—He is nothing less than a venal traitor

Venditioni exponas. Law Lat.—"You shall expose for sale."—The name of a writ, directing a sheriff to sell certain property therein mentioned.

Venenum in auro bibitur. Lat. SENECA.—"Poison is generally drunk out of gold."—Those who use less costly utensils, are not liable to such murderous attempts.

Venienti occurrite morbo. Lat. PERSIUS.—"Meet the approaching disease."—Do not let the malady strike root, but seek the proper advice and remedy, on its first approaches.

Venire facias. Law Lat.—"You shall cause, or order to come."—The judicial writ by which the sheriff is empowered to summon a jury.

Veniunt a dote sagittæ. Lat. JUVENAL. "The darts were shot by the dowry."—The suitor was smitten with her property, not with her person.

Veni, vidi, vici. Lat.—"I came, I saw, I conquered." —This was the brief account transmitted by *Julius Cæsar* of a victory.

Ventis secundis. Lat.—"With prosperous winds."—With uniform success.

Ventre affamé n'a point d'oreilles. Fr. Prov.—"A starved belly has no ears."—An hungry audience is not to be satisfied by mere argument.

Verba animi proferre, et vitam impendere vero. Lat. JUVENAL. "To speak the words of the mind, and to stake one's life for the truth."—To speak with honest frankness, and to prefer liberty to life. An admirable summary of the duties of a good citizen.

Verba homicidium non excusant. Lat. Law Max.—"No words of provocation will excuse the commission of manslaughter."

Verba ligant homines, taurorum cornua funes. Lat.—"Words bind men, but ropes are necessary to bind the horns of a bull."

Verba provisam rem non invita sequentur. Lat. HORACE

"Words will spontaneously offer themselves to him, who has well-arranged ideas of his subject." —This is of nearly the same import with the quotation from Cicero, *Rerum copia*, &c., which see.

Verbatim et literatim. Lat.—"Word for word, and letter for letter."—A faithful and exact copy.

Verbosa ac grandis epistola venit
A Capræis. Lat. PERSIUS.
"A verbose and turgid epistle comes from Capreæ."—This is applied by the poet, to the haughty mandates issued by Tiberius in his retreat. It is now used to mark a lofty tone, assumed by the opposite party, in any polemic discussion

Verbum verbo reddere, fidus
Interpres. Lat. HORACE.
"As a faithful interpreter, to translate word for word;"—to give a translation strictly literal.

Verbum sat sapienti. Lat.—"A word is sufficient to a wise man."—He can take a hint.

Veritas, a quocunque dicitur, a Deo est. Lat.—"Truth, by whomsoever it is uttered, comes from God."

Veritas cum libertate. Lat.—"Truth with liberty."

Veritas nihil veretur, nisi abscondi. Lat. Law Max. —"Truth is afraid of nothing but concealment." —The characters of truth are plainness and frankness.

Veritas odium parit. Lat.—"Truth often causes hatred."

Veritas vincit. Lat.—"Truth conquers."

Veritas visû et morâ, falsa festinatione et incertis valescunt. Lat. TACITUS.—"Truth is confirmed by investigation and delay: falsehood avails itself of haste and uncertainty."

Veritatis simplex oratio est. Lat. SEN.—"The language of truth is simple."

Vérité sans peur. Fr.—"Truth without fear."

Ver non semper viret. Lat.—"The spring does not always flourish—or, *Vernon* always flourishes.'

Vero verius quid sit, audi. Lat. MART.—"Now listen to what is more true than truth itself,"—to what is most sacredly correct.

Versate diu, quid ferre recusent,
Quid valeant humeri. Lat. HORACE.
"Consider well what your strength is equal to, and what exceeds your ability."

Versus. Lat.—"Against."

Versus inopes rerum, nugæque canoræ. Lat. HOR. "Verses devoid of substance, melodious trifles." Or, as a modern poet has it,
"Your filmy, gauzy, gossamery lines."

Verum atque decens. Lat.—"That which is true and proper."—Or, just and honourable.

Verum illud est, vulgo quod dici solet;
Omnes sibi malle melius esse quam alteri.
Lat. TERENCE.
"The common assertion is certainly true, that we all wish matters to be better with ourselves, than others."—Whatever may theoretically be said of philanthropy and benevolence to others, self-love will be found to be the prevailing principle.

Verum opere in longo fas est obrepere somnum. Lat. HORACE.—"But in a long work, it is allowable that sleep may creep on."—A degree of negligence is pardonable in a long work, which in a brief production would be highly reprehensible.

Verum putes haud ægre, quod valde expetas. Lat. TERENCE.—"You believe that easily, which you hope for earnestly."—Men are led without difficulty into the belief of that, which they passionately desire.

Vestigia nulla retrorsum. Lat.—"There are no traces backward."—All the footsteps lead to the lion's den, but there are no marks of any returning. It is a danger from which there is no retreat.

Vetera extollimus, recentium incuriosi. Lat. TAC. "We extol the ancients, regardless of those of later date."—We are more ready to give praise to the deeds, or writers of antiquity, than to do justice to contemporary merit.

Veterum non immemor parentum. Lat. VIRGIL. "Not forgetful of his ancestors."

Veto. Lat.—"I forbid" it.

Vetustas pro lege semper habetur. Lat. Law Max.—"Ancient custom is always held as a law."—Where there is no positive law, the custom, if from time immemorial, may be pleaded.

Viamque insiste domandi,
Dum faciles animi juvenum, dum mobilis ætas
Lat. VIRGIL.

"Take the course of strong rule, whilst the mind of youth is flexible, and capable of strong impressions."—Vigorous methods, but divested of harshness, should be early called into use by those, to whom the education of youth is committed.

Viam qui nescit, quâ deveniat ad mare,
Eum oportet amnem quærere comitem sibi.
Lat. PLAUTUS.

"He who knows not his way to the sea, should take a river as his companion."—By this figure it is intimated, that a tedious, but certain course, to any given object, is preferable to one which may possibly be more brief, but is at the same time uncertain.—The savages of America thus steer their course through its immense deserts: when the windings of the river are marked and numerous, they know that they are approaching to the sea.

Via trita, via tuta. Lat.—"The beaten path is the safe one."

Vice versâ. Lat.—"The terms being exchanged."—Thus—the generous should be rich, and *vice versâ* the rich should be generous.

Vicinus urit Ucalegon. Lat. VIRGIL.—"Your neighbour Ucalegon's house is on fire."—The danger is approaching to you so nearly, as to demand your utmost exertion.

Victor, volentes per populos, dat jura. Lat.—"He, as a conqueror, dictates his laws to a willing people."—This is a compliment generally paid to a victorious leader. The will of the people subdued, though it does not actually follow, is presumed as a thing of course.

Victrix causa Diis placuit, sed victa Catoni. Lat. LUCAN.—"The victorious cause was adopted by the Gods, that of the vanquished by *Cato.*"

Victrix fortunæ sapientia. Lat. JUVENAL.—"Wisdom frequently conquers fortune."—A wise man will often parry or subdue the reverses of chance.

Vide. Lat.—"See."—*Vide ut supra.* "See the preceding statement."

Vide et crede. Lat.—"See and believe."—If any thing like incredulity remains, convince yourself by ocular demonstration.

Videlicet. Lat.—"To wit—that is to say."

Videndum est, ne major benignitas sit quam facultates. Lat. CICERO.—"We should be careful that our benevolence does not exceed our means."—A caution, which there are *very few* occasions for urging.

Video meliora proboque,
Deteriora sequor. Lat. OVID.
"I see and approve of better things, but I follow the worse which I condemn."—This is frequently used by the speaker or writer, as a sentence of self-condemnation.—It may also be applied to a third person, where his conduct is directly opposite to his known sentiments.

Vi et armis. Lat.—"By force and arms."—By a force not sanctioned by law. By main force.

Vigilantibus. Lat.—"To the watchful."

Vigilantibus non dormientibus servit lex. Lat. Law Max.—"The law regards those only who watch, and not those who sleep."—The law is only for the protection of those, who take due care of their property. It notices not those, who may suffer from their own neglect.

Vigueur de dessus. Fr.—"Strength is from above."

Vilius argentum est auro, virtutibus aurum. Lat. HORACE

"As silver is worthless compared with gold, so is gold when compared with virtue."

Vim vi repellere, omnia jura clamant. Law Lat.—"All law permits a man to repel force by force."

Vincit amor patriæ. Lat.—"The love of my country overcomes."

Vincit omnia veritas. Lat.—"Truth conquers all things."—It must ultimately prevail over every cavil, and every objection.

Vincit qui patitur. Lat.—"He conquers who endures."—He succeeds by patient perseverance.

Vincit, qui se vincit. Lat.—"He conquers who overcomes himself."

Vincit veritas. Lat.—"Truth prevails."

Vino tortus et irâ. Lat. Hor.—"Though tortured both by wine and anger."—The poet is speaking of a man who can keep his friend's secret, though the *lene tormentum,* or gentle compulsion of wine, or the more forcible excitation of anger, were both employed to wrest it from his bosom.

Vir bonus dicendi peritus. Lat.—"A good man skilled in the art of speaking."—By this, which was the ancient definition of an *Orator*, it appears that none could rank as such, but men of probity. Our modern notions are rather more relaxed.

Vir bonus est quis?
Qui consulta patrum, qui leges juraque servat.
Lat. Horace.

"Who is a good man? He who respects the decrees of the legislature, and bows to every positive law, and every moral obligation."

Vir bonus et prudens dici delector. Lat. Horace.—"I love to be called a good and a wise man."—All wish to *possess,* but few strive to *deserve,* this character.

Vires acquirit eundo. Lat.—"She acquires strength in her progress."—This is spoken by the poet of fame or rumour.

Virescit vulnere virtus. Lat.—"Virtue flourishes from a wound."

Vir haud magnâ cum re, sed plenus fidei. Lat. Cic. —"A man possessed of little wealth, but of incorruptible integrity."

Viri infelicis procul amici. Lat. Sen.—"Friends are always distant from a man who is unfortunate." —Misfortune occasions a shyness, even amongst friends the most professed.

Vir sapit, qui pauca loquitur. Lat.—"He is a wise man, who speaks but seldom."

Virtus ariete fortior. Lat.—"Virtue is stronger than a battering-ram."

Virtus est medium vitiorum, et utrinque reductum. Lat. Hor.—"Virtue is the middle between two vices, and is removed from either extreme."—Thus, generosity is the middle virtue, the extremes of which are avarice and prodigality.

Virtus est per se ipsa laudabilis, et sine quâ nihil laudari potest. Lat. Cicero.—"Virtue (or purity of intention), is, in itself, praiseworthy, and, without it, no action can be laudable."

Virtus est vitium fugere, et sapientia prima
Stultitiâ caruisse. Lat. Horace.
"It is a virtue to avoid vice, and the first step to wisdom, is to be free from folly."

Virtus in actione consistit. Lat.—"Virtue consists in acting."—It does not rest on cold theory, but on positive exertion.

Virtus in arduis. Lat.—"Virtue (or valour) in difficulties."

Virtus incendit vires. Lat.—"Virtue kindles the strength."

Virtus laudatur et alget. Lat. Juv.—"Virtue is praised and freezes."—Virtuous efforts are viewed with cold admiration, and often meet only with sullen neglect.

Virtus mille scuta. Lat.—"Virtue is equal to a thousand shields."

Virtus, repulsæ nescia sordidæ,
Intaminatis fulget honoribus. Lat. Horace.

"That virtue which is unconscious of a base repulse, shines with unstained honours."

Virtus requiei nescia sordidæ. Lat.—"Valour which knows not ignoble repose."

Virtus semper viridis. Lat.—"Virtue is always flourishing."

Virtus vincit invidiam. Lat.—"Virtue overcomes envy."—The virtuous man is, in the end, sure of his reward.

Virtute et fide. Lat.—"By virtue and faith."

Virtute et labore. Lat.—"By virtue and toil."

Virtute et operâ. Lat.—"By virtue and industry."

Virtute non astutiâ. Lat.—"By virtue, not by craft."

Virtute non viris. Lat.—"From virtue, not from men."

Virtute officii. Lat.—"By virtue of his office;" which, in a legal sense, makes an act good, and justifiable.

Virtute quies. Lat.—"Content in virtue."

Virtutem incolumem odimus;
Sublatam ex oculis quærimus invidi. Lat. Hor
"We hate virtue when it is safe and flourishing; but when removed from our sight, even envy itself regrets it."—Such is the nature of man.

Virtutem primam esse puta, compescere linguam.
Proximus ille Deo est, qui scit ratione tacere.
Lat. Cato.
"Account it a great virtue to be able to govern the tongue. He possesses a god-like quality, who can be silent, although he is in the right."

Virtutem videant, intabescantque relictâ. Lat. Juv.
"Let them (the wicked) see the beauty of virtue, and pine at having forsaken her."—This is the greatest curse that can befall them.

Virtuti nihil obstat et armis. Lat.—"Nothing can resist valour and arms."

Virtuti, non armis, fido. Lat.—"I trust to virtue, and not to arms."

Virtutis amor. Lat.—"The love of virtue."

Virtutis amore. Lat.—"Through the love of virtue."

Virtutis avorum præmium. Lat.—"The reward of the virtue of my ancestors."

Virtutis fortuna comes. Lat.—"Fortune is the companion of virtue."

Vis a tergo. Lat.—"A propelling force from behind."

Vis à vis. Fr.—"Opposite—over the way, facing."

Viscera. Lat.—"The bowels or intestines."—*Viscus,* (in the singular,) denotes any one of the different organs of the human body, having an appropriate use, as the brain, the stomach, the heart, &c.

Vis conservatrix naturæ. Lat.—"The preserving power of nature."

Vis, consilii expers, mole ruit suâ. Lat. HORACE.—"Force, not directed by wisdom, falls by its own weight."—Brutal force is as nothing, when it is not guided by the counsels of reason.

Vis inertiæ. Lat.—"The power of inertness."—In physics, this is applied to the power of a stationary body, resisting that which would set it in motion. In morals, it has a figurative application, and serves as another name for indolence.

Vis medicatrix naturæ. Lat.—"The healing power of nature."—That effort which nature constantly makes to overcome disease, and restore a healthy action to the system.

Vis preservatrix. Lat.—"The preserving power."

Vis unita fortior. Lat.—"Force or power is strengthened by union."

Vitâ cedat, uti conviva satur. Lat. HORACE.—"Let him take leave of life, as a guest satisfied with his entertainment."

Vitæ est avidus, quisquis non vult,
Mundo secum pereunte, mori. Lat. SENECA.
"He is greedy of life, who is not willing to die, when the world is perishing around him."

Vita enim mortuorum in memoriâ vivorum est posita. Lat. CICERO.—"The life of the dead is placed in the memory of the living."—They survive in remembrance, and still exist, as a biographer would say, in fair report.

Vitæ post-scenia celant. Lat. LUCRETIUS.—"They conceal that part of their life which is passed behind the scenes."—They throw a veil over their private life, and hide it from the world.

Vitæ summa brevis spem nos vetat inchoare longam. Lat. HORACE.—"The short span of our lives forbids us to encourage a lengthened hope."—Such is the brief term of our existence, that he who looks to remote prospects is generally disappointed.

Vitæ via virtus. Lat.—"Virtue is the way of life."

Vitam impendere vero. Lat.—"To stake one's life for the truth."—Stated as the best character of a good citizen.

Vitam regit fortuna, non sapientia. Lat. CICERO.—"Fortune, and not wisdom, governs human life."

Vitanda est improba Syren—Desidia. Lat. HOR.—"That destructive Syren, Sloth, is ever to be avoided."—The man who devotes himself to indolent habits, must be considered as lost to himself and to society.

Vita, sine literis, mors est. Lat.—"Life without learning is death."—The uncultivated mind is unable to enjoy the real pleasures of life.

Vitavi denique culpam;
Non laudem merui. Lat.
"I have been careful to avoid censure, if I have not deserved commendation."—This is a suitable motto for a very numerous class of poets, who seem to aim at no higher praise than that of faultless insipidity.

Vitia otii negotio discutienda sunt. Lat. SENECA. "The vices of sloth are only to be shaken off by business."—The mind will rust and canker without employment.

Vitia nobis, sub virtutum nomine, obrepunt. Lat. SEN.——"Vice steals into our minds, under the name and guise of virtue."

Vitiant artus ægræ contagia mentis. Lat. OVID. "When the mind is ill at ease, the body is also in a certain degree affected."—The converse of this proposition may be asserted with equal justice.

Vitiis nemo sine nascitur. Lat.—"No man is born without his faults."—We owe every allowance to the faults of others, being conscious that every human being has his share of imperfection.

Vitium commune omnium est,
Quod nimium ad rem in senectâ attenti sumus.
Lat. TERENCE.
"It is a fault which is common to all, that in advanced age, we are too much attached to our property and interest."—As prodigality is proverbially said to be the fault of youth, so is avarice that of later years.

Vitium fuit, nunc mos est, adsentatio. Lat. SYRUS.
"Flattery was formerly considered a vice, but it is now grown into a custom."—It has become so familiar, that it no longer provokes our detestation.

Vitium, tanto conspectius in se
Crimen habet, quanto major, qui peccat, habetur. Lat. JUVENAL.
"Depravity assumes a degree of criminality, proportionate to the rank of the offender."

Vivat Respublica. Lat.—"May the Republic long continue."

Vivâ voce. Lat.—"By the living voice."—By oral testimony, as opposed to written evidence. Electors are said to vote *viva voce,* when they *call out* the names of their candidates, instead of *silently* depositing them, on a ticket, in a ballot-box.

Vive la bagatelle! Fr.—"Success to trifling!"

Vive memor lethi. Lat. PERSIUS.
"Live ever in the remembrance of death."—This solemn recollection will be the best preservative from vice and error.

Vivendi rectè qui prorogat horam,
Rusticus expectat dum defluat amnis. Lat. HOR.
"He who postpones the hour of living rightly, is like the rustic who waits till the river shall have passed away."—He defers his reformation to a period which can never arrive.

Vivendum est rectè, cum propter plurima, tum his
Præcipuè causis, ut linguas mancipiorum

Contemnas—nam lingua mali pars pessima servi. Lat. JUVENAL.
"You should live virtuously, for many reasons, but particularly on this account, that you may be able to despise the tongues of your domestics. The tongue is the worst part of a bad servant."

Vivere rapto. Lat.—"To live by plunder."

Vivere sat vincere. Lat.—"To conquer is to live enough."

Vivere si nequis rectè, discede peritus. Lat. HOR.
"If you know not how to conduct yourself properly, show sense enough to leave the company of those who do."

Vive sine invidiâ; mollesque inglorios annos
Exige, et amicitias tibi junge pares. Lat. OVID
"Live free from envy; and without a wish for glory, desire only placid years, and to live in friendship with your equals."—Seek the quiet shade of life, and avoid the friendship of the great.

Vive, vale—Si quid novisti rectius istis,
Candidus imperti; si non, his utere mecum.
Lat. HORACE.
"Farewell, and be happy—if you know of any precepts better than these, be so candid as to communicate them, if not, partake of these with me."
———"If a better system's thine,
Impart it freely, or make use of mine."

Vivida vis animi. Lat.—"The strong force of the mind."—The lively *impetus* of genius.

Vivite felices, quibus est fortuna peracta
Jam sua. Lat. VIRGIL.
"May those be happy, whose fortunes are already completed."—Though struggling through life, I can see those without envy, whose efforts have had a successful termination.

Vivit post funera virtus. Lat.—"Virtue survives the grave."

Vivitur exiguo melius—natura beatis
Omnibus esse dedit, si quis cognoverit uti.
Lat. CLAUDIAN
"Men live best upon a little—nature has granted

to all to be happy, if the use of her gifts were but known."

Vivo et regno, simul ista reliqui,
Quæ vos ad cœlum effertis rumore secundo.
Lat. HORACE.
"I live and reign within myself, since I have abandoned those things, which you by your praises extol to the skies."—I have been happy, since I have resigned to you the pleasures of sensuality, and betaken myself to those of reflection.

Vivre ce n'est pas respirer, c'est agir. Fr. ROUSSEAU.
"Life does not consist merely in breathing, but in action."—The man can scarcely be said to live, who does nothing but obey his animal impulses.

Vix ea nostra voco. Lat.—"I can scarcely call these things my own," (alluding to ancestry.)

Vixere fortes ante Agamemnona
Multi: sed omnes illachrymabiles
Urgentur, ignotique longâ
Nocte, carent quia vate sacro. Lat. HORACE.
"Many heroes lived before Agamemnon, but they are all unmourned, and consigned to long oblivion, because they are without a sacred bard," to sing their praises.—This quotation is used in showing the value of poetry, in consecrating and embalming the deeds of virtue and of valour.

Vocem Comœdia tollit. Lat.—"Comedy carries the day."—The public show a greater inclination for amusement and ridicule, than for any thing serious.

Voilà pour l'achever de peindre. Fr. Prov.—"But to finish his picture."—To give the last and strongest feature of his character.

Voilà une autre chose. Fr.—"There you see another thing."—The circumstances of the two cases are wholly different.

Voilà tout. Fr.—"That's all."—There ends the matter.

Voir dire. Law Fr.—A witness is said to be examined upon a *voir dire,* when he is sworn and examined, whether he be not a party interested in the cause.

Voir tout en couleur de rose. Fr.—"To see every thing under a favourable aspect."

Volenti non fit injuria. Lat. Law Max.—"An injury can not be done to a willing person."—None can complain of wrong in a proceeding, when the measure had their previous assent.

Volo, non valeo. Lat.—"I am willing but unable."

Volti subito. Ital.—"Turn over quickly."—A direction to the performer, given at the bottom of a page of music, when the piece is continued on the following page.

Voluptates commendat rarior usus. Lat. JUV. "Our pleasures have an higher relish when they are rarely used."—The keenest sense of pleasure is blunted by a too frequent repetition.

Vota vita mea. Lat.—"My life is devoted."

Votorum summa. Lat.—"The very extent of one's wishes."

Vous me fites, seigneur,
En m'attaquant, beaucoup d'honneur. French. "You did me, Sir, by attacking me, a great deal of honour."—The reproaches of such an adversary, I consider rather as a compliment than a disgrace.

Vous y perdrez vos pas. Fr.—"You will there lose your steps."—You will find that your labour and pains are thrown away.

Vox et præterea nihil. Lat.—"A voice and nothing more."—An empty and unavailing sound. A fine speech without matter. A mere display of words.

Vox faucibus hæsit. Lat. VIRGIL.—"The voice stuck in the throat."—Spoken of a person struck dumb with amazement.

Vox populi, vox Dei. Lat.—"The voice of the people is the voice of God."—A strong expression of the sovereignty of the people.—An exclamation often used by demagogues, when that voice can be brought to favour their covert and sinister views.

Voyer dire. See *Voir dire.*

Vulnus alit venis, et cæco carpitur igni. Lat. VIRG. —"She (or he) nourishes the poison in her veins.

and is consumed by a hidden fire."—Applied very frequently to a secret passion, where, according to our immortal bard:

——"Concealment, like a worm i' the bud,
Feeds on her damask cheek."

Vulnus immedicabile. Lat.—"The incurable wound"—an irreparable injury.

Vultus animi sensus plerumque indicat. Lat. Cic.—"The countenance, most generally, betrays the secret workings of the mind."—and,

Vultus est index animi. Lat. Prov.—"The countenance is the index or portraiture of the mind."—So say the disciples of Lavater, but like other general rules, it is liable to many exceptions.

Z

Zest. Fr.—An interjection.—"Pshaw, stuff, ridiculous."

Ζωη και ψυχη. *Zoe kai psuche.* Gr.—"My life and soul."

Zonam perdidit. Lat. Hor.—"He has lost his purse."—He is desperate, through the want of money.

Zonam solvere. Lat.—"To unloose the virgin zone, or *cestus.*"

THE END.

www.ingramcontent.com/pod-product-compliance
Lightning Source LLC
LaVergne TN
LVHW020231110826
845151LV00003B/890

* 9 7 8 1 4 2 5 5 3 0 8 2 2 *